Living

Stories

Fortress Press Books by
Donald Capps

Deadly Sins and Saving Virtues (1983)

Reframing:
A New Method in Pastoral Care (1990)

The Depleted Self:
Sin a Narcissistic Age (1993)

Agents of Hope:
A Pastoral Psychology (1995)

Living Stories:
Pastoral Counseling in Congregational Context (1998)

Living Stories

Pastoral Counseling in
Congregational Context

Donald **Capps**

Fortress Press

DEDICATED TO TROELS NØRAGER

"Like cold water to a thirsty soul,
so is good news from a far country."
—Proverbs 25:25

LIVING STORIES
Pastoral Counseling in a Congregational Context

Scripture quotations from the New Revised Standard Version of the Bible are copyright © 1989 by the Division of Christian Education of the National Council of Churches in the United States of America and are used by permission.

Cover design: Brad Norr Design
Text design: David B. Lott

Library of Congress Cataloging-in-Publication Data

Capps, Donald.
     Living stories : pastoral counseling in congregational context /
     Donald Capps.
          p.   cm.
     Includes bibliographical references and index.
     ISBN 0-8006-3073-4 (alk. paper)
     1. Pastoral counseling. 2. Pastoral theology. 3. Parishes.
     4. Storytelling—Religious aspects—Christianity. I. Title.
     BV4012.2.C265   1998
     253.5'2—dc21   98-9235
                                                            CIP

The paper used in this publication meets the minimum requirements of American National Standard for Information Sciences—Permanence of Paper for Printed Library Materials, ANSI Z329.48-1984.

Manufactured in the U.S.A.   AF 1-3073

02   01   00   99   98   1   2   3   4   5   6   7   8   9   10

Contents

Preface

B ecause we find ourselves on the verge of the next century, we are prone to think more about how things will be changing than how they will stay the same. As I consider pastoral counseling as it exists today and the form it may take in the future, I anticipate that it will undergo major changes in the years to come, almost to the point of becoming unrecognizable to those who practice it today. This anticipation stems in part from the fact that, as Yogi Berra is said to have said, "The future ain't what it used to be," to which we might add, "And it never was." One takes few risks when one predicts that in the future things will be different as long as one does not specify exactly *how* they will be different. But this anticipation also derives from the fact that, in the case of pastoral counseling, we have been working with much the same paradigm, with a few variations, for several decades, and, as the experience of other professional fields teaches us, it is common for a reigning paradigm to persist for several decades and then to be replaced by a new paradigm which will, in its turn, persist for several decades, only to be replaced by another. There is every reason to believe that pastoral counseling will undergo a similar paradigmatic revolution. In fact, I believe that we are already in the midst of such a revolution, and that efforts to revise the existing paradigm have already given way to attempts to envision a new one.

In light of these anticipations, this book is certainly not a definitive book on pastoral counseling. It *is*, however, an effort to make a strong, convincing case for the importance of pastoral counseling to the life of the congregation. Much of what gets written or presented in lecture form about pastoral counseling has greater applicability to the work of those for whom pastoral counseling is a specialized ministry than to the work of those for whom it is one of many pastoral tasks. The establishment of pastoral counseling centers in recent decades, and the development of a population of trained specialized pastoral counselors, has placed pastors in the congregational context in something of a quandary as far as pastoral counseling is concerned. The existence of acclaimed preachers who crisscross the country and preach to large audiences at church conventions, pastors weeks events, and the like, has *not* prompted pastors of congregations to give up the practice of preaching on a regular basis. On the contrary, these acclaimed preachers have served as role models for pastors of congregations and have inspired them to work at the preaching craft with even greater appreciation for preaching's power to affect the lives of their congregants. The development of pastoral counseling specialists has had virtually the opposite effect on pastors of congregations. Rather than being inspired by the fact that pastoral counseling is now a well-established specialized ministry, they have found it intimidating and daunting, or have viewed this as providing a defensible rationale for not engaging themselves in much pastoral counseling but instead to "leave it to the professionals, who (apparently) know what they are doing."

This book is written for the pastor who, on the one hand, wants to continue to engage in pastoral counseling or finds it impossible not to do so, but, on the other hand, does not want to become so invested in pastoral counseling that he or she would be unable to perform the many other tasks of ministry that are expected of the parish pastor. The basic argument of this book is that pastoral counseling is essential to the life of the congregation because it responds to a fundamental human need to give systematic, constructive attention to the ways that individuals "story" their lives so that they may develop new, more fulfilling life stories. It introduces the narrative approach to counseling, and then focuses on three noted brief therapists who offer three different, but mutually supportive, approaches to the "re-storying" of the counselee's life: Milton H. Erickson, proponent of the inspirational story; Paul Watzlawick, advocate of the paradoxical story; and Steve de Shazer, who favors the miracle story. These narrative models involve the employment of counseling "arts" that pastors may also use—the arts of using the power of suggestion, untying knots, and identifying exceptions. These arts are as ancient as they are contemporary. They are found in various folk traditions, and are especially manifest in Gospel accounts of the teaching and healing ministry of Jesus. These arts are powerful tools that pastors may use as they listen to parishioners tell their personal stories and look for guidance in the revisioning of their lives.

This book also makes the case that pastoral counseling, when responsibly done, provides a positive communication model for the larger life of the congregation. To develop this point, I give considerable attention to the issue of gossip, for this is undeniably a common feature of congregational life and one that can be very destructive. I advance the argument here that gossip is not an unmitigated evil, however, and that pastoral counseling may be that place in the life of the congregation where the positive features of gossip are enhanced and the negative features are minimized. In this way, it models for the congregation better craftsmanship in communication.

Throughout this book, I make connections between the contemporary psychotherapeutic and social-scientific literature and the ministry of Jesus. My purpose in doing so is not to claim that the contemporary literature is inherently or fundamentally Christian, nor is it to make the case that Jesus was a psychotherapist. Rather, my purpose is simply to encourage readers to envision ways in which they may appropriate the "living stories" of the Gospels in their engagement in pastoral counseling. If psychotherapists rely heavily on the *Diagnostic and Statistical Manual of Mental Disorders (DSM-IV)* to guide them in their work, one can only hope that pastors will make comparable use of Gospel stories to assist them in the work of enabling others to live more abundant lives.

I express my appreciation to Cynthia Thompson for shepherding this book through the review process and for her helpful editorial suggestions. I am also grateful to J. Michael West and Henry French at Fortress Press for completing the editorial process and seeing that the book came out in a timely fashion. David Lott has done an exceptional job in its production. Joan Blyth-Lovell typed the final manuscript with extraordinary efficiency. Karen Capps, who has been my reliable companion through what we call our "thirty-odd years" of marriage, provided just the right amount of support and encouragement. I have dedicated this book to Troels Nørager, Professor of Psychology of Religion and Pastoral Theology at Aarhus University in Aarhus, Denmark. Our conversations about metaphor, narrative, and communication have helped me to clarify my own views on these issues, especially as they have bearing on the issues addressed in this book. Our personal friendship has been a great blessing to me.

Finally, my book would not be complete without acknowledgment of my indebtedness to the work of Milton H. Erickson (particularly as reflected in Sidney Rosen's edited volume of his stories, *My Voice Will Go with You: The Teaching Tales of Milton H. Erickson*, several of which appear in this book), Steve de Shazar, and Paul Watzlawick. Without the prior research of these great brief therapists, my own work would not be possible. I hope the approaches I offer here honor their own narrative models and increase the reader's interest in further reflection on their contributions.

Introduction

Counseling in the Congregational Context

Much is being written these days about the importance of narrative for theological reflection, and the narrative sermon is still widely used. The pastoral care and counseling field has also taken up the issue of narrative, with several books having been written on the uses of narrative in pastoral counseling.[1] Many articles published in the major journals in pastoral care and counseling begin with a personal story, such as the author's experiences in childbirth, or struggle with a debilitating illness, or sexual abuse.

Another important development is that several books have been written on the value of brief therapy methods for pastoral counseling.[2] These authors have shown how brief therapy, an important movement within family therapy, can be a valuable resource for pastors who are involved in counseling their own parishioners.

For the most part, these two important developments in the pastoral care field have taken shape independently of one another. There are various reasons for this, but perhaps the most significant is that many of the authors who are writing on narrative employ the perspective of psychoanalytic object relations theory, which emphasizes the ways in which we internalize and project parental and other culturally transmitted models and images. This theory has proven a valuable psychological resource for these authors, as it has enabled them to explore such issues as how a religious tradition, especially its representations of God, is internalized by the individual self and externalized in the form of essentially patriarchal religious institutions.

These authors are certainly not writing in opposition to family therapy. Indeed, several employ systemic language when they write about
the relations between the self, the family, the church, the community,
the nation, and the natural world. But, by and large, these texts have
not directly addressed the matter of pastoral counseling itself, especially what a narrative model may have to contribute toward a new
understanding of how pastoral counseling may occur in the congregational setting.

The texts on brief therapy do address this latter issue, as they are
mainly written for the parish minister, and their purpose is to explain
how pastoral counseling may be conducted in a responsible manner
in the parish context by setting appropriate limits to the length and
the goals of counseling. These books, however, do not take significant account of the narrative interests of the brief therapists themselves, or of the fact that brief therapists are part of a larger movement among family therapists toward a privileging of story.

One of the purposes of this book is to bring these more or less independent trends in pastoral care closer together, with the expectation
that, in doing so, a new understanding of how pastoral counseling
may occur in the congregational setting will emerge. A perennial complaint of parish ministers is that the books that are written about
parish ministry often fail to reflect the reality of parish ministry itself.
In *Language, Structure, and Change*, Jay S. Efran et al. tell about their
conversation with a colleague who writes books on how to study.
When one of the authors asked him whether he follows his own
advice (that is, does he sit upright in a chair, the book flat on the table,
and a light behind his right shoulder, and so forth?), he said no, that
he studies in bed, with the TV on, and a stack of cookies at his side.[3]
The authors confess that, like their colleague, they frequently fail to
use their own therapeutic model when actually engaging in therapy.
In a sense, any book that is written about parish ministry will miss the
mark to some degree simply because parish ministry itself is so
diverse. What may be relevant to one congregational setting has little
or no relevance to another. Yet, unlike preaching, which occurs with
regularity in virtually all congregations, pastoral counseling is either
not done with any regularity in some congregational contexts or, if it
is done, the approach is very different from what the books on pastoral counseling tend to advocate.

Many of my former students have come back to the seminary reporting that, as far as pastoral counseling is concerned, they simply do not do very much of it. "I do a lot of pastoral care," they will say, "but very little pastoral counseling." The "counseling" they say they do—in a tone of voice that suggests they do not consider it to be real counseling—usually occurs during coffee hour or before or after a committee meeting. Sometimes it is conducted over the phone. A mother wants to know what the pastor knows about a religious group that her daughter has become involved with at college, or a husband has just been informed that his wife has cancer and he wants the pastor to know about it and keep him in his prayers. In these instances, it does not make much sense for the pastor to infer that behind these requests there is an implied request for counseling as well. It may be that the mother's request for information about a campus religious group masks a deeper set of ambivalent feelings about her relationship to her daughter, and it may be that the husband's requests for prayers for his wife's recovery masks some deeply ambivalent feelings about his marriage that have now begun to surface as his wife's life is threatened. But is the pastor justified in acting on these possible implications?

The vast majority of pastors will say that they have no right to make such inferences. To suggest that the mother "needs" counseling herself or that the husband might want to come to the pastor's office where they can talk "in a more relaxed atmosphere about the tragedy that has befallen him" seems presumptuous and invasive. The responsible pastor will provide the information that the mother is asking for. If he knows the answer, he will tell her on the spot. If he doesn't know, he will promise to find out. Later he will make a point of asking her how her daughter is doing, whether she is still involved in the religious group, and so forth. The responsible pastor will promise to pray for the man's wife and will inquire as to how much is known at this time about the cancer, when more will be known, and various other questions designed to enable her to respond to the husband's disclosure in an appropriately caring way.

Pastoral care has taken place. But pastoral counseling? No. Not, at least, as it is currently defined. What has taken place is not comparable with what is being described in the books that use the brief therapy model to set forth principles, procedures, and processes for

how the pastor might counsel a couple who is having marital problems or a family that is being torn apart by their teenage son's drug
use. Nor is it comparable to the cases in the books on narrative in
which the counselor (often the author) has been seeing a depressed
client for several weeks or even months, during which the two of
them have been exploring such issues as the client's image of God
and how changes in this image have paralleled changes in the client's
sense of self. Such cases may be very informative for the pastor in
indirect ways, influencing how one preaches and conducts worship,
or how one responds to the felt need for the church to provide
opportunities for members to talk about how their theologies affect
their daily lives. Yet, helpful as these cases may be for the pastor's
ministry, they often accentuate the gap between how pastoral counseling is portrayed (that is, as a deep and ongoing process) and the
experience of pastors whose caring ministry is more often informal
and focused on a single issue or problem.

I have been a seminary professor for twenty years, long enough to
know how I typically respond to students when they make an
appointment to see me about a personal matter. I have also talked
with many parish ministers over the years, and, from these conversations, I think I have a pretty good idea of how they typically
respond to parishioners who make an appointment to see them
about a personal matter. It seems to me that I, as a seminary professor, and parish ministers have more in common with each other in
how we respond to such situations than we do with those who
engage in full-time counseling or therapy. More often than not, we
(seminary professor and parish minister) have only one or two meetings with an individual. If we were to suggest more, we suspect that
the student and the parishioner might think that we didn't have
enough to keep us busy or that we have some ulterior motives or
inappropriate needs of our own that we are seeking to satisfy. Our
role seems to be a rather informal one of providing some moral support, perhaps some clarification about a problem or issue, and this
seems, in turn, to be pretty much the extent of what the student or
parishioner is seeking from us.

Usually, those who are engaged in counseling on a full-time basis
have a more elaborate agenda, and this is usually true of the person
who comes to them for help. In fact, one reason individuals tend to

resist going to a counselor or psychotherapist is that they assume they will be getting into something that will be time-consuming and will involve significant adjustments to their daily schedules. Few assume that the counselor will declare them cured or their problem solved after only one or two sessions.

There are, of course, instances in which psychotherapists see certain clients for only one or two sessions. A psychotherapist in New York City specializes in one-session counseling, a practice he adopted after he found that about two-thirds of the clients who had failed to return for their second scheduled visit (and were thus declared "failures") felt, on the contrary, that the initial visit had been so clarifying for them that they did not need more counseling. Yet, for the most part, the counseling that is done by full-time professionals differs significantly in scope and expenditure of time and effort from what parish ministers and seminary professors typically do. My point is simply that seminary professors and parish ministers are more alike in this regard than they are different. So the question that I will be raising in this book—"Is pastoral counseling essential to parish ministry?"—is much the same question that I ask myself, "Is pastoral counseling essential to seminary teaching?" My answer in both instances is yes, but to say that something is essential does not necessarily mean that one does it every day, or that one devotes many hours to it every week.

The issue that this book addresses is the viability of pastoral counseling in the congregational setting. Is pastoral counseling, as distinct from pastoral care, a viable feature of congregational ministry? I realize that for some pastors the answer to this question is easy. Some will say that they have never believed that it was appropriate for them to engage in pastoral counseling, so they have developed skills in making good referrals. On the other hand, others will say that pastoral counseling in the congregational setting is certainly viable; after all, they do a lot of it. While these are not trivial answers to the question that I am raising here, they are not the answers that we need, because they basically give an empirical—and personal—response to what is a deeper, more substantive question. By asking about the viability of pastoral counseling, I am not so much asking whether there are pastors who do it, but whether it is so integral to the ministry of the church that, without it, the Christian life itself is impoverished.

By putting the issue this way, I raise the challenging question that pastoral counseling's detractors have been able to avoid when they declare that pastoral counseling is simply evidence of the degree to which the secular world has made inroads in the church itself. Also, by putting the question this way, I make clear that an affirmative answer to this question means that we will need to find more effective ways for parish pastors to engage in pastoral counseling. If pastoral counseling is an essential ministry of the church, then the fact that many pastors are not engaged in it, or assume that they are not, is a serious problem. If, on the other hand, it is not an essential ministry of the church, then we should seriously question the current assumption that books on pastoral counseling are written for parish pastors. They may still be written, but the fact that they are for pastoral counselors in specialized ministries should be made clear.

That the answer to this question is not obvious alerts us to the fact that pastoral counseling has always had a somewhat anomalous position in congregational life. While we never even raise the question whether congregational life would be seriously impoverished if there were no preaching, this "taken-for-grantedness" does not apply to pastoral counseling. Even though pastoral counseling has been a feature of church life for a half-century, and has roots in various traditional pastoral acts of hearing confession, admonishing the wayward, and so forth, its legitimacy as a ministry of the church is still being questioned, and there is little consensus among parish ministers or laity as to whether pastoral counseling is integral or vital to the church's ministry. Yet, the fact that pastoral counseling is relatively new should not, in itself, be used to challenge its legitimacy, for there are many features of contemporary congregational life that do not have a long tradition behind them. Sunday schools, for example, were not a regular feature of American congregational life until the latter half of the nineteenth century, and the impetus for adoption of the Sunday school in mainline Protestantism was a defensive one, for independent Sunday schools were threatening to draw the children (and thus their parents) away from the more established churches. A century later, the church school is now a "taken- for-granted" feature of congregational life, and there is a very broad consensus that it is integral to the ministry of the church. Thus, the fact that pastoral counseling is something of a Johnny-come-lately is not, in itself, a sufficient argument against the view that it is an essential ministry of the church, especially if it has replaced earlier forms of pastoral counsel.

That a vast network of pastoral counseling centers now exists across the nation, staffed by full-time professional counselors, many of which are only tangentially related to congregations, is also an insufficient argument against the view that pastoral counseling is essential to the life of the congregation itself. While it is now well established that pastoral counseling can be done effectively outside the congregational context, this does not necessarily mean that it is therefore expendable as far as congregational ministry is concerned. Even though preaching is done in a variety of noncongregational settings—athletic stadiums, nursing homes, prisons, street corners—no one has seriously suggested that, in light of this, there is no need for preaching to occur in the congregational context.

I argue here that pastoral counseling is indeed essential to the life of the congregation, and that where it is missing from the congregation's ministry, the life of that congregation is, in consequence, impoverished. But I also want to make the corollary argument that our understanding of what pastoral counseling is or entails needs to be shaped by the setting in which it occurs, that is, its *congregational* context. Probably the major reason that pastoral counseling has continued to seem to many to be of marginal importance to the life of the congregation is that the congregational setting itself has had little influence on how it has been conceived or designed. All too often, a practice that was developed in other social contexts has been inaugurated, with very little modification, in the congregational context. Is it any wonder that many, feeling its "foreignness," have complained that it is merely symptomatic of the secularization of congregational life? What is therefore needed, and what I place before my readers here, is a careful consideration of what pastoral counseling that is truly shaped by its congregational context might become. I set forth my own vision of what pastoral counseling in the congregational setting might look like, and I am prepared to defend this vision, but most important is that we address the issue itself. So far, there has been remarkably little envisioning of what pastoral counseling in the congregational setting might look like, and how it might assume its own distinctive form vis-à-vis the pastoral counseling that occurs in pastoral counseling centers.

My proposed vision for pastoral counseling shaped by the congregational setting in which it occurs involves a linking of the narrative theme that is now so much a part of the pastoral theology literature with the innovative forms of counseling that are emerging from
the brief therapy movement. In this vision I draw on those features
of brief therapy that are themselves informed by a concern for story,
but I also contend that pastors, unlike full-time counselors in pastoral counseling centers, cannot simply apply the brief therapy model
to their pastoral counseling ministry, for the models that parish ministers employ need to be shaped by the congregational context itself.
Thus, the pastoral counseling that I envision pastors engaging in may
not look like what we normally take to be "pastoral counseling" and
may differ significantly from the pastoral counseling that is performed in pastoral counseling centers. It may, in fact, differ so much
from what we have traditionally taken pastoral counseling to be that
some readers will question whether it is even appropriate to use the
term "pastoral counseling" in naming it. Yet, in my view, it is very
important that we use this label, because I want to make a case for
replacing what we have known as pastoral counseling with this
newer, more radical model. This will be impossible if we merely say
that what we have always taken to be "pastoral counseling" is what
it is, and this new model is simply something else (in other words, a
concentrated form of pastoral care). A congregationally shaped pastoral counseling approach will not become widely adopted unless we
are successful in claiming that it is, indeed, pastoral counseling, and
deserves to be recognized as such. Otherwise, the present conception
of what it is will continue to prevail, and some pastors will practice
it while many others will decide that it is better left to others, to those
who have specialized training.

By framing the issue in terms of whether pastoral counseling is
integral to the life of a congregation, I am also taking the view that
pastoral counseling is more than a service that the congregation,
through its minister, may provide its members. Congregations often
provide services, such as chartered tours of the Holy Land, that are
not generally considered to be essential to congregational life as
such. These are, if you will, added benefits of membership in a given
congregation. The question I am posing, however, is whether the
experiences that pastoral counseling provides are so essential to the

life of a congregation that, if these experiences do not occur, the life of the congregation itself is thereby impoverished. It is unnecessary for us to claim that the experience it provides is as essential, say, as the experience that occurs in the worship service, but we would want to be able to claim that the experience afforded by pastoral counseling is at least as essential as that provided by the educational ministry of the church.

I realize that the very idea that pastoral counseling might offer an essential experience is difficult to entertain because we immediately think of several practical objections to it: How could a pastor find time to counsel every member of the congregation? And would this not have a very negative effect on the congregation, as it would create relationships between the pastor and individual counselees, or suspicions of favoritism, that would reverberate negatively throughout the whole congregation? Indeed, is it not the case that pastoral counseling succeeds to the degree that it is *not* considered vital to the life of the congregation? Were it to seem essential or vital, it could easily go from being incidental to the life of the congregation to being inimical to it.

These objections, however, are based on assumptions about the nature of pastoral counseling that reflect how pastoral counseling is currently conceived. They do not necessarily apply to pastoral counseling that is genuinely shaped by the congregational setting itself, for we do not as yet know very much about what pastoral counseling that is truly native to the congregational context will look like, or of what it will consist. It is therefore important for us to suspend these objections until we have a better idea of what might result from an attempt to take seriously the question whether pastoral counseling offers an experience that is integral to the life of the congregation, the absence of which would significantly impoverish this life. If this question is answered in the affirmative, then the practical questions about how pastoral counseling might be made an integral part of the church's ministry would need to be addressed. But these practical questions should not be allowed to preclude the exploration itself. If we allow them to do so, no re-visioning of what pastoral counseling may become in the life of the congregation will ever occur.

What, then, is the experience that pastoral counseling affords, which is integral to the life of the congregation? My answer is simple:

It is the experience of telling stories within a constructive framework.
Pastoral counseling, like all other forms of psychotherapy, involves
storytelling, but also, like other forms of psychotherapy, it involves
giving some prior thought and continuing attention to the framework
in which this storytelling occurs. In contrast to much gossip, which
also involves storytelling, pastoral counseling is attentive to the fact
that, while storytelling can be a very worthwhile thing, there are certain dangers involved in it as well, and the counselor's responsibility
is to see that these dangers are minimized so that the benefits of the
storytelling may be maximized. This entails creating a constructive
framework within which personal storytelling takes place.[4]

Storytelling also occurs in pastoral care. It typically occurs when
a pastor goes to visit a member who is in the hospital or homebound.
It also occurs when a member mentions a personal problem to the
pastor during the after-worship coffee hour, or before or after a committee meeting. Such events are usually not viewed as pastoral counseling, but as acts of pastoral care. The distinction is a valuable one
as it allows us to ask whether pastoral counseling provides an experience that is integral to the life of the congregation which is different from the experience that pastoral care provides. Pastoral care has
a tradition that is as long and distinguished as that of preaching, and
is not in any danger of being considered incidental to the life of the
congregation. But pastoral counseling is in a much more tenuous situation, and one way to frame our question of whether it provides an
experience that is integral to the life of the congregation is to ask
whether the experience that pastoral counseling offers is distinct
from that which pastoral care provides.

I believe that the answer to this question is yes, and that the difference is that, in pastoral counseling, the persons involved in the
storytelling event agree that there will be a systematic effort to interpret the story so that new understandings of the story will occur. In
pastoral care, the minister listens to the story that is being told and
responds to its basic factualness. If a homebound person tells the
pastor about how she feels today in contrast to how she felt last
week, the pastor has no reason to question or challenge the veracity
of her story. The pastor is there, by and large, to listen and to offer
assurances that the congregation is keeping her in their prayers. If a
mother tells the pastor at coffee hour that she is concerned about the

religious group with which her daughter has affiliated herself at college, this story, too, is pretty much taken for what it is represented to
be, and the pastor responds accordingly (that is, by offering or soliciting information about the religious group in question).

Thus, while pastoral care also affords a constructive environment
for the storytelling, it tends to take the other's story at face value, and
does not make an effort to connect the present story to an implicit
story that may lie behind it. This is surely not to minimize the value
of pastoral care, for there is often a need for the experience of having
our story taken at face value and responded to accordingly. In fact, we
often resent the efforts of a listener to make more of the story we tell
about ourselves than appears to be there. We expect the other to
respond to its matter-of-factness, and not to try to read between the
lines. If we are in the hospital, or homebound, we want the pastor to
listen to our account of our illness and to assure us of God's presence
with us. We do not expect any more—or less—than this.

With pastoral counseling, the storytelling has a different purpose.
In this context, we *are* asking for something more than a listening ear
and a word of assurance. We want the pastor to join with us in interpreting the story we tell, and we hope that the pastor, by virtue of her
training and experience, will be able to see things in the story that we
cannot see. On the basis of this interpretation, we may also expect
that the pastor will offer some suggestions or advice. If the pastor
believes there is no real problem there, or nothing really to be concerned about, we want this also to be said. When our stories about
ourselves are interpreted, we feel that we ourselves are being interpreted. We have this experience of being interpreted when we hear a
sermon that truly relates to our own situation. But, in this case, what
we are experiencing is a connection or relationship between our own
story and the sermon story—whether a biblical story or a story about
other persons or even a hypothesized "typical" person—whereas, in
pastoral counseling, the story *is* our own story.

Is the experience of telling one's story and opening it up for interpretation truly integral to the life of the congregation? I believe that
it is, but that, heretofore, we have not made a strong case for this, in
part because pastoral counseling has not been widely understood in
terms of storytelling. It is only in recent years that therapists have
made the point that all forms of psychotherapy or counseling involve

storytelling, and thus all counseling is at least to some degree hermeneutical (that is, concerned with interpretation). I want to make a case for the importance to the congregation's life of the opportunity to tell one's story in a constructive context, one in which constructive interpretation occurs. Then, having made this case, I want to make some practical suggestions for how this may occur in the congregational setting. These suggestions will address the objections noted earlier relating to the issue of the pastor's limitations in terms of time and training.

The approach to pastoral counseling I present here is quite congruent, at least in time and effort expended, with what most parish ministers are already doing. I have no desire whatsoever to challenge or persuade pastors to spend a lot more time doing pastoral counseling, for this would be counterproductive, as it would be in my own situation as a seminary professor. Not only would it endanger one's effectiveness in other aspects of one's ministry, but it would also increase the danger that the counseling may take an inappropriate course, or result in a compromising situation between a pastor and a parishioner. While reliable data is hard to come by, one study shows that about 13 percent of parish clergy have been sexually involved with a parishioner. In contrast, 5 percent of psychotherapists have had such involvements.[5]

Most of the situations that I will present in this book involve one or two counseling sessions. Those that exceed this number either involved serious trauma (for instance, a young girl who was sexually molested at a shopping mall) or involved a disciplinary problem that necessarily played itself out over the course of the school year (in this case, counseling sessions were not scheduled weekly, but were spread out over several months). This means that at least in terms of expenditure of time and energy, what parish ministers customarily do and the way narrative-oriented therapists go about their work is quite similar. Obviously, these therapists see more clients, and have more specialized training in knowing what makes problems persist, but, in terms of form and scope, the similarities are greater than the differences. These similarities do not, in and of themselves, establish the value or usefulness of these particular therapeutic approaches for the congregational context, but they do encourage us to give serious thought to this very possibility.

What we need to ask is, *In what ways* might these narrative counseling approaches be valuable and useful for counseling in the congregational context? By framing the question in this way, we avoid any suggestion that pastors need to take these approaches whole, or that they need to identify themselves as Ericksonian, Watzlawickian, or de Shazerian (the three models explored in this book). I think we learned from the experiences of the 1960s, when pastors were self-identifying with various counseling models (client-centered, logotherapy, rational-emotive, and so forth), that it is not a good idea for pastors to become wedded to a particular counseling model or approach. For one thing, pastors have the freedom, which many full-time counselors do not have, *not* to identify with any particular model or approach, and this freedom should not, in my view, be easily or unthinkingly sacrificed. For another, there is always the danger that one may come to believe that one's chosen model is inherently expressive of the Christian faith, a situation not unlike that of ethicists who believe that a particular economic system (capitalism, socialism, and so forth) is inherently Christian. My own personal view of the matter is a pragmatic one, that is, if an approach is effective and is congruent with fundamental Christian values, one may well choose to use it. If it fails either of these two tests, then we should not use it, and, in any case, we are under no obligation to confine ourselves to a single method or approach.[6]

I believe that what makes the narrative approaches to be explored here valuable and useful for counseling in the congregational context is that they invite us—as pastors—to reflect on how we "story" our own lives and those of the persons to whom we seek to be of some assistance. In the following chapters, I will discuss three ways in which lives get "storied." One is *inspirationally*, another is *paradoxically*, and a third is *miraculously*. The value of all three is that they are inherently hopeful; that is, they do not accept the view that our lives are to be ultimately despaired of.[7] But each has a somewhat different, if not entirely distinctive, way of envisioning what it means to have hope in the face of life's inevitable problems and adversities, and these differences will be highlighted in our discussion of these approaches.

Some of us are especially moved by "inspirational" stories. We resonate deeply with stories about persons who met a challenging situation in their lives and not only overcame it but were made stronger in the process, and thus are better prepared to face the next difficulty or crisis. Others of us are especially captivated by the paradoxes of life. We find these paradoxes challenging, not only intellectually but also emotionally. We find ourselves or someone we know caught in a dilemma and we wonder if there is any truly graceful way out of it, and, if so, will we or they be able to find it? Still others of us live for the miraculous. We are impressed by the fact that miracles have been known to occur and that they often happen to persons who have been willing to contribute to their realization. When they happen, we are especially impressed with how a problem that had felt so weighty and interminable has so completely resolved itself.

I believe that of these three ways of "storying" lives, each of us has our own favored type, largely because it is the way in which we see our own lives evolving. We need make no apologies for this perception of our own lives to those who see their lives evolving in another mode. By the same token, when you and I engage in pastoral counseling, we have an obligation to maintain a kind of free-floating attention to all three types, neither denigrating or attempting to redirect our counselees toward our own personal viewpoint. In this sense, our very awareness of these three story types may enable us to be more "text-focused" than "reader-focused" (as de Shazer puts it), thus allowing the one who has come to us to determine how the broad outlines of our conversation together will itself be storied. This does not, however, mean that we have no power to guide or influence the process, for perhaps the most important thing we gain from our awareness of these story types is not the type itself, but the art that is manifest in and through it. As pastoral counselors, our primary task is to be attentive listeners—to hear the counselees' stories in all their experiential richness and complexity—but, secondarily, we also want to be of help to the degree that we are able. Three ways of being helpful, which are directly related to the three story types, are the judicious use of (1) the arts of the power of suggestion, (2) the untying of paradoxical knots, and (3) the discernment of the exceptions. Many of the problems and issues that parishioners bring to parish pastors can be ameliorated by the self-conscious use of one or another of these forms of artistry. And let us not forget that these are the very arts that Jesus used to heal the sick, to encourage the discouraged, to adjudicate disputes, and to proclaim that there are already signs that a new world is dawning.

In short, the preferred story world of the person or persons who seek our assistance has an important influence on the objectives that we set for our counseling work. But this does not mean that we cannot make use of our own individuality, including our own preferred ways of thinking about problems, and our own creative ideas for how to work toward solutions. One problem with many of the pastoral counseling texts written for pastors in the past was that they were so precisely and schematically laid out that they threatened to stifle the individuality of the pastor who tried to apply them.

The figures whom I will discuss in this book—Erickson, Watzlawick, and de Shazer—allow their own individuality to express itself in their counseling work, and no doubt their personality differences account to a large extent for their differences in style and approach. As I will demonstrate, each one's individuality is reflected in the type of story he tells or privileges. Even as a novel by Jane Austen is immediately recognizable, and distinguishable from a novel by, say, Henry James, so an Erickson story is readily distinguishable from a Watzlawick story, and a Watzlawick story from a de Shazer story. This is true in spite of the fact that they share some common assumptions about what makes for effective therapy, and in spite of the fact that they are seeing persons with similar problems. These differences between the three figures discussed in this book should disabuse us of the idea that there is one right way to do pastoral counseling, or that there is a certain standard against which we need to evaluate our individual achievements as counselors.

The figures whom I will discuss in this book are also *innovative*. They are not reluctant to try something that they haven't tried before, even realizing that it may be ineffective. Some years ago, a student whom I had gotten to know quite well through classes came to me with a request. He and his fiancée were to be married during the summer, and his home pastor had agreed to officiate at the wedding. But the two of them felt the need for some premarital counseling, and he wondered if I would do this for them. I agreed, and suggested that we plan to meet together three times, at roughly two-week intervals.[8] Then I suggested that it might be nice for us to do this at a local restaurant, and I proposed that I would pay for our dinners, this being my "wedding gift" to them. I no longer recall what my reasons were for this suggestion. It might have been a selfish one—that is, because I don't especially like to return to my campus office in the evening. (If so, Oscar Wilde's aphorism "Selfishness is not living as one wishes to live, it is asking others to live as one wishes to live" is apropos).

What I discovered from this "experiment" is that I felt I learned much more about how the two of them related to one another in this real-life setting than I could possibly have learned by talking with them in my office. There was the way he helped her on with her coat, the way they ordered their meals, the way each of them responded to the waiter—many, many things that I would not have noticed otherwise. As for the objection that the setting was too public and would inhibit discussion of very personal matters, this was simply not the case. No doubt it helped that we had a private booth in the back corner of the restaurant, but neither of them felt inhibited from talking about the personal issues that they, and I, wanted us to cover. An unexpected dividend was that when one or the other went to the restroom, I was able to ask one, in their partner's absence, whether we were discussing the issues that most concerned them, and whether there might be something each would like to share with me privately.

For me, at the time, this was an innovative approach to doing premarital counseling. For some pastors, this may be something they are already doing, or perhaps they have devised some other innovation. The point is not that I am advocating that every pastor do premarital counseling in a local restaurant, but that we exercise our freedom to innovate, to try different ways of doing counseling. Jay Efran et al. say this:

> There is nothing sacred about an office. Sometimes there are other locations that provide more suitable environments for moving an inquiry forward. We have no hesitation about leaving the office when necessary. For instance, we have taken a number of phobic clients to a nearby amusement park—Six Flags *Great Adventure*. It is a phobic's nightmare. There are giant Ferris wheels, sky rides, roller coasters and "free-fall" machines—and it's all safety-checked and well-insured. Our aim in going there is *not* to extinguish fears or systematically desensitize clients, but rather to make available to phobic clients the adult equivalent of monkey bars. There are opportunities to test and

challenge oneself—to conduct mini-experiments in reactivity and survival methods. A person can confront his or her belief systems and study the strategies by which they were formed and sustained. We think of it as an elaborate laboratory facility with sophisticated equipment. Best of all, it has been made available to us at low cost—the price of admission.[9]

I realize that most parish pastors' schedules are already so full in the evenings that they simply could not spend three rather leisurely evenings in a restaurant doing premarital counseling. But my point is that I had done something that was, for me, quite innovative, and I think that we all felt—I certainly did—that there was something spiritual about our having done premarital counseling in the context of table fellowship.[10]

There is also the issue of *intimidation*, of how easily we become intimidated when we face the prospect of becoming involved in pastoral counseling. I have spoken with countless pastors who have told me that what they learned to do early in their careers was to make good referrals. This meant, of course, that they met with a troubled parishioner once, and that the purpose of this meeting was for the pastor to gain a sufficient sense of what the problem was so that he could refer his parishioner to a professional therapist in the community. I do not wish to denigrate the idea of making good referrals, and I have no desire to criticize a pastor who sees a parishioner only once. In fact, several of the successful cases I will present in this book involved only one counseling session. But I *do* think that a certain amount of intimidation lies behind the "good referral" model of pastoral counseling, especially when it is used exclusively. It is certainly true that, in using this method, these pastors have been able to avoid the danger of becoming inappropriately involved with a parishioner. But what this "good referral" model communicates is that pastoral counseling is *not* an essential aspect of pastoral ministry, for the referral of everyone who comes to the pastor to talk about a personal problem carries the implicit message that there is no real place for counseling in the ministry of the church. It is also, I believe, a defensive, reactive stance, for which the pastoral counseling movement itself is partly to blame. If pastoral counseling "specialists" present parish pastors with very unrealistic pastoral counseling models (in terms of time and energy required), we should not be surprised when pastors respond by choosing to do as little pastoral counseling as possible: "If I can't do it 'right' [that is, the way the experts say it must be done], then no one can blame me for choosing not to do it at all."

In this book, therefore, I will set forth an image of what pastoral counseling can be that not only is realistic, but also recognizes that many of the problems which parishioners bring to their pastors may *not* require a referral. Referrals are often based on the pastor's acceptance of the parishioner's own diagnosis of the problem. But what if this is not in fact the problem? What if the parishioner's self-diagnosis is based on an inappropriate assumption? When a pastor makes referrals routinely, there is the risk that a parishioner will not follow through on it and thus get no help whatsoever. It may also communicate, whether intentionally or not, that a parishioner's problem is a very big problem, requiring specialized treatment. Whenever a pastor is tempted to make a routine referral, she should be aware that the problem itself may come to be reconfigured in the very process of exploring the client's story.

Another form of intimidation comes from those who insist that counseling must be distinctively, uniquely Christian, and who therefore make a firm distinction between "Christian" and "secular" counseling. Even pastors who do not subscribe to this distinction may find themselves feeling intimidated by the Christian counseling movement, as it may cause them to doubt whether what they are doing is "pastoral" if, for example, they do not cite the Scriptures or pray with a counselee. In this book, I will make frequent allusions to the similarities between Erickson, Watzlawick, and de Shazer and the healing ministry of Jesus. If such similarities come readily to mind, we need not feel defensive when we choose *not* to cite the Scriptures or engage in prayer with our counselees. It is not the formalism, but the form, of what we do that ultimately matters.

But perhaps the greatest intimidation of all comes from within ourselves, from our fears and uncertainties about whether we have the capacity to listen with genuine empathy to the stories that our parishioners have to tell about themselves. There is something about talking with another person about their life story that makes us feel unusually vulnerable. Will I be able truly to listen? Will I be able to respond appropriately and helpfully? Will the conversation reveal my own inadequacies, my own blind spots, my own shallowness? I think that such fears derive from an imaginary boundary that we have created between ourselves and the one with whom we are conversing. Especially helpful to me toward minimizing (if not overcoming) my own fears and uncertainties is an observation by Carl R. Rogers in his autobiographical essay "This is Me" in *On Becoming a Person*. In discussing the various things he has learned from his experience of listening to clients, he notes:

> Somewhere here I want to bring in a learning which has been most rewarding, because it makes me feel so deeply akin to others. I can word it this way. *What is most personal is most general.* There have been times when in talking with students or staff, or in my writing, I have expressed myself in ways so personal that I have felt I was expressing an attitude which it was probable no one else could understand, because it was so uniquely my own. . . . In these instances I have almost invariably found that the very feeling which has seemed to me most private, most personal, and hence most incomprehensible by others, has turned out to be an expression for which there is a resonance in many other people. It has led me to believe that what is most personal and unique in each one of us is probably the very element which would, if it were shared or expressed, speak most deeply to others. This has helped me to understand artists and poets as people who have dared to express the unique in themselves.[11]

Thus, when we listen to another tell her story, we are listening to our own. I would not want my own fears and uncertainties to deprive me of this unique opportunity to hear my own story from a different perspective, from a different voice.

If pastoral counseling involves the telling of personal stories within a constructive framework, it follows that pastors will be helped in their "hearing" of these stories if they have some knowledge of how stories, especially personal life stories, actually work. There are at least two ways by which one may acquire such knowledge. One is by reading autobiographies, as the reading of autobiographies helps us to see how people tell their life stories and especially how they place their life experiences within an interpretive framework. Another is by becoming familiar with some of the work that therapists are now doing in the area of story. I believe that we are currently witnessing a shift of emphasis among family therapists from a systemic model to a narrative or story model, and that it is valuable for pastors of

congregations to know something about these more recent developments. This is not to say that the systemic models are obsolete or of
doubtful value, for many of the situations that pastors encounter
continue to lend themselves to systemic analysis and interpretation.
But it is to say that a great deal of attention is now being paid by
family therapists to the fact that therapy involves storytelling. Much
of this new literature can be very useful to the pastor for pastoral
counseling purposes, especially in clarifying what it means to say
that pastoral counseling in the congregational context involves locat-
ing personal stories within a constructive interpretive framework.

In this book, I have chosen to focus on the second of these two
resources, as I believe that most pastors will perceive that the therapy literature has a greater practical utility than the autobiographical literature. I hope in the future, however, to write another book
in which I explore the uses of written autobiographies for pastoral
ministry, as I believe that autobiographies provide an important
conceptual bridge between the story approach to counseling and the
master story that frames the life of every Christian, the biblical text
itself.[12]

In chapter 1, I will introduce some of the new work being done on
story by authors trained in the family therapy tradition. Besides introducing these representative examples of the current interest of family
therapists in story, I also attempt in this chapter to reconcile family
therapy and client-centered therapy, the latter of which played a very
significant role in the 1950s through 1970s in supporting the very
idea that parish ministers may legitimately engage in the activity
called "pastoral counseling." Chapters 2–4 will focus on selected figures in the brief therapy movement, a major force within family therapy. I suggest that each of these figures works out of a particular story
frame, and thus tends to elicit a particular type of story from his
clients. In others words, when they listen to their clients tell about
their reasons for seeking counseling, they hear the story in a certain
predetermined way and have a certain prejudgment as to how they
would expect or hope to have the story come to a satisfactory conclusion. Thus, Milton H. Erickson privileges the *inspirational* story;
Paul Watzlawick, the *paradoxical* story; and Steve de Shazer, the *miracle* story. All three are committed to helping their clients find new
grounds, or recover old grounds, for hope, but they do so through the

different lenses provided by their preferred story type. By presenting all three types, I signal that I favor an eclectic approach on the part of the pastoral counselor, as this enables the pastor to be more responsive to the uniqueness of each individual counselee, or to their unique circumstances at the moment they seek the pastor out for counseling.

Chapter 5 addresses the problem of gossip, a common form of storytelling within the life of the congregation. While gossip is usually detrimental to congregational life because it involves storytelling that is inherently destructive, this is not always the case. Sometimes it plays the same constructive role in the life of a social group that I am claiming for pastoral counseling. Thus, gossip provides a valuable lens through which to identify both the constructive role of pastoral counseling as well as the dangers that are inherent in it.

An epilogue on the paradox of pastoral power focuses on the need for pastoral counseling to be appropriately limited, especially in terms of its objectives, so that it avoids ascribing too much significance to the counselor–counselee relationship in effecting change, and too much reliance on the counseling process to do for the counselee what the congregation does through its other expressions and forms of life.

Finally, a word about the title that I have chosen for this book: When I began going to movie theaters as a boy, all of the films were in black and white. When films in color began to appear, advertisements in the newspapers would announce that they were in "living color." What did this phrase "living color" mean? "Living" as opposed to what? I imagine that those who coined the phrase wanted to make the point that these new films, unlike those in black and white, would look true to life, for the world itself appears to us in color (even on the gray days). But the phrase "living color" also has a note of hyperbole, of melodrama, that somehow the same *events* that we previously viewed in black and white will now somehow come alive, become more vivid and dramatic. These events will now "live" on a plane previously unrealized in the black-and-white films.

My title, *Living Stories*, has similar connotations. On the one hand, it suggests that our lives are stories—and that what each of us lives, each in our own ways, is a story—or, better, a whole lot of stories loosely strung together to make a sort of whole. This is the real—or realistic—meaning of the title. It simply says what is true. But the title has another more hyperbolic meaning, containing the suggestion that lives—yours and mine—can come alive, become more vivid and dramatic, less humdrum and boring, more fully realizing of their potential. The difference between meaning A and meaning B is captured in these two reactions to a story: "That's a pretty interesting story" and "My, what a powerful story!" The exclamation point speaks volumes. This book, then, is about helping persons in our congregations to experience life as a living story, and seeks to provide some guidance to pastors about how they may help others experience the movement from meaning A to meaning B. It is my hope that this book will assist pastors in coming to a greater conscious awareness of how and why this movement occurs, thus enabling them to help to make it happen more often than it happens merely by chance, and to articulate more effectively to their congregations why pastoral counseling is a good use of the pastor's time and a good thing for the whole congregation, including those who may never request it for themselves.

Chapter 1

The Stories Clients Tell

T he narrative approach to counseling advocated by family therapists is reflected in the work of Janine Roberts, Patricia
O'Hanlon Hudson and William Hudson O'Hanlon, and Alan
Parry and Robert E. Doan, authors whose writings I will discuss in
this chapter.[1] These are only three of the many books that have been
written in recent years on a narrative-oriented therapy, but they
demonstrate the fact that story has become a widely used construct,
especially among family therapists, and is being used in a variety of
constructive and creative ways. The authors that I will present here
have different ways of accounting for this new interest in narrative.
Parry and Doan are especially concerned to locate this interest within an analysis (and critique) of postmodernism, while Roberts is especially concerned with the fact that clients come to therapy with very
different "cultural stories," and thus very different assumptions about
how their future stories might evolve. In other words, she tends to
focus more on the multicultural aspect of contemporary society in the
United States. While Hudson and O'Hanlon are less inclined to
attribute interest in narrative to cultural factors (indeed, they point to
the fact that they have found acceptance for their ideas in many countries throughout the world, suggesting that "In relationships it seems,
to echo Harry Stack Sullivan, that we are all simply more human than
otherwise"[2]), they *do* note that they have been much influenced by
social constructivist theories, and that this accounts both for their differences from behaviorism and their emphasis on narratives:

Couples come to us with views that have been influenced by their social/familial interactions and language-based constructions of their situations. We are attempting to enter into those constructed views and to influence them in certain directions. Couples have written certain love stories. We help them rewrite those stories.[3]

Janine Roberts begins her book, *Tales and Transformations*, with a story about how she came to be interested in storytelling as a resource in family therapy. She was working with the nurse in a school in Newark, New Jersey, as a VISTA volunteer. Twin brothers in the school, Kevin and Keith, had rickets. The nurse wanted Janine to work with their mother, Lavinia, to see if the boys could get medical treatment. The family had no phone, so the next day she walked over to their apartment.

Lavinia invited Janine in, and went to get her purse. She took an old plastic sheet from her purse and handed it to Janine. Inside was a yellowed piece of newspaper. At the top of the clipping was a picture of Lavinia holding Kevin and Keith when they were born. The story told how she had more children than anyone else in the city—twenty-two—including three sets of twins. Lavinia watched Janine carefully as she read this introduction to this woman who had been born in the South to a sharecropper's family and had come north as a young woman looking for a better life. Roberts comments on this story:

We all need to be seen and heard, to be known for our unique life experiences. We all carry our stories with us and when we tell them to others they have the power to link us together. Over the years that I have been an actress, teacher, then family therapist, the story of Lavinia and her children has stayed with me as a reminder of how central a role our stories play to pull together the events of our lives and connect us to others. As Lavinia watched and listened to see how I would hear and react to her story, and I in turn watched and listened to her response, we began to see what kind of relationship we could have together.[4]

As a family therapist, Roberts has found that story plays a very prominent role in family therapy: "Since it is impossible to talk about a problem without telling a story, stories are central to therapy."[5] As clients tell, write, and read the texts of their lives, their stories become a wonderfully versatile tool that helps them to reflect on where they have been, where they want to go, as well as creates a collaborative therapeutic relationship. In this mobile society, regardless of the changes of locations and varieties of transitions in families, people always have their stories with them. Furthermore, work with stories can be done with any model of treatment and is a dynamic technique that can be used with a wide range of ages.[6]

The focus of her book is not on teaching therapists how to create and tell therapeutic stories, but on evoking the client's reflective and inventive capacities for making use of their own tales. She is especially interested in family stories that capture the particular events of a group of people as they live through the larger social, political, and economic changes of an era. These stories offer possibilities for interpreting and making meaning of individual lives and family dynamics, and to take account of the influences of historical events (for instance, economic depression, national wars, and so forth) on their respective lives.

Roberts notes that each member of a family usually tells the story of an event differently. In couples therapy, one often finds that the two individuals look at the same set of events very differently. In one case, the wife told the story of a marriage that involved their moving year after year because of her husband's employment. She felt as though she had followed him, uprooting for the sake of his career, and now she wanted him to pay more attention to her and her needs. But, according to his story, she had wanted the upward mobility that his job promotions guaranteed, and her current dissatisfactions came at the worst possible moment because the national recession that had forced job layoffs in his company meant that he was actually working two jobs within the organization. Roberts suggests that the therapist's role is to let the number of perspectives that clients bring be told, and then to help them construct new meanings that work better for them. Clients report that what therapy did for them was to provide a place where they could put out their different views and not get into a fight over them. Because the therapist did not take sides, it enabled them to listen to the story as the other told it. As one couple expressed it, "We needed someone like you who didn't already have a set version of the right story."[7]

In counseling *individuals*, the fact that there are two sides to every story may not be the issue, but this does not mean that the therapist is any less concerned with alternative versions of the story. As Roberts points out, we, as individuals, have our characteristic ways of telling our individual or family stories, and oftentimes what we need is to be able to tell stories in a way that is more helpful. She identifies the various "story styles" that she typically encounters in therapy with individuals, couples, and families.

Six Types of Stories

Intertwined. The intertwined story style is where one story is linked to another, but the storyteller may not be aware that she is connecting them, or, even if she is aware, she many not know the real basis on which she is doing so. A young mother who was unmercifully teased as a child by her older sister reacts to a similar situation involving her two children by jumping into the middle of their disagreements to protect the youngest child. Her two stories—one as a child and one as a mother—are intertwined, but, in this case, the storyteller was unaware of the connection between them until it was pointed out by her therapist. Then the therapist helped her to respect the integrity of each story, allowing it to stand on its own, so that she could make a more informed judgment as to what her role should be in relation to her children's disagreements.

Roberts notes that stories may be intertwined by virtue of their similarity, as in this particular case, but they may also be intertwined because they are perceived as opposites to one another. A client may tell a story about how her mother was intrusive and controlling toward her when she was a child, and then relate how she has bent over backwards not to violate her children's privacy or tell them what to do. In this case, the woman is aware of the opposition between the two stories, because she vowed she would never do to *her* children what her mother had done to her. She has succeeded in keeping her vow, but Roberts cautions that

> When stories are too richly cross-joined, the first story seems to over-whelm the second story with interpretations of behavior and actions and with its own emotional field. People involved in the second story then find few possibilities of coming to their own meaning-making of

the events of their lives. The meaning has already been passed on from the first story.[8]

Roberts suggests that the therapist might ask the client how the two stories influence one another and whether the influence is helpful or not. She may also invite the client to consider how her telling of the story would be different if it did not trigger the other, earlier stories.

Distinct/Separated. A second story style is the distinct/separated story. It represents the opposite end of the continuum from intertwined stories. Stories that are connected are not perceived as such, and the client therefore lacks access to an important level of meaning about his life. A man who was ten years old when his father abandoned the family after serving in the Vietnam War finds himself wanting to spend very little time on family activities and experiencing powerful urges to go off on his own. When the therapist makes the connection between the two events, noting that his sons are about the same age that he had been when his father left the family, the man saw things he had never recognized before. He realized that his father's departure left him without any ideas about how to be a father to his two sons. Roberts recommends that the therapist encourage the client to explore the significance of the earlier experience for the current life story, and to consider how the current story, when viewed in light of the earlier story, might be different in emotional tone, expected outcome, or possibilities for the future.

Minimal/Interrupted. A third story style is the minimal/interrupted story. Here the problem is that the client does not have much access to stories concerning an aspect of her life that has bearing on her present complaint. A woman—an only child—in treatment for depression had very little to tell about her growing-up years or her parents. Both parents were older and had died when she was in her early twenties. As it seemed to her and her therapist that her depression might be connected to her childhood, especially to how feelings were expressed in her family, finding out from living relatives that her parents were ecstatic when she was conceived because they had been trying for a number of years to have a child encouraged her. As her collection of family stories multiplied, she was able to envision a wider range of possibilities for her own current and future life story.

Roberts' notes that contacting relatives and old acquaintances and reading old family letters may be helpful in resurrecting buried stories. Photographs and other artifacts are also valuable tools to stimulate one's own recollections. Some stories are minimal or interrupted because they relate to traumas or estrangements. But even in the case of stories that cannot be retrieved, the therapist may still ask the client to imagine the lost story and to ask herself what difference this way of imagining the events makes for her current life story.

Silenced/Secret. The fourth style, silenced/secret, has to do with stories, usually family stories, that are hidden and secret. What makes them not only fascinating but powerful is that the themes associated with these silenced stories play central roles in family dramas. Roberts tells about her brother Mark who left the alcohol treatment center where he had been staying and disappeared from family contact for nine years. The family imagined that he might be dead. Then one night Roberts received a phone call from Mark and, as they talked, he kept telling her how he had always felt so left out and alone in the family. In the meantime, she had learned that her parents had decided to give Mark up for adoption when he was born because they were having a very serious marital crisis—her father had moved out and was living with another woman. But the obstetrician was very upset with their decision to put the child up for adoption, and insisted that the mother nurse her newborn baby while she remained in the hospital. Four days after the birth, the parents decided to try to reconcile their differences and they brought the baby home. Yet, though they remained together, they could not agree on how to parent Mark, and these disagreements went far beyond the usual parental discord. If Mark felt left out and alone in the family, this was an accurate perception of the reality of the situation. In a sense, it was a minor miracle that he was in the family at all.

Mark did not know about any of this, but when his sister Janine told him the story the night that he called, events in his life that were otherwise meaningless or strange began to fit together. Roberts emphasizes the complex issues of safety involved in the decision to bring these secret stories out into the open. Besides the decision how, whom, and when to tell, there are questions that the therapist may ask the client to help discern the meaning of the story for his life today. These include asking why and by whom the story was silenced, and what effect this silencing has had on the client and on other family members.

Rigid. A fifth story style is the rigid story. These are stories that are told over and over in much the same way. The text is known and there are set interpretations. Frequently, two or more family members tell it in exactly the same way, though it is also frequently the case that one person is considered to be in a privileged position to tell it, and no other persons are allowed to tell it, nor is anyone permitted to challenge this official version. In one family, the father told his son Tom many times how no one came to his own high school graduation to hear him play the trumpet, and how he worked like a servant in the family restaurant. Tom had heard these stories so many times that he knew them by heart. It seemed to Tom, who is the client, that his father was so stuck on the theme of his own childhood deprivations that he couldn't get into his own fathering role. The therapist suggested that Tom gently interrupt his father's stories of deprivation and ask him about times in his life when he had felt supported by others. Roberts also suggests that the therapist take the same story and provide it with a different meaning, even a different ending. If Tom has suspected that his father tells the story as a way to communicate to him about his own parenting, Tom might consider other possible meanings to the stories. His father may be unaware of some of these meanings, such as his belief that he had to develop a great deal of self-reliance, and has, perhaps, in his own way, helped Tom to develop qualities of self-reliance too.

Evolving. A sixth type of story is the evolving story. This involves recognition that the story is different at different times in life, that the meaning of the story is always open to reinterpretation. The same event—for example, parents divorcing when the client was a small child—may be understood very differently as the client goes through life and acquires new experiences and perspectives that allow her to reinterpret the story or place it in a new context of meaning. How we reinterpret the stories of experiences that happened in the past provides insight into what we are becoming, and how we ourselves are changing over time. As Roberts points out,

"Stories are relatively simple formats that illuminate complex inter-actional patterns. They locate us in our lives. They tell us where we have come from and articulate central themes and values." At the same time, these stories from the past "can provide the foundation for new stories, new ideas, and beliefs to be shared."[9] The therapist may support and stimulate this idea that our stories are always evolving by asking how the stories have changed over time, what in the client's family or community life has supported this evolving process, and how these stories might be told at some future time. It is clear that Roberts values the evolving story type because she believes in the importance of change, both at the individual and the family level. Rigid stories keep individuals and families locked in the past. Evolving stories open them to new future possibilities. But her openness to change does not mean that she thinks the old stories that clients carry with them are of no worth. On the contrary, "Understanding what has been given to us through the stories in our lives, while having an ongoing dialogue about the new stories that are being created, lets us both hold the past and move on with the present and future."[10]

Theme Stories and Cohering Stories

In addition to these six story styles, Roberts identifies two ways in which the therapist may help the client achieve a storytelling focus. One is to encourage *theme stories*. These are stories that center around the content of the problems that clients bring to therapy. This is a common technique used by stand-up comedians, who may tell several stories on the theme of spousal relationships, then tell sever-al more on the theme of politics, and then complete their routine with stories on the theme of their own lack of self-esteem. In thera-py, of course, the problems that clients have brought to therapy are no laughing matter, but therapists often do find that several small stories having a common theme may lead to more significant insights than one blockbuster of a story.

Roberts tells about an older couple whose marriage was the second for both. They had been married five years when they came for ther-apy. The problem that they brought to the first session was that they were constantly disputing with one another over financial matters.

They were especially conflicted over the fact that they had moved into Albert's house when they were married but the house remained in his name only. The therapist asked each of them to tell a story about what money had meant in the family when they were growing up, including how money may have been experienced differently by the men and women in their respective families. Both told stories of growing up in families where money always seemed to be a problem, but there were differences. In Albert's family, his father was an immigrant who always squirreled his money away for fear he would run short, and never told his wife about how it was being acquired or spent. Bernadette told of how her parents lost their house and their savings in the Great Depression of the 1930s and never recouped. She felt they were ambivalent about money, that having money usually brought trouble down on them rather than security. Once these differences were identified, the therapist helped Albert look at why it might be hard for him to be clear about what he had and to share it with Bernadette, while Bernadette began to recognize her own ambivalent feelings about money—why she wanted to press Albert to be more straightforward with her about money, but also why she wanted to avoid the subject altogether. Having identified these differences, they then set about finding an amicable solution, one that involved having Albert give Bernadette a monthly accounting of their financial situation so that she would not worry or suspect that Albert was hiding something from her.

By *cohering stories*, Roberts means stories that help clients cope with breaks or ruptures in their lives owing to family deaths, separations, trauma, or several difficult or stressful changes coming one right after the other. The cohering story is one that a client tells in order to communicate what is happening to her and to explore ways in which she might begin to put her life back together again. These are not well-crafted stories because the client is in too much emotional pain or confusion to be able to put a *coherent* story together. But it *is* a *cohering* story, one that is pulling threads from here and there as a way of making sense of what is going on. Where the thematic story is quite clear as far as basic content, the cohering story is more diffuse. Yet it is, in its own way, a narrative, as it tells a story about how one is experiencing the change that is occurring, and how things seem so different from what they were before the crisis or loss took place.

Cultural Stories: The Crucible for Personal Stories

Roberts devotes a whole chapter to the complex relationship between personal stories and cultural stories. She notes how for some members of our society the story style with which they grew up was the *silenced/secret* style, not because there was some carefully concealed family secret (for instance, illegitimacy, alcoholism, bankruptcy), but because there was a cultural matter that the family preferred not to talk about. A daughter whose father was in a barren desert internment camp near Delta, Utah, during World War II knew little about his experience as she was growing up, as the story was talked about neither in the larger society nor at home. She realized only years later the large impact this event had on her family and on herself.

In the United States at various times, it has been dangerous for people to acknowledge that they are members of certain groups. Gay and lesbian persons who have not openly declared their sexual orientation constantly monitor what parts of their stories to tell in the various social contexts in which they participate. They often experience an underlying tension between their fear of accusation and their quest for integrity and integration. But Roberts points out that it is not just a matter of whether there is danger in sharing stories, for it is important to have the possibility of a resonance between personal stories and cultural stories:

> It is hard to link past, present, and future in one's life when the cultural stories that frame one's experience are storied in stereotypical, inaccurate, narrow, and rigid ways. For instance, it is difficult for young Native Americans to imagine a multidimensional future when their . . . past life has been storied in a banal manner.[11]

Roberts emphasizes that therapy should not focus on the therapist's interpretation of cultural events, and that the client should interpret cultural events in order to determine how they resonate in her own life. But it is also important that the client experiences the therapist as having empathy for the cultural story, as well as a desire to help the client determine how she will use this story in her own life. A method that Roberts has found useful is to ask the client to imagine that she is from a very different cultural background and to think of how she might tell her personal story from this other point of view. An Asian American woman who was passed over for job promotions because she was not considered assertive enough was encouraged to think about how her experience would be different if she were, say, an Anglo American woman, an Asian American man, or an Anglo American man. The purpose of this method is not to put down other groups or encourage clients to see themselves as victims but to help the client articulate the role that culture plays in her personal story and perhaps to imagine other ways that she might deal with the problems she brings to therapy.

Roberts also discusses the responsibility that therapists have to go beyond the role of ethnographer of the individual lives of clients and to share clients' experiences with the larger society, especially those stories that have been silenced. Therapists who take stories outside the therapy room can break silences, help overcome individuals' sense of isolation, and help to create a social climate in which people do not blame themselves for larger social and cultural failures. She opposes the sensationalizing of personal stories by television talk shows, and argues instead for the style of disclosure that we find in responsibly written autobiographies and biographies. The stories need not be written down. They may be presented orally or even dramatized. But what autobiographers and biographers have traditionally done is to understand personal dilemmas within a wider cultural field. Looking at this larger frame

> often offers people opportunities to move out of blaming cycles— cycles in which they blame either themselves or others. As they see the various constraints or beliefs that affected people's lives, they begin to empathize with family and individual dilemmas and become less judgmental. It can also help them to see other kinds of interventions that may be needed, such as political or community action.[12]

Facts, Stories, Experience

Another valuable perspective on the stories that clients tell is found in *Rewriting Love Stories: Brief Marital Therapy,* by Patricia O'Hanlon Hudson and William Hudson O'Hanlon. They distinguish between three different aspects of people's situations: the *facts*, the *stories*, and *experience*.[13] The *facts* are those aspects of the situation that could be agreed upon by most observers by consensus. They constitute what most anyone would perceive with one's senses in any particular situation. The *stories* are the meanings and interpretations we give to those facts. The authors call them stories to make the point that they are not truths, but theories, constructs, and made-up hypotheses. *Experience* is the label they use to describe internal feelings, sensations, fantasies, automatic thoughts, and the sense of self that each person possesses.

In their brief marital therapy work, Hudson and O'Hanlon operate on the assumption that facts and stories (the interpretations we place on the facts) need to be clearly differentiated. One method they use to establish a factual baseline is what they call "video talk," or getting the client not to go beyond describing what one could see or hear on a videotape about the situation. This is an alternative to using vague words that are open to different interpretations or telling just so much of what happened that only one's own interpretation is possible. For example, a man has been seen having lunch with a woman who is not his wife on several occasions. This is the fact of the matter. The video-talk method is an attempt to establish this factual baseline. Everyone can agree on this. When we move beyond the observable fact, we begin to tell a story.

Another approach to achieving a distinction between facts and stories is to interrupt the storyteller when an interpretation is being made by saying, "or not." If the storyteller says, "These lunches are the beginning of an affair," the therapist may say, "But perhaps they are not. There may be some other explanation." This is an appeal for open-mindedness, for tentativeness, at this point in the conversation. A related approach is simply to say to the client, "For the moment, do not add any meanings to your description of the situation. I want us to be as clear as we can be about what happened." While these approaches might appear to be offensive to the client— "The therapist doesn't care what *I* think"—the effect is almost always the opposite. The client relaxes when she understands that the process will be conducted in an orderly fashion. First we will focus on the facts, then we will take up what the facts mean. The only client who is likely to be offended by this approach is one who believes there is only one way to understand the situation, and this is *his* way. (There are obvious parallels in this case with Roberts' *rigid* story type.)

If facts are the "what," stories are the "why." Stories, according to Hudson and O'Hanlon,

> are part of our ways of understanding the world and what happens in our lives. Each of us puts our experiences together in our own individualized way. We have different maps for the same terrain. One person might be looking at a topographical map while the other has a road map, yielding very different views—yet the territory remains the same."[14]

We also use stories "to explain what happens in our relationships and to guess at the future."[15] When problems develop, or when people disagree, it then becomes a matter of "dueling stories." Whose story is right and whose is wrong? This, say the authors, is itself the wrong way to approach it because, in relationships, when one person loses the right/wrong battle, the relationship itself usually loses. Stories are never neutral. They are *not* merely descriptive, merely an accounting of the facts. Sometimes the stories we tell are inflated, making it seem as though what happened was better or greater than it was. We tell such idealized stories about ourselves and we tell them about our spouses, children, and grandchildren as well. Oftentimes we tell stories that demean or discount others and ourselves as well. In a relationship, such stories, whether told out of frustration, anger, or hurt, can poison the relationship: "You're just like your mother!" "You care for *your* family more than you care for me." "You always need to be in control." These are, at best, half-truths (we probably *are* like our mothers in some ways but unlike them in others), and it may be the differences, not the similarities, that we most value in ourselves. If so, we feel discounted when only the similarities are pointed out.

In their practice, Hudson and O'Hanlon have found that there are "typical stories" that people use to explain relationship issues to themselves and others. *Mind reading* involves one person deciding that he knows what the other is thinking, feeling, experiencing, or intending, without having been given this information by the other person. A couple agreed (fact) that their fights usually began in the kitchen. According to the husband, they began when his wife gave him her "get-out-of-the-kitchen" look. The therapist (Patricia Hudson) suggested he check out this impression by asking her, each time she had this look, what she was actually thinking. When the couple returned the following week, they reported that about half the time she had this look she wasn't thinking of her husband at all but was eavesdropping on the children in the next room or thinking about some ingredient she had forgotten to buy for the dinner she was preparing.

Causal explanations involve deciding why something is happening or why oneself or someone else is doing or experiencing something. A wife explained her husband's lack of sexual demonstrativeness toward her on grounds that he came from a family of five brothers and no sisters: "He never learned how to behave around girls." When the therapist responded, "Then I would gather from this that he was never demonstrative," she thought for a moment, and said, "Well, come to think of it, he was very affectionate toward me when we were dating." When she abandoned her causal reasoning, she proceeded to tell how her husband was more affectionate toward his dog than he was toward her. The therapist, intrigued by this observation (fact), asked her to say more about how it was between her husband and his dog. "Well, when he comes home after work, the dog hears the car outside and runs to the door to meet him. Before you know it, the two of them are wrestling together on the living room floor." After a moment's pause—involving a sudden flash of insight—she laughed and said, "I think I'll try outracing that old mutt to the front door."[16] (Roberts would refer to this as making a connection between two seemingly unrelated stories, the one about how her husband was demonstrative when they were dating and the one about how her husband was demonstrative toward his dog.)

Predictions are statements that proclaim what will or will not happen in the future: "He'll never stop drinking." "If she gets a job, she won't stay with it for more than a few months." The mood is usually grim when one person says about another that the other will never change, but the sense that the future *could* be different from the past.

Labeling (or characterization) involves deciding what characteristic another person manifests and then stating it as a fixed, set quality: "He's narcissistic." "She's a moody person." "She has low self-esteem." "He's very stubborn." These are not necessarily wrong perceptions, but when they are used to define a person, they inevitably leave out other important qualities and they neglect to say that much of the time the other person is not narcissistic, or moody, or lacking self-esteem, or stubborn. In what ways are these terms appropriate and in what ways are they inappropriate? Under what conditions is he very stubborn? Might the fact that his stubbornness may be discerned in certain conditions be attributed to the equally important fact that in most other situations he is flexible and open to change? His stubbornness in this particular regard may be related to some underlying story from his past, for example, a situation when he felt very threatened or endangered. In light of this earlier story, his "stubbornness" might be interpreted by him as "resoluteness," "standing his ground," and so forth. For him, it may not have the negative characterological connotations that the word *stubborn* tends to convey.

Generalizations involve exaggerating to universals like "always," "never," "nobody," "everybody," "all the time": "Nobody cares about how this house looks but me." "He is never on time." "She's always charging up the credit cards." An interesting fact about generalizations is that if the therapist can get the storyteller to think of a single exception, then the generalization itself is challenged. If he was on time once, then "never" does not fit. If the storyteller responds by saying that the exception only proves the rule, the therapist's response to this is that the existence of the exception is evidence that the one being generalized about is fully capable of doing what the storyteller says he or she cannot do. While the therapist may seem here to be taking the side of the accused against the accuser, this defense of the accused always contains an implicit challenge: Will you now make it a point to be on time? Will you quit running up the charges on the credit card? The legitimacy of the complaint has not been contested, only the generalization itself has been. The fatalism that is often associated with such storytelling has also been implicitly challenged. The therapist has implied that the storyteller need not resign herself to the status quo. She need not be the only one who attends to the matter of making the house look nice.

Equivalences are where an abstract concept is assumed to have a simple, clearly defined meaning. "I just want her to be a *wife*—you know, cleaning the house, cooking, taking care of the kids." Or, "He isn't acting like a *husband* should. He thinks it's perfectly OK for him to go out with his buddies at night and leave me home alone." Or,

"*Love* is never having to say you're sorry." Or, "*Honesty* in a relationship means that you tell the other everything, even your inner-
most thoughts." The authors claim that exploring the equivalences
that people have for such abstract concepts as love, honesty, support,
selfishness, romance, fun, and so forth, takes up a large part of therapy. Sometimes they challenge the assertion. Is it really the case that
love is never having to say you're sorry? For one thing, this is a generalization, and, therefore, at a minimum, it should admit of at least
one exception, that is, where love has meant saying that one is truly
sorry. More difficult, perhaps, is challenging the storyteller's description of what it means to be a wife or husband. These are often deeply
rooted and they are usually not considered by the storyteller to be
open to challenge. "A wife who does not clean the house, cook, and
take care of the kids is not my definition of a wife." "A husband who
goes off in the evening to be with his buddies and leaves me home
alone is not my idea of a husband." The therapist, however, is not so
sure, as the therapist knows that there are in fact wives who do not
clean the house, cook, or take care of the kids. The therapist also
knows that there are *husbands* who clean the house, cook, and take
care of the kids. The very fact that such exceptions exist in the real
world challenges the equivalence that the storyteller is making
between the abstract concept and its supposedly clearly defined
meaning. This challenge, in turn, creates the opportunity for the couple to discuss together what *wife* and *husband* will mean for *them*
and for their own marriage.

Evaluations involve deciding that certain things are right or
wrong, good or bad, valuable or worthless. "Why do you watch
those stupid shows—they're such junk." "Your mother is a bad person." "Looking at pornography is wrong." The authors say that they
often help couples come to appreciate their differences about values,
for while there can be compromises in the area of actions, sometimes
differences in values, even with changes in actions, do not change:
"Difficulties often arise when one person forgets that values can differ and assumes his or her values are true and the partner is wrong
for not agreeing."[17] Also, when values do change, they tend to
change slowly and, over the course of a marriage, one person may
change more in one area while the other changes more in some other
area. The wife, for example, might become a vegetarian while the

husband continues to believe there isn't anything wrong with eating meat. Conflict may arise if she treats him as a moral inferior or if he complains that she is no longer the woman he married. The therapist can help them see that it is not imperative that they share all values in common (that is, that they are not expected to present a united moral front to the world), but also emphasize that we all change through the years, and it is hardly fair or appropriate to expect that the other will remain the person she was some twenty years ago, as though she were some inanimate statue.

Hudson and O'Hanlon refer to these as "typical stories" that clients use to explain situations that are causing difficulties or problems. The key word here is "explain," as these are all attempts to provide an explanation for what is taking place or going on. The problem is that these explanations are either incorrect, or, if there is some truth to them, they are not contributing much (if anything) to the resolution of the problem. In most instances, they actually exacerbate the problem, making it more difficult for the couple to find a solution that will be satisfying to both. This implies that most of us, especially when we are upset or angry, tell rather "bad" stories. Most of the typical stories that Hudson and O'Hanlon identify here would probably fall under Robert's heading of the "rigid" story type, as they are stories that refer to presumably fixed traits and behaviors, that portray the other characters in the story in stereotypical, one-dimensional ways, and that are almost totally lacking in imagination. These stories do not envision a changed future, but only explain, or attempt to explain, why the present is so grim and unacceptable.

On the other hand, the authors emphasize that stories are not all bad. Stories may hurt a relationship but they may also support it: "Clients will continue to generate stories after our treatment. We just want them to take their stories less seriously or generate ones that support their relationships and help them resolve their conflicts."[18] Their own job, as therapists, is to acknowledge each person's story and gently challenge those stories, so that they may develop new and better ones. They also acknowledge each person's experience (or core self) and respect it. They do not try to change it, and they try to persuade each of them to cease trying to change the core self of the other: "Instead, we focus our (and their) change attempts elsewhere. The elsewhere is on changing actions and changing stories."[19]

Several of Hudson and O'Hanlon's illustrations from their own sessions with clients support Janine Roberts's description of story styles. For example, William O'Hanlon had worked with a couple who had experienced physical violence in their marriage. The violence stopped, but about eight months after the couple had stopped seeing O'Hanlon on a regular basis, the wife came back alone because she wanted to be able to deal better with her husband's "moodiness." When they unpacked the word *moodiness*, it involved her husband's yelling at her and calling her nasty names. When O'Hanlon suggested that this, too, could change, the woman expressed doubts, indicating that she had decided she would just have to get used to it if she wanted to remain married to him. O'Hanlon knew that she was an excellent horse trainer, so he asked her what she would do if she were brought a horse that was impossible to train. She immediately answered, "There's no such thing as an impossible-to-train horse!" When he asked her how she trained difficult horses, she described the four simple principles that she followed. When she finished, O'Hanlon told her that she knew everything she needed to know about how to "train" her husband to stop being so "moody" and to speak respectfully toward her. For the authors, this example illustrates the uses of an analogy—horse training—to help a client find a view that would help her solve her marital problems.[20] But this case also fits with Roberts's view that when stories that are not perceived to be connected, but are *distinct* or *separated*, the client lacks access to an important source of insight into the story that brings her to therapy. The client's story of how to train a horse was very relevant to her story of her husband's moodiness and verbal abuse, but she had not seen the connection before. Once it is seen, it seems quite obvious, and one may well wonder why she did not see it beforehand.

In another case, a couple came for therapy because they felt that they were drifting apart. Karen was consumed by a career that she did not like but felt trapped in because the money was excellent. Earl was an elementary school teacher who found conversation difficult. The therapists asked them when they had found it easiest to talk together in the past. They agreed that they had their best conversation while on walks. The therapists suggested that they walk at least twice before their next session. They came back and reported that they had been talking much more easily both on walks and at home. They decided the problem was not so much their marriage but Karen's dissatisfaction with her job.[21]

For the authors, this case illustrates the process of looking for exceptions to the problem, for times when the current difficulty did not exist. Assuming that there *have* been times in the past when they were able to communicate (for, otherwise, they would not now be feeling that they were drifting apart), how did these times occur? What was peculiar or unique about them? In effect, the therapists were acting on their experience that generalizations are hardly ever totally true, that there are almost always exceptions. But this case also illustrates Roberts's idea that an experience in the past may have bearing on the present if only this earlier experience can be retrieved. Since both Karen and Earl could recall times when they had had good conversations, and agreed that these were times when they were on walks, this story, previously unspoken, now becomes of key importance to the story that they are telling now, about how they feel they are beginning to drift apart. A connection was made, and a reassessment of the story they had told the therapists resulted. Now that the focus will be Karen's dissatisfaction with her job, there will probably be another connective story from the past that is relevant to her dissatisfaction, and what she might do about this dilemma (that is, of not liking the job but liking the pay she receives for doing it).

Helping Clients Become Authors of Their Own Stories

In *Story Re-Visions*, Alan Parry and Robert E. Doan view therapy as a means of helping people become the authors of their own stories.[22] Therapy provides a space "for the deconstruction of a client's story so that it can be viewed as only one interpretation among many possible ones (both past and present)."[23] This is not to say that the client's story is trivial, for it is the story that has been "inhabiting" the client in the form of meanings and views of the world. But once the client begins the process of telling the story, this permits it to be viewed as a highly influential text that the client did not totally author. When this discovery is made, the work of story deconstruction may begin, and this creates the space for story revision.

The authors emphasize the importance of the phase of story revision. In fact, it cannot be overemphasized:

> It is one thing to be a catalyst in the deconstruction of clients' or families' mythology; it is another to provide them with the opportunity to revise their stories in such a way that these will be more in line with what they want. To omit the re-vision process is to leave the clients in a state of "psychological free fall." Alternately stated, it is to leave them outside of a story [and] there is not much safety outside of a story; instead, there are only feelings of disconnection, lack of frame of reference, and uncertainty about where people belong and how they are to know. Without a sense of being part of a "shared story," people's lives seem to have little direction or meaning.[24]

Like Janine Roberts, Patricia Hudson, and William O'Hanlon, Parry and Doan are family therapists, but their view of family therapy is quite different from the "traditional notions that family therapy means having as many members of the family in each session as are willing to attend, and that a family therapist does not see individuals."[25] Their view of family therapy refers to "a way of thinking" rather than "a particular type of treatment." As they see it, individuals compose families, families compose cultures and sociopolitical systems, and cultures and political systems compose countries. There are individual stories and story interactions at each of these levels. Thus, family therapy may be viewed as a frame of reference that emphasizes the interconnectedness of all stories, and may therefore be done with individuals, families, and even larger social groupings. Some of the authors' most successful work has been done with individuals whose family members were unwilling or unable to attend therapy. These cases were informed, however, by a narrative family therapy frame of reference, and much of the therapeutic outcome was probably attributable to the relationship changes the clients began to initiate in their families. This, in their view, *is* family therapy.

But how does deconstruction of the old story and re-visioning of a new story actually work? The authors begin with the basic premise that the old story is largely shaped and informed by the narratives and meanings of others. But how, in practical terms, does the therapist work with the old story? They recommend that the therapist listen for the dominant themes in the story that the client tells.

Examples are religious affiliations, racial or ethnic ties, gender orientation, professional identity, and family tradition and history. For the story revisioning to take place, these themes need not be abandoned in the new story, but they do need to be reinterpreted on the basis of the client's own personal experiences rather than the experiences and stories of others.

To illustrate, one of the authors was seeing a client who had placed a great deal of importance on his job. But then he lost his job, apparently because of another person's jealousy. In the wake of his job loss, he became unhappy, then depressed, and eventually quite suicidal. Then, however, he began to turn things around, and managed to get another job. As the therapist said to him, "You are on your way to regaining control of your life." But then he suffered a stroke and was again out of a job because of lingering health problems. The doctors had since been telling him to take things easy, and the therapist took this to mean that the client would not be able to work professionally as he had done in the past.

Clearly, a dominant theme in the therapeutic conversation is the client's professional identity and how much it has been critical to his self-worth throughout the years. When stripped of his professional identity the first time, he became depressed and almost took his own life. The second job loss was a double blow and he now seems more demoralized than ever. The old story is no longer working, no longer relevant, and the new story is yet to be conceived or plotted out, much less written. The therapist suggests that the client is being invited to come up with some other standard besides that of work by which to judge and evaluate himself. Are there other things in the story of his life that are important, things that give meaning to his life? When the client responded uncomprehendingly—"What do you mean?"—the therapist suggested some things, other than the client's job, that might have given his life some meaning, such as religion, family traditions, or male friendships. The client responded, "No, not really. I've never been very religious, and the men's movement just doesn't interest me. The family tradition was all about work . . . that's all there was." So the therapist tried again, "How about what it means to be a good human being. Has that been important to you all along?" "Well, yeah, sure. I've always tried to be a good person." As the conversation continued, therapist and client focused on the task of defining what a "good person" would be if it did not include work, as this was how "good person" was defined in the old story. The old story based on work, and maintaining a sense of self-worth through work, has been deconstructed. The issue before them is how the client might find other criteria and other grounds for viewing himself as a person of worth. The authors conclude:

> This example represents a case where not many dominant themes had emerged (other than work!), and this had served as a major stumbling block in the client's progression. Hunting for and finding another dominant theme proved very useful in the client's story revision.[26]

Parry and Doan's approach has certain affinities with Roberts's. A strong similarity is their idea of re-visioning the story and her emphasis on the evolving story. Like Roberts, Parry and Doan believe it is important to respect the old stories because these provide the basis for eliciting the new story. If, as they suggest, the old and new stories tend to collide, there is nonetheless a thematic connection between the old and the new story, as well as a need to begin formulating a new cohering story.

My concern in this chapter has been to establish that story has become a widely used construct among family therapists, augmenting and even, at times, replacing family therapists' traditional emphasis on the family system. If there is a basic weakness in this approach, it is that it gives relatively less attention to what Hudson and O'Hanlon call "experience" than some other therapeutic traditions do. Hudson and O'Hanlon identify experience as "the label we use to describe internal feelings, sensations, fantasies, automatic thoughts and sense of self that each person has." But they do not give nearly as much attention to the relationship between experience and story as they give to the link between fact and story. In fact, they do not really discuss experience at all. This is also true of Parry and Doan. Like Hudson and O'Hanlon, they affirm that there is a "sense of self" or "core self" that gets expressed through stories, and they seem to believe that, even if this core self does not exist independently of stories, it is somehow more than the sum of the stories one tells about oneself. But they do not address this issue in any systematic way, and as a result, the reader may feel as though these texts themselves are in a sort of "psychological free-fall."

If this were merely a conceptual problem, we might choose to ignore it. But this tendency to downplay experience as such seems to be reflected in the therapeutic process itself, at least as it is represented in these three texts. The internal feelings, sensations, fantasies, and automatic thoughts of the clients are not much commented upon, and this is in spite of the fact that they are telling some very personal stories about themselves.

Is There a Self in This Story?

I believe that we need to look outside of these texts, perhaps even outside family therapy itself, to find conceptual resources for dealing with this very important aspect of therapy. Because a sense of self seems to be involved in this experiential dimension of the therapeutic process, we could turn to the psychoanalytic tradition for these resources, as Michael P. Nichols has done in *The Self in the System*, a book that weds family therapy and psychoanalytic self psychology and object relations theories.[27] But another therapeutic tradition that is able to take account of the "experiential" dimension in a way that is compatible with the story approaches developed by the family therapists presented here is client-centered (or Rogerian) therapy. This is what I recommend. Admittedly, this proposal may seem odd in light of the conflicts that ensued between the family systems therapists and client-centered therapists in the 1960s and 1970s. But, by now, at least some of the major disagreements between the two schools are no longer relevant (that is, they are an "old story" awaiting the birth of a "new story"). One of the most obvious of these disagreements was over the fact that client-centered therapy was typically individual therapy whereas family therapists (as Parry and Doan point out) were seeing as many family members together as they could get to come to therapy. The old individual vs. family controversy has faded away, and, as Parry and Doan note, they do not see any incompatibility between counseling individuals and claiming that they are in fact doing family therapy.

Another point of controversy was that client-centered therapy focused on the internal experience of the client whereas the family therapy approach was interactional, concerned with interpersonal relationships. Carl R. Rogers addresses this difference in his article

"The Implications of Client-Centered Therapy for Family Life."[28] In this article, Rogers identifies "some of the ways in which clients change in their family living as a consequence of client-centered therapy." He suggests that they become more expressive of their true feelings to other members of their families, that they discover that relationships can be lived on the basis of real feelings rather than defensive pretense, that they learn something about how to initiate and maintain real two-way communication, and they tend in the direction of permitting each member of the family to have her own feelings and to be a separate person. He includes in this article several excerpts from the case of a woman whom he had seen on an individual basis. She was a single parent, living with her ten-year-old daughter and her seventy-year-old mother, who dominated the household by her "poor health." The client was controlled by her mother, and unable to control her daughter. She knew that most people thought she would be much better off if she left her mother, but she could not bring herself to leave her mother, in spite of her awareness that her mother had made her feel guilty all her life for her ill health. She felt she was being cowardly, but also felt that her hands were tied. As she observed how Rogers responded to her feelings of frustration, and how his quiet acceptance of her negative thoughts toward her own mother made her feel better about herself, she began to wonder if the same approach might work in her relationship with her mother, and in creating a better emotional climate between her daughter and her mother. By treating her mother and her daughter in a "client-centered" way, she witnessed a dramatic change in the relationships between the three of them and a marked change in the emotional climate of the home.

It is true that therapy as such was interactional only in the sense that it gave considerable attention to the relationship between therapist and client. It was not primarily concerned to change the family system itself. Such changes, when they occurred, were a by-product of changes in the client's own self-experience. Yet, precisely because client-centered therapy focuses on the individual's own experiencings, it is nicely positioned to augment the story approaches that are now being formulated by the family therapists.

The most accessible and relevant resources for this therapy are Rogers's chapters on "What It Means to Become a Person" and "To

Be That Self Which One Truly Is: A Therapist's View of Personal Goals" from his most popular text, *On Becoming a Person*.[29] In the first of these two chapters, Rogers notes that he has had the opportunity of working with people who present a wide variety of personal problems, but that

> Below the level of the problem situation about which the individual is complaining—behind the trouble with studies, or wife, or employer, or with his own uncontrollable or bizarre behavior, or with his frightening feelings, lies one central search. It seems to me that at bottom each person is asking, "Who am I, *really*? How can I get in touch with this real self, underlying all my surface behavior? How can I become myself?"[30]

Rogers proceeds to identify the changes that occur in a person when she encounters a therapist whose purpose is to understand the way the client feels in her own inner world, to accept her as she is, to create an atmosphere of freedom in which she can move in her thinking and feeling and being in any direction she desires. How does she use this freedom? What typically happens is that the client seeks to get behind the false fronts, or the masks, or the roles with which she has faced life and to discover something more basic, something more truly herself. She also finds herself experiencing feelings that she did not realize were within her, and this, in Rogers' view, "is really the discovery of unknown elements of self."[31]

This process of opening oneself to new feelings, whatever these may be, leads to the discovery of an

> underlying order, which exists in the ceaselessly changing flow of her experience. Rather than to try to mold her experience into the form of a mask, or to make it be a form or structure that it is not, being herself means to discover the unity and harmony which exists in her own actual feelings and reactions. It means that the real self is something which is comfortably discovered in one's experiences, not something imposed upon it.[32]

Thus, Rogers is not reluctant to use self-language, but he wants to understand this as integral to experience, inseparable from it. It is not an entity as such, but an orderliness or formfulness that inheres in all of the complexities of an individual's experiencing.

He identifies the person who emerges from this process as having these characteristic trends: openness to experience (less defensiveness and rigidity); trust in one's own organism as a basis for decision making (less fear of the emotional reactions that one has); an internal locus of evaluation (less looking to others for approval or disapproval, for standards to live by, for decisions and choices); and willingness to be a process (less expectation that therapy will result in the achievement of a fixed state or goal).

In the second of these two chapters, Rogers says that every individual asks herself at one time or another, sometimes calmly and meditatively, sometimes in agonizing uncertainty or despair, what her goal is in life, what she is striving for, or what is her purpose. One is asking, in the words of Kierkegaard, what it means "to be the self which one truly is," and how one might discern this more truly or accurately, and realize it more fully. On the basis of his work with "troubled and maladjusted individuals," he believes that he "can discern a pattern, a trend, a commonality, an orderliness, in the tentative answers to these questions which they have found for themselves."[33] These include many of the changes and characteristic trends that he identified in the earlier chapter, but he presents them as ways of being toward which one is moving. Thus, there is a tendency to move away from facades, from "oughts," from meeting the expectations of others, from pleasing others, and toward self-direction, being a process, being complexity, openness to experience, acceptance of others, and trust of self. In this movement away and movement toward one is not trying to be more than one is, with the attendant feelings of insecurity and defensiveness that this creates, but one is also not trying to be less than one is, with the attendant feelings of guilt or self-deprecation.

Rogers acknowledges that some people object to "the path of life" that he describes because they and he have real differences in values, differences that he respects. But he has also found that sometimes the objections are based on certain misapprehensions, and these he wants to address in hopes of clearing them away. One is that the phrase "To be the self which one truly is" implies fixity, a static or essentialist view of the self. He rejects this view because he is convinced that "change is facilitated, probably maximized, when one is willing to be what he truly is."[34] It is only as one can become more like oneself that there is any prospect of change. Another misapprehension is that the process he has been describing could mean that persons would become bad, evil, uncontrolled, destructive. He says that this view is well known to him because he finds it in almost every client. They worry that if they let the feelings flow that have been dammed up in them, they will experience a personal catastrophe, that all hell will break loose. Yet, the whole course of one's experience in therapy contradicts these fears. Clients discover that the more they are able to permit previously blocked or unacknowledged feelings to flow, the more these feelings, when one lives "closely and acceptingly with their complexity, operate in a constructive harmony rather than sweeping [one] into some uncontrollably evil path."[35]

Rogers does not deny that many of the previously unexpressed feelings have been curtailed because one was trying to meet the expectations of other persons or of the culture. To express them may cause others to get upset, and may place one at odds with one's culture. But this does not mean that the individual has become some sort of monster, an antisocial creature in whose company no one else can bear to be. On the contrary, when we are open to all of our experience, we have better access to all of the available data in the situation on which to base our behavior: "Thus, an individual may persist in the concept that 'I can handle liquor,' when openness to his past experience would indicate that this is scarcely correct."[36] In Rogers's view, one becomes more truly social when one becomes more truly the self that one is. It is the individual whose experiencing is rigid and compartmentalized who is truly dangerous to others.

Rogers concludes this chapter by noting that he recognizes that the "path of life" that he is outlining is a value choice which is quite at variance with the goals that individuals usually choose or follow. But he commends it because it "springs from individuals who have more than the usual freedom to choose, and because it seems to express a unified trend in these individuals."[37] In effect, he is arguing that as individuals become more free to become the self that they feel, internally, is true for them, they will manifest these trends.

I believe that there are some common threads between Rogers's depiction of the experiential process leading to a more fully realized self and Roberts's emphasis on the goal, in family therapy, of moving from rigid storytelling to a more evolving story mode. There are also parallels between his emphasis on affirming one's experiential complexity and her emphasis on the value of moving from disconnected and silenced stories to more connected ones. Both see the problems involved in the splitting of experiences off from one another, and view as a positive development the recognition of how the various features of one's life cohere and interrelate. The differences are that Roberts focuses on the narratives that her clients tell whereas Rogers focuses on the experiential process that lies beneath these stories. These differences, however, are not contradictory but complementary. The therapist can be responsive to both at once.

If, for example, a client is telling a story illustrating how she is always doing what her mother expects of her, the therapist can focus on the story itself and be responsive simultaneously to the feelings that the telling of this story evokes in the client. These may be feelings of anger that she has allowed her mother to have a dominating influence in her life, but they may also include feelings of resignation, that she will not be able to change the situation as long as her mother is alive. There may also be feelings of fear over what would happen if she did begin to make her own decisions: Will she have the competence to do so? What if she should fail (that is, make a stupid or bad decision)? Beneath every story there is an experiential substructure, and it is the client-centered approach that is perhaps the best available one for sensitizing us to this underlying structure.

Rogers's views are also compatible with Parry and Doan's emphasis on replacing the old story with a new story, and with seeing this as a process in which previously denied aspects of the self are allowed to emerge. In reporting on what occurs in client-centered therapy, Rogers describes a process that is very similar to the process that Parry and Doan describe. Their example of the man who can no longer work productively is an excellent case in point. In the "old story" of his life, his valuation of himself was directed solely toward work, a value that he had derived from his family, who also placed high and virtually exclusive emphasis on the importance of work. Now that he can no longer work, he is being challenged to identify other aspects of himself that he can value. The shift that the therapist in this case is advocating is one that moves from valuing himself in terms of what he can do to valuing himself in terms of what he can be. To go from being a "good worker" to being a "good person" may not appear to be freeing, as it could simply mean that he is now meeting external definitions of what it means to be a "good person," but the point is that there is a process occurring here, a movement from one story to another story, and in this process, there is a more complex sense of self emerging.

The question that the story approach raises for the client-centered approach is whether an exclusive focus on the experiential process leaves the client with insufficient clarity as to what has been realized by virtue of the therapeutic process itself. While Rogers is able to identify the characteristic trends that occur when the process is going well, the client may need to be able to articulate these changes in the form of a story, especially a story whose contrast with the stories that the client brought with her to therapy may be noted and celebrated. In point of fact, most of Rogers' counseling cases have such stories. The client who effected a dramatic change in the emotional climate that had prevailed between herself, her mother, and her ten-year-old daughter is an excellent example. Here is one of the stories she tells:

> Well, I've made a stupendous discovery, that perhaps it's been my fault entirely in overcompensating to mother . . . in other words, spoiling her. So I made up my mind like I do every morning, but I think this time it's gonna work, that I would try to . . . oh, to be calm and quiet, and . . . if she does go into one of her spells, to just more or less ignore it as you would a child who throws a tantrum just to get attention. So I tried it. And she got angry over some little thing. And she jumped up from the table and went into her room. Well, I didn't rush in and say, oh, I'm sorry, and beg her to come back, and I simply just ignored it. So in a few minutes, why, she came back and sat down and was a little sulky but she was over it. So I'm going to try that for a while.[38]

Thus, Rogers's cases include many such stories, but he himself does not draw attention to the fact that counseling involves storytelling.

My purpose in this chapter has been to make a case for the story approach to therapy by providing several examples of such approaches. I have also made a constructive proposal, based on Hudson and O'Hanlon's own model (of facts, stories, and individual experience), for augmenting the story approach with the client-centered focus on internal experiencing. If anyone had recommended linking family therapy and client-centered therapy a decade or two ago, that person would have been deemed either crazy or ignorant of their respective views. But therapeutic models change over time, as their own rigid stories become more evolutionary ones, allowing increasing freedom to consider an alliance that would have been considered impossible some twenty years ago. This is itself a testimony to the life-changing properties of stories.

Chapter 2

The Inspirational Story

The Art of the Power of Suggestion

The preceding chapter showed that the stories that clients tell may be identified according to types (intertwined, distinct/separated, silenced/secret, rigid, and so forth). Therapists also may be differentiated from one another by virtue of the stories they tell about their therapeutic work. In this and the two following chapters, I will discuss three therapists whose differences from one another are reflected in the types of stories they tell. While all three have a great deal in common as far as therapeutic theory is concerned, each one's uniqueness is expressed in the types of stories they tell about what they are trying to accomplish as therapists. The therapeutic art of each is also reflected in the stories they tell. Thus, I suggest that Milton H. Erickson uses the *inspirational story* to demonstrate the art of the power of suggestion, that Paul Watzlawick employs the *paradoxical story* to demonstrate the art of untying knots, and that Steve de Shazer uses the *miracle story* to demonstrate the art of identifying exceptions.

My purpose in viewing these therapists' work in this way—as exhibiting a preference for a particular kind of story—is not to suggest that these are the only types of story that a therapist might evoke from their clients. There are surely many other types of stories that we might identify by considering other therapists. But what I do want to contend is that these therapists help us to see that there is more to counseling than identifying the type of story that a client brings to the initial session. Additionally, one must consider the story of the counseling experience itself, and the different ways in which therapists seek to en-story this experience. We need to be self-aware of how we envision the story that we hope will emerge out of our own counseling efforts. We need to know how we subtly, or not so subtly, influence our counselees to tell the story we want them to be able to tell.

The fact that each of these therapists favors a particular story type tells us something about them and how they individualize their role as therapists. The very plurality of story types found in their collective writings suggests that the counselor plays a profound role in determining what makes a good story, that is, a story that, in his or her opinion, reflects a positive counseling outcome. Most pastors are already aware that theirs is the role of "attentive listener," as most have been introduced through basic courses in pastoral care and counseling to one or another text on listening skills.[1] In presenting these three story types, I seek to alert pastors to their own story preferences, thus prompting them to ask themselves why they prefer this or that type of story. How does this preference affect—for good or ill—their capacity to listen helpfully?

In this chapter, I focus on Milton H. Erickson, a rather eccentric man who was a master at telling inspirational stories. Everyone who knew Erickson attests to the fact that he was a remarkable person. His influence on the current generation of brief therapists can hardly be exaggerated. Yet he is not widely known outside of family therapy circles, and is often confused with Erik H. Erikson, the famous psychoanalyst whose career, chronologically speaking, paralleled Erickson's own. One reason for his relative obscurity is the fact that he spent much of his professional life in private practice in Phoenix, Arizona, where he went to live in midcareer due to health problems resulting from his lifelong struggle with the effects of polio, which he contracted in 1919. Another reason for his obscurity is that his career also paralleled those of the major pioneers in family therapy—Virginia Satir, Carl Whitaker, Salvador Minuchin, and various others—whose writings enjoyed a greater popularity because they addressed family therapy issues more directly. Erickson was best known in his own time as the author of books and articles on hypnosis, a technique that he frequently used in therapy with individuals, but one that was not seen to have immediate value for family therapy, as putting a whole family in a trance simultaneous-ly was quite unthinkable. Also, as Erickson viewed it, hypnosis was designed to influence the unconscious mind of the client, and sys-tems theorists were not very favorable to the idea of the uncon-scious, which they considered a relic of the psychoanalytic tradition. By now, however, the climate in family therapy has changed, and Erickson's techniques, including hypnotic suggestion, have been enjoying considerable popularity.

Another problem was that he was not, in fact, a systems theorist. Stephen R. Lankton and Carol H. Lankton have recently pointed out that Erickson never formulated his work in terms of family systems theory. They ask,

> Is there a particular Eriksonian attitude, theory, and behavior towards individuals and families formulated within a systems framework? Many family therapists would be satisfied with a formulation of his diagnosis and intervention strategies that relied upon general systems theory, ecosystems theory, or cybernetic-type theory. However, Erickson himself never offered such a formulation. . . . If one looks in the indexes of Erickson's collected writings, or article titles of any book written by Erickson (and co-authors), or any edited collection of articles authored by Erickson, not a single entry will be found entitled "family" or "systems," etc. It is intriguing that he is well known for his creative and pioneering contributions to family therapy . . . and still not a single entry in books *by him* refer to "family."[2]

The Lanktons note that books edited by Jay Haley, including *Uncommon Therapy: The Psychiatric Techniques of Milton H. Erickson* and *Conversations with Milton H. Erickson* are notable exceptions,[3] but this is because the "emphasis on families was added by the editor and not by Erickson." Instead, Erickson's own orienta-tion "is shown by the entries in the index that reflect the language he used. That language was psychodynamic!"[4] They explain Erickson's use of psychodynamic rather than systems language on the grounds that when he began his career, "the language of systems theory just didn't exist! He couldn't use it."[5]

If Erickson was not a systems theorist, he *was* a gifted storyteller. As David Gordon points out in *Therapeutic Metaphors*, he was the type of storyteller who discovered that "when he tells his tales, those who listen actually *live those adventures* inside of themselves."[6] As

Haley writes in his introduction to *Uncommon Therapy*, "Generally, Dr. Erickson describes his approach with remarkable clarity, at times adding a touch of drama, *since he tends to see the world in that way.*"[7] As Haley's edited volumes demonstrate, it is certainly possible to locate Erickson's case stories within the "family life cycle" framework that Haley provides in *Uncommon Therapy*, seeing these stories as illustrative of certain family life issues such as courtship, young adulthood, marriage, childbirth, and the weaning of parents from their children. Yet, as the Lanktons point out, these are not Erickson's but Haley's constructs, and they locate his stories within a structure that it did not occur to him to provide.

Sidney Rosen's more recent editorship of *My Voice Will Go with You: The Teaching Tales of Milton H. Erickson* allows the stories to speak for themselves, and permits Erickson to speak for himself via the stories.[8] The fact that Erickson had intended to be the coauthor of this book and that his wife, after his death, spent days "going over the manuscript . . . insisting on accuracy, even in the smallest details,"[9] indicates that this project was close to his heart, as it would be a living testimony to what his life's work was all about.

In her foreword to *My Voice Will Go with You*, Lynn Hoffman reports that she first became aware of Erickson's "amazing exploits" when she began to work as a writer and editor at the Mental Research Institute in Palo Alto in 1963. She was putting the material together for Haley's book, *Techniques of Family Therapy*: "Haley, who had taped hours of conversation with Erickson, told me story after story about him, while I listened entranced." She compares Erickson's stories with those of Mark Twain:

> Milton Erickson's teaching tales—the stories he told his patients and the stories he told the pilgrims who came to sit at his feet—are ingenious and enchanting. They are extraordinary examples of the art of persuasion. Some people would say that they are much too good to be tucked away on the psychiatric shelf, since even though their intention was therapeutic, they are part of a much larger tradition: the American tradition of wit and humor whose great exemplar is Mark Twain.[10]

As one who participated in his teaching seminars, Hoffman says that the written word fails to capture what Erickson was like in person:

Because of the curious way Erickson stands on the line between healer and poet, scientist and bard, it is difficult to describe his work.
Transcripts of his seminars, though wonderful, are to some extent
unsatisfying. The written word simply cannot convey the pauses,
smiles, and piercing upward glances with which Erickson punctuates
his narratives, nor can it record his mastery of voice and tone. The
written word, in short, cannot give any idea of the way Erickson *insinuates* himself.[11]

In his editor's note, Rosen recalls a conversation in 1978 between
Erickson and one of the psychiatrists who attended his seminars: "At
one point Erickson had turned to the psychiatrist and, with a slight
smile, had asked, 'Do you still think that therapy is just telling stories?'" Rosen adds, "Now, it is obvious that even though Erickson's
therapy was not *only* 'telling stories,' the telling of what I call his
'teaching tales' was one of the major elements in his therapy."[12] In
discussing Erickson's method of what he calls "strategic therapy,"
Haley identifies several of Erickson's motivating techniques, including encouraging resistance, providing a worse alternative, effecting
change by communicating in metaphor, encouraging a relapse, eliciting a response by frustrating it, and so forth.[13] These are the very
techniques and strategies that storytellers use to hold the attention of
their audiences and are integral to the stories that Erickson himself
told. Thus, for Erickson, there is no clear division between story and
technique, or story and strategic intervention, for the "methods" of
storytelling already anticipate these methods of therapeutic intervention. His therapeutic approach may not be "just telling stories," yet
stories and how they are made and told are the very heart of his therapeutic approach.

Rosen refers to the stories in *My Voice Will Go with You* as
"teaching tales" because they were stories that Erickson frequently

told to patients and students over the years. For the last six years or
so of his life he met with groups of psychotherapists almost every day,
for uninterrupted four or five-hour sessions, during which he would
discuss hypnosis, therapy, and life, and would generously call on
"teaching tales."[14]

Because he told these stories to his clients, primarily for the purpose of motivating them to make the changes in their lives that they

desired but found themselves resisting for any number of reasons, I like to think of them as "inspirational stories," as they "inspire" the listener to make changes in her own life. To persuade a counselee to act in a beneficial way, Erickson would sometimes tell one client a story about another client or about a personal family incident. In this way, the motivation was indirect. By telling a story about another person or situation he could plant the suggestion that the present client might do something similar. If it had been done before by someone else, it could be done again.

The Art of the Power of Suggestion

As Erickson discovered early in his career, storytelling is the subtle art of persuasion, of the power of suggestion. By telling a story, he could inspire clients to do something that they would not do if directly advised to do so. He understood that if he advised a client directly, he would need to support his advice with reasons: "You should do such-and-such because . . ." The client may, in turn, challenge the reason given for why she should do such-and-such, and the reason might then become the focus of conversation, often creating disagreement and dispute. The "why" that the therapist gives may, in any case, be misguided or irrelevant. Thus, Erickson did not advise, but he used the power of suggestion, and stories proved a valuable way to exercise this power. By telling a story, he did not have to give reasons and explanations. The story has its own powers of suggestion, its own implied reasons and explanations. Unlike a directive, a story allows the client to feel that she remains in control of her life, for she is free to decide whether or not the story will have relevance for her. The story also allows the client considerable freedom to improvise, to act within the story's broad framework but not to follow it slavishly in every detail. After all, the story is not to be taken literally but is meant to inspire the listener to act in a way she has not heretofore been acting.

Those who had the experience of hearing Erickson tell his stories attest to how powerful they could be, and, therefore, how much power Erickson himself could wield as a counselor. He once told Jay Haley that he was not at all reluctant to exercise his power as a therapist. Haley adds:

With his willingness to take and use power, I think it is fortunate that he was a benevolent man. If the kind of influence he had was turned to destructive purposes, it would have been most unfortunate. He was not only benevolent, but he was consistently helpful to people, both in and out of his office. . . . I never had a doubt about his ethics or his benevolent intentions and I wasn't concerned about his exploiting anyone for any personal advantage.[15]

His willingness to be a strong influence in another person's life was partly due to the fact that he was a medical doctor who specialized in psychiatry, and therefore believed that he had a moral obligation (had taken an oath) to do everything in his power to help his counselees. Yet, even his professional identity as physician was placed within a story context. As illustration, he sometimes used the word *prescribe* when suggesting that a counselee take a certain course of action ("This is what I prescribe. . . ."). The word *prescribe* is actually more directive than *advise*, yet, in the context of psychotherapy, it functions metaphorically, not literally. After all, he does not actually write out a prescription to be filled by the local pharmacist. The "prescription" is an imaginative fiction: "Supposing I play the doctor in this scenario and you play the patient. As your doctor, this is what I would prescribe. . . ." In the context of therapy, to "prescribe" is to use metaphor to effect a change, for the therapist does not literally "prescribe," and is in no position literally to "order" or "command." As we will see from his inspirational stories, Erickson's "prescriptions" and "orders" are typically received as valued gifts, as evidence that he values clients so highly and takes their desire to live a healthier life so much to heart that he gives them precisely what he believes they need. They are, of course, free to decline the gift.

A story that illustrates both the "prescription" technique and Erickson's use of the art of the power of suggestion is the following.[16]

The African Violet Queen

A student once approached [Erickson] with concern about a maiden aunt who had made multiple suicide attempts. Instead of attempting to arrange an appointment at his office, Erickson simply showed up at the woman's home the next day where she lived alone with her maid. When she came to the door, he introduced himself and asked to be given a tour of the house. Surprised but intrigued, she agreed to show him around.

In the sun porch, he noticed a row of pots containing African violets. The lady informed him that one thing she had a touch for was growing these plants. He also learned that she went to church every Sunday, but other than that had no meaningful social life. Upon leaving, therefore, he said to her, "Madame, here is your prescription. I want you to send your maid to the nursery to purchase many more pots and every strain of African violets they carry. Furthermore, whenever a child is born to a member of your congregation, I want you to give a pot of African violets to the parents at the baptism. And whenever a wedding is celebrated, I want you to give a pot of these flowers to the bride."

Twenty years later, he recalled, he clipped an article from the local newspaper, "THE AFRICAN VIOLET QUEEN DIES AT AGE 76 . . ." it began, and went on to recount a touching tale of how appreciated this woman had been in her church and community. In telling this story to a group of therapists shortly before his death, Erickson concluded with the remark, "I never did know what was wrong with that woman"—A disingenuous statement, perhaps, but one that underscored his emphasis on results rather than explanations.

This story, reported by Harvey Mindess, illustrates how Erickson used the device of the "prescription" to inspire the woman to do as he suggested. It surely helped that his "prescription" was part of a "house call," as this lent support to the fiction that he was a doctor who had carried out a careful "examination" of his patient. This is also why his concluding observation—"I never did know what was wrong with that woman"—seems so disingenuous, for what kind of doctor writes out a prescription without first finding out what is truly wrong with the patient?

The fact that she did as Erickson suggested also illustrates how the art of the power of suggestion works. Erickson would tell his students to "enter the patient's world" and "use the patient's own language." Here, he literally enters the woman's world by asking her to give him a tour of her home. This very request intrigues her; she did not expect him to show up at her door, and was doubly surprised that he would ask for a tour of her home. During the tour, however, he learned what her interests were: growing African violets and going to church. His "prescription" effectively links these two seemingly unrelated interests. Before he linked them, she hadn't seen the possible connections between these interests. By connecting them, he addressed her suicidal threats, which derived from her feeling that her life lacked any real purpose. By entering her world he was able to work within her own frame of life and not impose his onto hers. He did not ask her to change her way of living, but only suggested a variation on what she was already doing: "Do what you are doing already—growing African violets and attending church—but with more intentionality."

Note, too, that he does not overreact to the fact that she had threatened suicide several times. He might have assumed that because she was suicidal he should arrange to have her hospitalized. But his tour of her home, during which he observed her behavior, led him to conclude that there was nothing really wrong with her, or, at least, nothing that could not be immeasurably helped by having a reason to live. In this sense, his statement—"I never did know what was wrong with that woman"—is disingenuous in another sense, as it has the implication that there *wasn't* anything fundamentally wrong with her. One gathers that he struck upon the plan he proposed when he saw her African violets and perceived what these might mean metaphorically. What she shared with these African violets was life itself. How might one ensure that she would not take her own life? By inspiring her to share their beauty with others and thereby making herself beautiful in their eyes. That she became known as the "African Violet *Queen*" testifies to the fact that the flowers' beauty became ascribed to her as well.

One is reminded here of the biblical story of the woman, apparently a woman of the streets, who poured expensive ointment on Jesus' head. Especially noteworthy is his response to her act: "She has done a beautiful thing to me" (RSV) and "Wherever this good news is proclaimed in the whole world, what she has done will be told in remembrance of her" (Matt. 26:6-13). The woman who did this "beautiful thing" will always be known as the "Expensive Ointment Woman." She cannot be otherwise identified. So, too, the woman in Erickson's inspirational story will be known as the "African Violet Queen," and her life will always be associated with beautiful flowering plants. These qualities become attached to her as well, as she becomes, for those who hear the story, a vital, beautiful woman for the "beautiful things" she did for others. Moreover, when this story is told to others, it becomes an inspiration for them as well. They may imagine themselves in a comparable story, germane to their own life world, and may feel their own lack of purpose addressed as well.

In the following story from *My Voice Will Go with You*, Erickson again makes a point of entering the client's own world.[17]

Walk a Mile

A medically retired policeman told me, "I have emphysema, high blood pressure, and, as you can see, I am grossly overweight. I drink too much. I eat too much. I want a job but my emphysema and high blood pressure prevent that. I would like to cut down on my smoking. I'd like to get rid of it. I'd like to quit drinking about a fifth of whiskey a day and I'd like to eat sensibly."

I said, "Are you married?"

He said, "No, I'm a bachelor. I usually do my own cooking, but there's a handy little restaurant around the corner that I often visit."

"So, there's a handy little restaurant around the corner where you can dine. Where do you buy your cigarettes?"

He bought two cartons at a time. I said, "In other words, you buy cigarettes not for today but for the future. Now, since you do most of your own cooking, where do you shop?"

"Fortunately, there is a little grocery right around the corner. That's where I get my groceries and cigarettes."

"Where do you get your liquor?"

"Fortunately there is a nice liquor store right next to that grocery."

"So you have a handy restaurant right around the corner, a handy grocery right around the corner, and a handy liquor store right around the corner. And you want to jog and you know you can't jog. Now, your problem is very simple. You want to jog but you can't. But you can walk. All right, buy your cigarettes one pack at a time. Walk across town to buy your pack. That will start to get you in shape. As for your groceries, don't shop at the handy grocery around the corner. Go to a grocery a half-mile or a mile away and buy just enough for each meal. That means three nice walks a day. As for your liquor, you can drink all you want to. Take your first drink at a bar at least a mile away. If you want a second drink, find another bar at least a mile away. If you want a third, find another bar a mile away."

He looked at me with the greatest anger. He swore at me. He left raging.

About a month later a new patient came in. He said, "A retired policeman referred me to you. He said you are the one psychiatrist who knows what he is doing."

The policeman couldn't buy a carton of cigarettes after that! And he knew that walking to the grocery was a conscious act. He had control of it. Now, I didn't take food away from him. I didn't take tobacco away. I didn't take liquor away. I gave him the opportunity to walk.

In his editorial comment on this story, Rosen says that the patient "was forced to reframe his behavior. He had to take it out of the category of involuntary behavior. He realized, as Erickson commented, that 'walking to the grocery was a conscious act.'"[18] Rosen also notes that "Erickson recognized that he was dealing with a man who had a long history of carrying out orders. Therefore, he gives him orders with the expectation that the man will carry them out. This is an important example of meeting the patient in his frame of reference. One would not necessarily treat other patients in this manner."[19]

There is also a fictional quality to his "ordering" of the man to do this and that because he knows that he cannot enforce these orders. The man is not under his direct control as he would have been were Erickson his supervising officer at the precinct. Yet, as Rosen points out, Erickson did enter the man's world by giving him orders, orders that, if he really wanted to, he *could* carry out. Furthermore, Erickson could anticipate that the man's immediate reaction would be one of anger, not because he was being "ordered" to do something that he did not want to do, but because he realized that Erickson had deprived him of his best alibi for *not* changing: "I do what I do because I have no choice in the matter. I am the victim of my circumstances." By planting the idea that the man *could* go about getting his food, cigarettes, and liquor in a new and different way, Erickson makes it impossible for him to believe that there is only one way to get these things, the way that is not conducive to good health. At the same time, he avoids getting placed in the situation of telling the man that he has to give up all the things that he enjoys. As Erickson puts it, "I didn't take food away from him. I didn't take tobacco away. I didn't take liquor away." Thus, the man's anger is also due to his understanding that Erickson has skillfully avoided becoming the focus of his anger. How can he justify being angry with

Erickson if Erickson has not instructed him to give up food, cigarettes, and liquor? Yet, he storms out of the office in a rage precisely because he knows that Erickson has checkmated him. As he thinks
in retrospect about what Erickson has done, his attitude changes
from his initial anger to admiring respect. Erickson is one psychiatrist who "knows what he is doing."

Rosen locates this story in a chapter of *My Voice Will Go with
You* entitled "Reframing." The reframing in this instance is in the
fact that Erickson does not try to deprive the man of the things he
wants, but offers a new way of going about obtaining these things.
Erickson also finds out what it is that the man wants to do but cannot—which is to get some much needed exercise so that he can lower
his blood pressure and his emphysema—and he inspires him to do
just that by teaching him a new way to go out and secure the things
he wants. Thus, as in the case of the "African Violet Queen,"
Erickson makes a link—in this case, between the things the man felt
he should try to give up but could not *and* the activity he believed he
should engage in but was not able to. Erickson made it impossible
for the man not to be aware—fully conscious—of this linkage as he
went out to get food, cigarettes, and liquor. As Erickson once said to
Rosen, "What you don't realize, Sid, is that most of your life is
unconsciously determined."[20] Rosen adds that Erickson believed the
unconscious can be changed and that what we do unconsciously may
be raised to consciousness. Thus, according to Rosen, what happened in this particular case was that the man had to reframe his
behavior and not view it as involuntary. As previously stated,
Erickson noted that the man realized "walking to the grocery was a
conscious act."[21]

If the "African Violet Queen" is reminiscent of the biblical story of
the woman who poured expensive ointment on Jesus, the biblical
story that "Walk a Mile" calls to mind is the story of the man who
had been lying near the pool of Bethzatha, having suffered from a paralytic condition for thirty-eight years (John 5:2-8). When Jesus asked
the man if he wanted to be healed, he explained to Jesus why he had
not been healed prior to this: "Sir, I have no one to put me into the
pool when the water is stirred up; and while I am making my way,
someone else steps down ahead of me." Jesus responded, "Stand up,
take your mat and walk." And the man did so. This story resembles

Erickson's case of the retired policeman in that both involve the paradox of grown men needing to learn how to walk. In the biblical story, the man who lay near the pool of Bethzatha had been expending his energies in getting himself into the water when it was stirring. If he had been doing this for thirty-eight years, this healing plan obviously was not working, and something else needed to be tried. If any of us were told that there is a cure for our problem, but it will take thirty-eight years for it to take effect, we would surely respond, "Then, that's hardly a cure at all. I could be long dead by that time!"

I can imagine that Jesus, on hearing that the man was expending considerable energy in trying to get himself into the pool, wondered what might happen if the man used the same energies in getting himself into an upright position. By "ordering" the man to stand up, he reframed the situation from one of futility—the thirty-eight years of trying something that was ineffective—to one of possibility. If the man had walked before, perhaps he could walk again. In Erickson's terms, Jesus recognized that much of our life is unconsciously determined, but that the unconscious can be changed. He took the man's paralysis out of the category of involuntary behavior and made it into a voluntary act, one over which he could exercise some control. His question of the man—"Do you want to be made well?"—plants the suggestion that healing in this instance *is* a voluntary, not an involuntary, matter. Also, Jesus' failure to comment on the man's explanation for why he had not gotten healed long before this creates doubt in the man's mind that this is an adequate explanation, as this explanation makes it seem that the man has no control over the situation, an assumption that Jesus, for the man's own sake, does not accept.

This biblical story is relevant to another story that Erickson tells, about how he himself learned to stand up and begin walking after he had lost the use of his legs due to polio. In this story he tells how he made a connection between his difficulty in relearning how to walk and his little sister's difficulty in learning to walk for the first time.[22]

Learning To Stand Up

We learn so much at a conscious level and then we forget what we learn and don't use the skill. You see, I had a terrific advantage over others. I had polio, and I was totally paralyzed, and the inflamma-

*tion was so great that I had a sensory paralysis too. I could move
my eyes and my hearing was undisturbed. I got very lonesome lying
in bed, unable to move anything except my eyeballs. I was quaran-
tined on the farm with seven sisters, one brother, two parents, and a
practical nurse. And how could I entertain myself? I started watching people and my environment. I soon learned that my sisters could
say "no" when they meant "yes." And they could say "yes" and
mean "no" at the same time. They could offer another sister an
apple and hold it back. And I began studying nonverbal language
and body language.*

*I had a baby sister who had begun to learn to creep. I would have
to learn to stand up and walk. And you can imagine the intensity
with which I watched as my baby sister grew from creeping to learning how to stand up. And you don't know how you learned how to
stand up. . . .*

*You learned by reaching up your hand and pulling yourself up.
That put pressure on your hands—and, by accident, you discovered
that you could put weight on your feet. That's an awfully complicated thing because your knees would give way—and, when your knees
would keep straight, your hips would give way. Then you got your
feet crossed. And you couldn't stand up because both your knees and
hips would give way. Your feet were crossed—and you soon learned
to get a wide brace—and you pull yourself up and you have the job
of learning how to keep your knees straight—one at a time, and as
soon as you learn that, you have to learn how to give your attention
to keeping your hips straight. Then you found out that you had to
learn to give your attention to keep your hips straight and knees
straight at the same time and feet far apart! Now finally you could
stand having your feet far apart, resting on your hands. . . .*

Commenting on this story, Rosen notes Erickson's suggestion that
a disability may give one a "terrific advantage over others." This is
the advantage of having given conscious thought to things that for
others are largely unconscious. Rosen also notes that Erickson has
often used this story metaphorically: "Paralysis is disabling, and a
patient is involved with things that are disabling. Erickson turns this
paralysis into something useful. He was alone and could rely on
nobody but himself, and he started watching."[23] He also plants the
idea that, if one is suffering enough or wants change enough, one will
become very attentive, very focused: "*You can imagine the intensity
with which I watched* as my baby sister grew from creeping to learning how to stand up." By watching her he would learn to walk again.

In effect, she was his inspiration, not because she did something unique (after all, virtually all healthy children her age learn to stand up and walk), but because she was learning to do what he would need to learn to do if *he* were ever to walk again. He took full advantage of their common predicament. Also implied in the story is Erickson's conviction that "people have, in their own natural history, the resources to overcome the problem for which they are seeking help. In this story, he reminds people that they have resources of which they are not yet aware."[24]

Another story related to the theme of learning to stand up and walk is one that illustrates Erickson's use of the technique of confusion, a common technique of story tellers, especially mystery writers, who create many possible suspects so that the reader will not guess the identity of the real murderer.[25]

Walking on Glare Ice

During the war I worked at the induction board in Detroit. One day, as I was going to the induction board, I saw a veteran who had returned with an artificial leg, looking at some glare ice and eyeing it suspiciously because he knew that he was likely to fall on glare ice.

"That's very smooth ice," I told him. "Stand where you are. I'll come over and teach you how to walk on glare ice."

He could see that I had a limp, so he knew I must be talking about what I knew. He watched me walk across that glare ice and asked, "How did you do it?"

I said, "I won't tell you, I'll teach you. Now, you just keep your eyes totally shut." And I turned him around, and walked him back and forth on the ice-free sidewalk. I kept walking him back and forth over longer distances and then shorter and shorter distances until finally I noticed his utter confusion. Finally, I got him clear across to the other side of that glare ice.

I said, "Open your eyes."

He said, "Where is that glare ice?"

I said, "It's behind you."

He said, "How did I get over here?"

I said, "Now you can understand. You walked as if the cement was bare. When you try to walk on ice the usual tendency is to tense your muscles, preparing for a fall. You get a mental set. And you slip that way. If you put the weight of your legs down straight, the way you would on dry cement, you wouldn't slip. The slide comes because you don't put down your full weight and because you tense yourself."

It took me a long time to find that out. Did you ever walk
upstairs one step too many? What an awful jolt it is! Walk down-
stairs one too many—you can break a leg. And yet you are totally
unaware of that set.

As Rosen explains, what Erickson has done here is to help the man
get "out of a fixed mental set. The first step is to confuse the subject.
The second step, during this confused period, is to lead the subject
over the obstacle so that the subject has an experience of success." In
this particular case, "the experience of success occurred when the subject failed to respond with his usual tightening, with his usual mental
set. The old set is replaced with a new one." Rosen also notes that the
man is likely to approach new "slippery" situations without carrying
over the fear associated with previous "falls." He also believes it was
important for the man not to use things he knows or perceptions that
he ordinarily would use. For this reason, Erickson had the man close
his eyes. Once the man stopped seeing, he could accomplish the task:
"Seeing had previously caused him to have a kinesthetic reaction that
caused him to adopt the wrong set."[26]

There are two other aspects of this story that Rosen does not comment on, but are also important. One is the fact that the man is a war
veteran who had lost his leg in battle, and now walks with an artificial leg. By observing that he was a war veteran, Erickson placed
himself in the man's own frame of reference. Perhaps he imagines the
man having his leg blown off by a landmine, or amputated as a result
of a wound suffered in close-range fighting with the enemy. Either
way, the ordeal of walking across the ice field is reminiscent of his
experiences in war. In other words, the man has a personal history
that Erickson takes seriously.

How does Erickson know that the man is a war veteran? One
assumes he knows this because he makes a connection between the
man's physical disability, his age, and the fact that a war is going on.
Also, since Erickson meets the veteran on his way to the induction
board, he noticed that he was heading toward the same building,
perhaps to pick up his disability check. This is all part of being
observant. But it helps Erickson in assessing the degree to which the
man fears crossing the ice and what kind of assistance he is likely to
accept or reject. His receptivity to help may also be due to the fact
that Erickson himself has a very obvious limp. He may not have

accepted help so willingly from someone who did not have a similar disability. But, in any event, it was important that Erickson, in his offer of assistance, did nothing to undermine the veteran's personal dignity and self-pride.

Another important aspect of the story is Erickson's repetition of the phrase "glare ice." While "glare" is not a very common word for a sheet of ice, it *is* in the dictionary ("glare: a smooth, bright, glassy surface, as of ice"). But "glare" has other meanings, including "to shine with a strong, steady, dazzling light," "to be too bright and showy," and "to stare fiercely or angrily." Thus, it also has certain more ominous or even sinister connotations ("to stare fiercely or angrily") as well as of excess ("too bright and showy"). It may also call to mind the phrase in our national anthem, "And the rocket's red glare, the bombs bursting in air." Its ominousness, its excess: these related connotations of the word *glare* connect it, metaphorically, to the battlefield. So, too, does Erickson's use of the confusion technique. Battlefields are obviously dangerous, but the fear they evoke is compounded by the atmosphere of confusion. What Erickson has done in this case is to use confusion constructively, to show that while confusion usually has very negative consequences, it may also have its positive ones. By disorienting the man, he helped him accomplish his goal of getting across the ice without falling.[27]

As noted earlier, Erickson's reputation was established on his work with hypnosis. In 1957 he founded the American Society of Clinical Hypnosis, and he edited the *American Journal of Clinical Hypnosis* from 1958 to 1968. Most of the therapists who consider themselves students of his are trained in hypnotherapy. The following story illustrates how he used hypnosis in his therapeutic work and, at the same time, shows that he did not consider hypnosis a substitute for the client's own agency in the solving of a personal problem.[28]

One counselee came to him because she had heard that he performed hypnosis. She hoped that this would be a relatively easy way for her to lose weight. As the story shows, he *did* use hypnosis with her; not, however, for the purpose of making it easier for her to achieve weight loss, but to make it more difficult. As the Lanktons point out, he used hypnosis with what Viktor E. Frankl termed "paradoxical intention."[29]

Reduce-Gain-Reduce

A woman came to see me and she said, "I weigh 180 pounds. I've dieted successfully under doctors' orders hundreds of times. And I want to weigh 130 pounds. Every time I get to 130 pounds I rush into the kitchen to celebrate my success. I put it back on, right away. Now I weigh 180. Can you use hypnosis to help me reduce to 130 pounds? I'm back to 180 for the hundredth time." I told her yes. I could help her reduce by hypnosis, but she wouldn't like what I did.

She said she wanted to weigh 130 pounds and she didn't care what I did.

I told her she'd find it rather painful.

She said, "I'll do anything you say."

I said, "All right. I want an absolute promise from you that you will follow my advice exactly."

She gave me the promise very readily and I put her into a trance. I explained to her again that she wouldn't like my method of reducing her weight and would she promise me, absolutely, that she would follow my advice? She gave me that promise.

Then I told her, "Let both your unconscious mind and your conscious mind listen. Here's the way you go about it. Your present weight is now 180 pounds. I want you to gain twenty pounds and when you weigh 200 pounds, you may start reducing."

She literally begged me, on her knees, to be released from her promise. And every ounce she gained she became more and more insistent on being allowed to start reducing. She was markedly distressed when she weighed 190 pounds. When she was 195 she begged and implored to be released from her own promise. At 199 she said that was close enough to 200 pounds and I insisted on 200 pounds.

When she reached 200 pounds she was very happy that she could begin to reduce. And when she got to 130 she said, "I'm never going to gain again."

Her pattern had been to reduce and gain. I reversed the pattern and made her gain and reduce. And she was very happy with the final results and maintained the weight. She didn't want to, ever again, go through that horrible agony of gaining twenty pounds.

Rosen explains what has happened here: "For this patient, the gaining of weight is no longer either rebellion or an expression of something she wants to do. It has become something she has been coerced into doing. Therefore, just as she had previously resented having to lose weight, she now resents having to gain weight."[30] What Erickson has shown, according to Rosen, is that it is often helpful to get patients to change their pattern. In this case, he simply had the woman reverse her pattern of reducing and gaining. Once she had done this she could no longer go through the same sequence repeatedly, as she had done all her life. She apparently had learned to be able to tolerate gaining weight only up to 180 pounds. We see this in many weight patients. They have a level of tolerance, at which point they urgently feel the need to reduce. Erickson succeeded in making this tolerance level intolerable because he made her go beyond it.[31]

Note that the woman had come to Erickson with the expectation that, through hypnosis, the loss of weight would be relatively easy. What he did, however, was to make it harder for her to lose weight and thus *harder for her to regain it again.* As she previously had been successful in losing a considerable amount of weight when she made the effort, she didn't need hypnosis to help her lose weight more easily. She had already proven that she could do *that* on her own. He judged that what would be hardest for her would be to gain additional weight beyond her current 180 pounds. The gaining of this additional weight proved such an intolerable experience that she was determined never to have to repeat it.

In another story, similar to the preceding one, Erickson uses an approach that Rosen places under the category of "prescribing the symptom."[32]

A Gorgeous Way to Diet

Now, another girl was overweight, and markedly so. I pointed out to her, "You're overweight and you've dieted and dieted, to no avail. And you tell me that you can stay on a diet for a week, or two weeks, even three weeks, and then you fall off and gorge. Then you're despairing and gorge some more."

"Now, I'll give you a medical prescription. Continue the diet given to you by your doctor in the past. Stay on that diet for two weeks and three weeks, if you can. And then, on the last Sunday of that third week, gorge like hell, because it's medical orders. You can't gorge enough to offset your losses in the three weeks. And you can gorge without a sense of guilt because you're under medical orders to gorge all day Sunday. And the following Monday go back to your diet. Stay on it three weeks, if you can, and then have another guiltless gorge day."

> *In my last letter from her she says that there has to be a better way to diet than saving up her hunger three weeks. She wants to be hungry each day, wants to enjoy food and enjoy the proper amount each day. The gorging days gave her the strength to be on the diet for those three weeks.*

Noting the fact that "you can't gorge enough to offset your losses in the three weeks," Erickson here deprives the woman of her belief that gorging after one, two, and three weeks of dieting is a "relapse," a belief that causes her to despair and gorge some more, eventually undoing the positive effects of the dieting. In this case, gorging is reinterpreted as doing what the doctor has ordered. The following day after the gorging, instead of continuing to gorge in the belief that she has failed, she returns to the diet for another two or three weeks. As Rosen points out, this is a story that illustrates the positive effects of "prescribing the symptom." Also noteworthy is Erickson's play on the words *gorging* and *gorgeous*. He takes away the negative connotations of the word *gorge* by associating it with the word *gorgeous*, thus implying that the method he has prescribed is a "beautiful" way to diet. She should not judge her gorging to be ugly or distasteful because it now fits into a dieting program that is a veritable work of art. The gorging is merely one aspect of this orderly, aesthetically pleasing process; it is the exception that proves that order reigns. Note, too, that he does not undermine the efforts of her medical doctor but supports these while only seeming to subvert them.

The fact that Erickson chooses Sunday as the day that she is allowed to eat all she wants is also significant. Since Sunday is the day when she would find herself most vulnerable to breaking the diet, telling her that this is the day that she has no choice but to break her diet effectively eliminates the guilt that eating on Sunday would otherwise generate. However, Sunday also has a deeper, metaphorical connotation, as it is the day we associate with religious observance, with demands for perfection. In this light, the biblical story that comes to mind is the story recounted in Matt. 12:1-8:

> At that time Jesus went through the grainfields on the sabbath; his disciples were hungry, and they began to pluck heads of grain and to eat. When the Pharisees saw it, they said to him, "Look, your disciples are doing what is not lawful to do on the sabbath." He said to them, "Have you not read what David did when he and his companions

were hungry? He entered the house of God and ate the bread of the Presence, which it was not lawful for him or his companions to eat, but only for the priests. Or have you not read in the law how on the sabbath the priests in the temple break the sabbath and yet are guiltless? I tell you, something greater than the temple is here. But if you had known what this means, 'I desire mercy and not sacrifice,' you would not have condemned the guiltless. For the Son of Man is lord of the sabbath."

A couple of chapters later, when the Pharisees and scribes complain that Jesus' disciples do not even wash their hands when they eat, Jesus points out that his critics have made a greater travesty of the tradition, and then says to the people gathered around, "Listen and understand: it is not what goes into the mouth that defiles a person, but it is what comes out of the mouth that defiles" (Matt. 15:1-10). Then, when the disciples reported that his critics took offense at what Jesus had just said, he replied, "Do you not see that whatever goes into the mouth enters the stomach, and goes out into the sewer? But what comes out of the mouth proceeds from the heart, and this is what defiles" (15:17).

This dispute between Jesus and his critics may seem light years removed from Erickson's story of the woman who is ordered to gorge on Sundays, but it makes explicit what is left implicit in Erickson's story, the fact that gorging oneself is not an offense against God, and neither is it self-defiling. What *is* an offense against God and *is* self-defiling is *verbal hypocrisy*—the lying and deceit that issues from the mouth. If Erickson removes her guilt by "ordering" her to gorge on Sunday, he also, more implicitly, addresses her shame for not being able to achieve absolute control over her eating, for her lapses, which appear to prove that she has a defective self. In removing her shame as well as her guilt, he reframes her situation as *not* a problem with her personally but with the original prescription—her doctor's dietary plan—which in its perfectionism and legalism required *refinement* so that it would have the effect that the doctor intended. Like "gorgeous," "refinement" has an aesthetic connotation, suggesting, metaphorically, that the gorging she does on selected Sundays is neither disgusting nor distasteful.

As Rosen points out, Erickson would vary his approach depending on how he perceived the counselee, and depending on how the counselee articulated the problem that brought him to Erickson's office. In the following story, Erickson tells us what he might normally have done in this particular case, and then relates how he decided to take a very different approach. Rosen views this as "a beautiful example of indirect suggestion, applied symbolically."[33]

Cacti

Usually I send alcoholic patients to AA because AA can do a better job than I can. An alcoholic came to me and he said, "My grandparents on both sides were alcoholics; my parents were alcoholics; my wife's parents were alcoholics; my wife is an alcoholic and I have had delirium tremens eleven times. I am sick of being an alcoholic. My brother is an alcoholic too. Now, that is a hell of a job for you. What do you think you can do about it?"

I asked him what his occupation was.

"When I am sober I work on a newspaper. And alcohol is an occupational hazard there."

I said, "Alright, you want me to do something about it—with that history. Now, the thing I am going to suggest to you won't seem the right thing. You go out to the Botanical Gardens. You look at all the cacti there and marvel at cacti that can survive three years without water, without rain. And do a lot of thinking."

Many years later a young woman came in and said, "Dr. Erickson, you knew me when I was three years old. I moved to California when I was three years old. Now I am in Phoenix and I came to see what kind of man you were—what you looked like."

I said, "Take a good look, and I'm curious to know why you want to look at me."

She said, "Any man who would send an alcoholic out to the Botanical Gardens to look around, to learn how to get along without alcohol, and have it work, is the kind of man I want to see! My mother and my father have been sober ever since you sent my father out there."

"What is your father doing now?"

"He's working for a magazine. He got out of the newspaper business. He says the newspaper business has an occupational hazard of alcoholism."

Now, that was a nice way to cure an alcoholic. Get him to respect cacti that survive three years without rain. You see you can talk about your textbooks. Today you take up this much. Tomorrow you take up that much. They say you do such and such. But actually you ought to look at your patient to figure out what kind of a man he is—or woman—then deal with the patient in a way that fits his or her problem.

What Erickson does here is similar to the suggestion he employs in the case of the "African Violet Queen." He makes an association between the man and the cacti. Both are living things, but the one fills himself with liquid until he is miserable while the other goes for months, even years, without any liquid whatsoever, and is thriving. Unlike humans, who often have a hard time "holding their liquor," the cactus is remarkably adept in "holding its liquid." (Cut into a cactus with a knife and you discover just how wet it is inside.) Erickson does not direct the man to quit drinking but instead suggests that he do a lot of thinking about how well the cacti do without continual liquid nourishment. In effect, he has told a parable, not unlike Jesus' parable about the lilies who neither sow nor spin, and yet are more beautifully clothed than Solomon himself (Matt. 6:27-30). As a parable, Erickson's proposal is suggestive but not coercive. He knows that he does not have the authority or power to compel the man to stop drinking. All that he can do (or chooses to do in this instance) is to plant the seed in the man's mind—"Can I live as the cacti live?"—and leaves it to the man to answer this question for himself. "Consider the lilies of the field. . . ." "Go out to the Botanical Gardens . . . *and do a lot of thinking.*"

Erickson says that he usually sends alcoholic patients to AA because they can do a better job than he can. He doesn't do that in this instance in spite of the fact that the man appears to be an especially good candidate for AA, and an especially poor risk for Erickson himself to try to help. In fact, until the man's daughter appears years later, Erickson doesn't know that he has actually helped the man. On the other hand, he prefaced his suggestion that the man go over to the Botanical Gardens with this preemptive comment, "Now, the thing I am going to suggest to you won't seem the right thing." Thus, he anticipates the man's reaction that he is being given bad or frivolous advice and effectively blocks it: "You think that what I am suggesting you do is a stupid idea. Well, I told you beforehand that you would think that." This implies that the man is not doing any great thinking himself if he thinks that Erickson's idea is not any good. Thus, it creates an odd sort of receptivity: "If he is about to give me what he thinks I'll think is bad advice, maybe I'll surprise him by taking his 'bad advice' seriously."

An underlying theme in this story is respect. Erickson says that he got the man "to respect cacti that survive three years without rain." But Erickson also got the man to respect *him* for *not* recommending the usual prescription for alcoholism (that is, referral to AA). One can imagine the man saying to himself if Erickson had followed his "usual" approach and recommended AA, "What kind of psychiatrist are you? Can't you be any more creative than that?" In deciding to take a different, even eccentric approach, one that could not have been predicted beforehand, Erickson was following his principle of entering into the client's world. The man, after all, was a writer. As such, he could appreciate Erickson's parable of the man who goes across town to sit alongside the cacti and does a lot of thinking. This is a creative little story, and one guesses that this man could see himself better in Erickson's story than in the usual AA story, which, while inspirational for many, is also rather predictable, and thus easily dismissed. The story of a man taking lessons from cacti is certainly unusual. For a writer, its very unorthodoxy would be intriguing. Unconsciously, if not consciously, it plays off the far more common story of the man who goes into a bar and sits on a stool, pours out his woes to a sympathetic bartender, and does "a lot of *drinking*." To sit and marvel at cacti is certainly a variation on *that* familiar and often hopeless tale.

Erickson's handling of the matter of the family's long history of alcoholism is also quite unorthodox. Here, again, he refuses to go by the book. Given the fact that alcoholism prevails in both the man's and his wife's families, one might have expected Erickson to take a family systems approach, focusing on the fact that alcoholism "runs in the family." Had he done so, however, he would have confirmed the man's own contention that, in light of this family history, he has presented Erickson with "a hell of a job. . . . What do you think you can do about it?" By refusing to get involved in exploring the family history and instead proposing a relatively simple course of action, Erickson placed the burden squarely on the man's own shoulders: "If you are an alcoholic, this is because you choose to be one. The family history does not interest me. It is a convenient excuse. Also, if history is the issue, then let us consider the history of the cacti, a type of plant which has survived for centuries in very inhospitable environments, yet members of which have lived for 300 years or more. The history of the cacti is infinitely more inspiring—and maybe more relevant—than the history of your particular family." An alcoholic who comes into a psychiatrist's office and immediately places the burden on the psychiatrist's own shoulders—"Now, that is a hell of a job for you"—can appreciate how skillfully the psychiatrist in this instance refused to be conned. Any self-respecting alcoholic would have to respect this particular psychiatrist, for Erickson did not let himself get caught in the trap that had been set for him.

On the other hand, by asking the man what he did for a living, he *did* enter the client's world. As the man explained to Erickson and later to his daughter, he *was* in a profession that posed particular hazards for an alcoholic. This, however, was a contextual factor that he could alter by leaving the newspaper profession and becoming involved with a magazine instead. In contrast to the family history, over which he had no direct control, he *could* exercise control in his profession, and Erickson implied as much when he parried the man's assertion that his family history presented *Erickson* with "a hell of a job" by asking, seemingly tangentially, what *his* "job" happened to be.

How did Erickson develop his unorthodox approach to psychotherapy? *My Voice Will Go with You* has several stories that go back to Erickson's early years as a psychiatrist at Worcester State Hospital in Massachusetts. In his introduction to these stories, Rosen states that "In dealing with psychotics, Erickson did not attempt to solve all of the patient's problems. As with other patients, he tried to bring about small changes that would lead to larger and broader ones."[34] He adds, "Erickson's first psychiatric experiences took place in a mental hospital, and he may have developed some of his important principles of therapy from work with psychotic patients. Certainly, this must have been true of two of his favorite maxims, 'Speak in the patient's language,' and 'Join the Patient.'"[35] In the following story, Erickson tells how he got a patient to give him a history.[36]

Inside Out

At Worcester I had a patient who always returned your greeting. If you asked him a question, he looked at you brightly. He was gentle,

docile, very quiet. He went to the mess hall, went to bed, was order-
ly, had nothing to say. He said "Hello" or "Goodbye." I got tired of
trying to interview him. I wanted his history. And he was obviously
in a world of unreality. It took me quite a while to figure out how to
get into his world.

One day I walked up to him and said, "Hello." He said, "Hello."
Then I took off my jacket, turned it inside out, and put it on backwards.

Then I took his jacket off, turned it inside out, put it on him
backwards, and said, "I'd like to have you tell me your story." I got
a history. Join the patient.

Rosen says that what Erickson did here was to "symbolically
enter" the patient's "inside-out" and "backwards" world of unreality: "Once the two of them were in the same 'world' (inside out and
backwards), they could talk to one another." Rosen also notes the fact
that the patient "always returned your greeting" was a good indica-
tor that he was likely to imitate the therapist's behavior. I wonder, too,
whether Erickson's putting his own jacket on "backwards" carried a
subliminal meaning, that he was "joining the patient" in the "back
ward," where the sickest patients were located. This would mean that
he would join the patient wherever he happened to be.

In another story, Erickson tells about a psychotic patient named
Herbert who, among his various symptoms, refused to eat solid
food. The first problem was how to get him to eat.[37]

Herbert

I knew that Herbert had once been a small child. I knew I had been.
I knew that all people were once small children and that they all had
human nature. I just employed human nature. How would you
make Herbert swallow solid food?

I had Herbert sit down at a table, with a plate full of food in
front of him. On one side was a deteriorated patient and on the
other side was a deteriorated patient. And they never ate food from
their plates. They always ate from somebody else's plate.

And Herbert knew that his plate was his. But the only way he
could keep it his was by swallowing it! He didn't want those damn
crazy fools to eat his food! That's human nature.

After he'd eaten his first solid-food meal, I asked Herbert how he
liked his dinner. He answered, "I didn't like it but I had to eat it. It
was mine."

I said, "I told you that you could swallow solid food."

Having gained this small victory, Erickson set about convincing Herbert that he had a real appetite for food. He sat Herbert next to the chef who, by prior arrangement, had twice as much food on her plate as she could possibly eat. As Herbert, without any food on his plate, watched her eat, getting hungrier by the minute, he finally asked her, "May I have some?" Next, Erickson rekindled Herbert's interest in card playing by forcing him to watch a game of cards being played by patients who were so deteriorated mentally that each was playing a different game, more or less—one poker, one bridge, one pinochle, and so forth. Their play so disgusted Herbert that he asked Erickson and the two attendants Erickson had used to compel Herbert to watch to join him in a game of their own. Erickson concludes: "A few months later Herbert was discharged from the hospital. He regained weight, to my knowledge, up to 180 pounds, and worked every day. All I did for him was correct his symptoms. [Actually,] I put him in a situation where *he* corrected his symptoms."[38]

Rosen comments that Erickson enabled Herbert "to recognize that he had an appetite for life as well as for food."[39] "Life," however, is an abstract idea, and what Erickson did was to link this desire for "life" to other living things, whether the African violet in the case of the woman who saw no purpose in living, or the cacti in the case of the man who was destroying his life through alcohol abuse. In the case of Herbert, Erickson simply exploited the fact that it is "human nature" to fight for the basic resources we need to sustain our lives. By placing him in the midst of patients who threatened to take these basic life sources from him, Erickson was guessing that Herbert would fight back.

Erickson also understood that we may become our own best allies when we are fighting for our lives. In the following story, he tells about his own struggle for life.[40]

The Boy Will Be Dead by Morning

I graduated from high school in June 1919. In August, I heard three doctors, in the other room, tell my mother, "The boy will be dead by morning."

Being a normal kid, I resented that.

Our country doctor had called in two Chicago men, as consultants, and they told my mother, "The boy will be dead by morning."

I was infuriated. The idea of telling a mother that her son will be dead by morning! It's outrageous!

Afterwards, my mother came into my room, bland of face. She thought I was delirious, because I insisted that she move the large chest in my room, in order for it to be at a different angle beside the bed. She put it beside the bed one way and I kept telling her to move it back and forth, until I was satisfied. That chest was blocking my view through the window—and I was damned if I would die without seeing the sunset! I only saw half of it. I was unconscious for three days.

I didn't tell my mother. She didn't tell me.

According to Rosen, this story conveys one of Erickson's therapeutic maxims: "Always look to a real goal, in the near future." In this case, "his goal was to see the sunset. Of course, before this goal could be achieved, it was necessary to move the obstacle."[41]

While Erickson was careful not to make excessive claims for his methods and techniques, his stories convey that problems, whatever their nature, may be overcome. Rosen believes this is because Erickson, through his stories, "helps a patient get in touch with her own unutilized knowledge."[42] As Erickson often pointed out, there are so many things we know but have forgotten that we know. His task as a therapist was to help his patients recall the knowledge that could help them in the situation at hand. Rosen also notes that Erickson's stories often include the theme of a quest. True, "The accomplishment of one of Erickson's assigned tasks may not have the heroic drama of the Golden Fleece, but the inner drama and feelings of accomplishment are comparable."[43] My own personal story illustrates both of these points.

A Lazy Way to Diet

Several years ago, I had a serious weight problem. I had gained several pounds a year over the space of five or six years, and there was seemingly no end in sight. Previously a rather thin person, weighing in the neighborhood of 160–165 pounds, I had gained forty-five pounds and weighed in the neighborhood of 210 pounds. I was troubled by this weight gain, my wife was concerned about it, and the doctor to whom I went for annual check-ups was beginning to issue definite warnings that I was on a dangerous path.

One evening I was reading Newsweek, *when I came across an article about powerful men in the U.S. Congress. As I read, the following phrase suddenly leaped out from the page, as if it were printed in bold letters: "Dan Rostenkowski, a big, burly man of 6'2" and 220 pounds, . . ." As I am exactly the same height as Rostenkowski, I realized that I had only ten more pounds to go—on my present schedule, about a year—and I would fit the description of "big and burly." On the one hand, I have often admired men who are "big and burly," as I associate them with "friendly and kind." But, having been very thin throughout my childhood, adolescence, and young adulthood, the phrase "big and burly" didn't square with my self-image. I decided, then and there, that I would lose weight.*

But how? I began making an inventory of the things that I was not very likely to do. I knew that I would not go to a diet center, mainly because I am too "frugal" to pay for something that I can do for myself. I also knew that I would not become the typical dieter, finding out about the calories and fat content of the foods I eat. I knew this because I recalled that when others talked about various foods having so-and-so many calories, my mind would wander and I wouldn't hear anything that was being said. The numbers meant nothing to me. Nor was I likely to begin exercising. The idea that I might join an athletic team, begin jogging, or try gymnastics was absurd. The doctor had advised me to get a dog because the dog would insist on going for walks. But, as I patiently explained to my wife, "Dogs prefer to go out and run around. Why confine them to a leash? If a dog wants to go for a walk, let him go on his own walk."

These sound like rationalizations. No doubt they are. But Erickson takes them at face value. He calls it "joining the patient's world," which is exactly what I was doing: viewing my problem from the perspective of the one who had the problem. I do not defend the "patient's world" in this case—his refusal to exercise, his distracted (superior?) attitude when others talked calories, his ridicule of his doctor's idea that he buy a dog—I simply identify it for what it was.

So what to do? Then an idea suddenly hit me. I drew on knowledge that I had forgotten I had. I recalled the years that I had spent as a visitor in hospitals and nursing homes: as a teenager peddling papers to patients, as a hospital janitor, as an orderly, as a student chaplain, as a pastor making visits. I recalled the numerous times that I had overheard one nurse saying to another, "I can't get Mrs. Smith to eat. All she wants to do is sleep. She'll waste away."

Could this be the answer? Is there an inverse relationship between eating and sleeping, such that a person who oversleeps becomes oblivious to food?

Erickson might say that I was simply identifying a fact about "human nature," though the fact that bears who hibernate in winter go without food suggests that, if so, it applies to other species as well. Also, I had made a *connection* between two experiences that were previously unrelated in my mind. There was my own undesired weight *gain* and there was my experience of overhearing nurses who were very frustrated by patients who were *losing* weight! This, too, is very Ericksonian.

I decided to try it. I began going to bed at eight o'clock every evening and remaining in bed until seven o'clock in the morning, a total of eleven hours of sleep every night. The first night I had great hunger pangs around ten or eleven o'clock, but these eventually subsided, and when I got up in the morning I had no desire for food whatsoever. Just for something to drink. By about eleven in the morning, I would be hungry, but not ravenously so. I would eat whatever appealed to me for lunch and this would sustain me to dinner, when I would eat whatever appealed to me, pretty much the same food that I had eaten before going on my new "sleeping program." (I refused to call it a "dieting program" because it wasn't that, though the goal—weight loss—was the same.) Then back to bed at eight o'clock. After two days of this new routine, I began to lose weight at a rate of a pound per day, sometimes two, and in the course of the next thirty days, I had lost thirty-five pounds.

I eventually returned to my former sleeping schedule, but somewhat reluctantly, as I had found to my surprise that I accomplished as much in thirteen waking hours as I had previously accomplished in sixteen or seventeen waking hours. But, I made a significant change in my eating habits to insure that I would not regain the pounds I had lost. I allotted myself one item of food for breakfast, two items for lunch, and three items for dinner. It didn't matter what these items were. All that mattered was the number. Unlike others who counted calories, I counted items. My reasoning here was that with an increasing number of items as the day progressed, my expectations were getting better, not worse. I was starting the day with one and ending with three. This method worked well. Not only did I not gain back what I had lost, but I lost another ten pounds.

I like to think of this as an inspirational story, an account of how one individual, who happens to be the storyteller, was faced with a weight problem and did something about it. I had taken stock of who I am ("entering the patient's own world"), I had made a connection between two experiences previously unrelated (my weight problem and my overhearing of nurses' complaints), and I had "prescribed" for myself something altogether unexpected, that is, going to bed when only small children and maybe a few Midwestern farmers still do. I also created for myself a working maxim: "I will sleep my way to better health."

What about the "diet" I adopted after the big weight loss had been achieved? This was a pure reframing, similar to Erickson's demand in "Reduce-Gain-Reduce" that the woman *gain* weight before losing so that the pattern becomes not losing-gaining but gaining-losing. Instead of the usual dieting pattern of having a "good healthy breakfast" and then, as the day progresses, giving up this or that, I wanted the sense that, as the day progresses, the situation gets better, not worse. By thinking in terms of "items," and giving them a numerical value only, I created a caricature, a parody, of the dieting plans I obviously disdained. Like the "calorie counters," I had my numerical system too, but it was something a five-year-old child could understand. No complicated math for me! Food had been converted into numbers, but the numbers didn't mean much. Also irrelevant was the question of whether the six items I had each day were "good" for me. All that mattered is that as the day unfolded my plate got fuller. I found I could live with that.

As one might expect, acquaintances who noticed that I was losing weight and were informed of how I was getting the job done would frequently offer theories and explanations for why it was working. But I found myself listening to these explanations with the same rapt *inattention* that I had previously greeted talk about the calories found in various foods. These theories and explanations may have something to them. I wouldn't know. What I *do* know is that Erickson makes a lot of sense to me when he tells his listeners at the conclusion of his "Cacti" story:

> You see you can talk about your textbooks. Today you take up this much. Tomorrow you take up that much. They say you do such and such. But actually you ought to look at your patient to find out what kind of man he is—or woman—then deal with the patient in a way that fits his or her problem, his or her unique problem.

Or, to paraphrase Erickson's conclusion to his story, "Walk a Mile": "Now, I didn't refer myself to a diet center. I didn't recommend that I buy myself a dog. I didn't tell myself I had to exercise. I didn't take away my favorite food. I just gave myself permission to sleep an inordinate number of hours each day." Did I treat myself like a child? If I did, I knew I could play *that* role better than these other roles because I had played it once before, more or less successfully. Given the nature of the task I assigned myself, it obviously did not, as Rosen puts it, "have the heroic drama of the Golden Fleece," but I would certainly agree with his subsequent statement that "the inner drama and feelings of accomplishment are comparable."

Life Imitates Art

In assessing what Erickson was able to accomplish as a therapist, it is important to recognize that *he* is the one who tells the stories about what he was able to accomplish as a therapist. These stories were primarily for younger therapists who placed themselves under his tutelage, though he also told them to patients, using stories of other patients to suggest ways in which current patients might address their own problems. Because Erickson is the identified storyteller, we might, however, fail to recognize that it was always the patient who initiated the storytelling. Without an initial story from the patient—usually a story about the problem that prompted her to seek his help and what she has already tried to do about it—there would be no story for Erickson himself to tell. As the case entitled "Inside Out" makes clear, Erickson could not help a patient who could not or would not tell him his personal story. Thus, his own stories build on the stories that his patients tell. *They* are the original storytellers. Then, following their lead, he tells two additional stories. One is the story he tells the patient about how she might do things differently, and the other is the story he tells others about the eventual outcome. In the "teaching tales" edited by Rosen, these three story layers are usually conflated into one single narrative.

For example, in the story entitled "Cacti," Erickson first listens to the story that the patient tells about being an alcoholic from a family of alcoholics. This story concludes with the patient saying to Erickson, "Now, that is a hell of a job for you. What do you think you can do about it?" Next, Erickson tells the patient a hypothetical story. It envisions the patient going over to the Botanical Gardens, taking a seat near the cacti and doing "a lot of thinking." This is a story told for the client's own benefit. Erickson knows that he cannot compel him to go to the Botanical Gardens. He also knows that even if the patient does go to the Botanical Gardens, it may not do any good, since the patient might continue drinking after doing "a lot of thinking." But the hypothetical story in this instance has a strong suggestion of quest, and somehow the patient knows that as he leaves the office and whatever he then decides to do, Erickson's voice—for better or worse—will go with him. This will be a voice that he cannot easily ignore precisely because it has "instructed" him to do something unusual and unexpected. Like the nobleman, Naaman, who was instructed by the prophet Elisha to wash himself in the River Jordan (2 Kings 5:10), the man finds this instruction difficult to counteract precisely because it violates his expectations.[44]

But Erickson does not tell us in so many words that the man actually went out to the Botanical Gardens. We only infer this from his daughter's statement, "Any man who would send an alcoholic out to the Botanical Gardens to look around, to learn how to get along without alcohol, and have it work, is the kind of man I want to see!" For all *we* know, the man may not have gone to the Botanical Gardens. Possibly, Erickson's hypothetical story was enough to effect the change, as the man saw himself in the story, and entered fully into it. Erickson is vague about the matter of whether the man actually went out to the gardens—purposely, in my view—because it may not matter all that much.

Then, instead of telling us that the man went to the Botanical Gardens and was immediately cured, Erickson moves to the third story, the story about how the man's daughter stopped by his office many years later, and how he learned through her that he had cured her father and mother too. This third story, like the story he tells of having read in the papers about the "African Violet Queen" on the occasion of her death, adds additional drama to the narrative, as it indirectly informs his listeners that it was not until many years had passed that he learned the outcome of his attempt to help the man with his drinking problem. He seems to say to his listeners that they may—or they may not—come to know the difference they have made in the lives of their clients, but when they do find out in some unexpected way, and it turns out to have been positive, this news comes as a nice, unexpected, but very welcome, gift. If Erickson used the unexpected to help his clients, consider the effect of this unexpected visit by the man's daughter on Erickson himself! It is reminiscent of Jesus' healing of the ten lepers (Luke 17:11-19). How does he know that all have been healed? Because one of them, a foreigner, came back to thank him. Especially inspiring in "Cacti" is that it was the daughter—the one who would most profit from her parents' sobriety—who came to give Erickson the good news. The story without end—a family that has been caught in the deadly grip of alcohol from generation to generation—has finally, with the daughter's story, found its own ending, and the ending is very good indeed.

We may, then, characterize Erickson's as a *three-story* universe. The first story is told by the counselee, and is usually a story of frustration and failure. The second story is told by Erickson to the counselee, and it is an imaginative story in which the counselee is the main character doing something very different from what she has previously been doing. The third story is Erickson's account of the outcome. His therapeutic, or strategic intervention is, of course, the second story. This is a story that discerns the possibilities for change that are already implicit in the story the client tells. For Erickson to be able to tell the second story, it is essential that he has listened attentively to the original story, for out of the details of the client's story he will formulate his own intervention, his own variation on the original story, a variation that envisions a very different ending.

It Is OK to Fail

As Rosen's collection of Erickson's stories makes clear, not all of his therapeutic interventions worked. Here is a story in which he was unsuccessful and accepted the fact.[45]

Sight-Seeing

A woman said she wanted me to do something about her weight. I looked at her fingernails. She had long, red fingernails. I think they're advertised as "Nails." You glue them on. They stick out. That amount of fat and those red fingernails!

*I said, "I can help you, but you'll have to cooperate. You climb
Squaw Peak."*

She said, "At sunrise?"

I said, "Yes."

She said, "Well, I'd like some company."

*I said, "You complain that your sixteen-year-old son is about a
hundred pounds overweight. Take him along for company. Set a
good example for him."*

*Next time I saw her she said, "You know, I don't believe I want
to lose weight and I know my son doesn't. Do you mind if I stop
trying to fool myself?"*

I said, "Not at all."

By commenting on the woman's nails, which he seems to take as
a sign that she is frivolous, Erickson prepares the listener for what
also seems to be a rather demanding "prescription" for her, that of
climbing Squaw Peak. Her perception of its difficulty is reflected in
her question, "At sunrise?" She ponders the prospect of getting up
early in the morning to climb Squaw Peak and begins to negotiate,
"Well, I'd like some company." Instead of saying, "Of course, take
along someone to make the climb more pleasant," he suggests that
she take her overweight son. As listeners, we assume this is not exactly the "company" she had in mind. As Erickson soon learns, the task
he set for her was too difficult and more than she had bargained for.
Yet, in spite of this failure, something *was* accomplished, for she
made an important self- discovery: "I don't believe I want to lose
weight. . . . Do you mind if I stop trying to fool myself."

The story does not have the successful ending that *we* wanted it to
have, but ending as it does—in self-discovery—how can we not have
respect for the client, as she came to a new insight about herself? This
story, of course, is reminiscent of the biblical story of the rich young
ruler (Matt. 19:16-22), one of the few instances in which Jesus is
reported by the Gospel writers to have failed. The early church tradition that identifies the rich young ruler as Paul and therefore suggests that Jesus did not ultimately fail indicates how much we want
our heroes to succeed every time. But the inclusion of failure stories
in *My Voice Will Go with You* is important, as they make the critical point that there are times when we cannot make everything turn
out as we want it to. Instructive for us in this particular case is that
Erickson does not chide or condemn the woman, but readily accepts

her decision to "stop trying to fool" herself. He can accept it because he recognizes that she has gained a true insight into herself, and why should we automatically assume that losing weight is more important than gaining such an insight?

This story also illustrates Carl Rogers's point that, at bottom, each person is asking, "Who am I, *really*? How can I get in touch with the real self, underlying all my surface behavior? How can I become myself?" In this light, the woman's decision to quit fooling herself and Erickson's acceptance of this decision may be viewed as an achievement that was, for her, as momentous as hiking to the top of Squaw Peak, for she moved away in her own self-experiencing from "oughts," from meeting the expectations of others, from pleasing others, and moved toward being a process, being complexity, openness to her own experience, acceptance of others, and trust of self. The "culture" may not approve of her decision because, after all, it idealizes thinness and treats women of her size as though they were moral degenerates. Such attitudes are found among Christians in spite of Jesus' own defense and preference for the company of persons who in his day were considered "gluttonous."[46] While Erickson's "That amount of fat . . ." comment suggests that he shared to some extent the prevailing "culture" of his time, nevertheless, he gave the woman "permission" to move away from "oughts" and "expectations" of others and toward not trying to be other than who she was, with the attendant feelings of defensiveness that this creates. If the story begins with a "prescription" to climb Squaw Peak and take her son with her, a prescription that is rather reminiscent of God's command to Abraham to rise up early and climb Mount Moriah with his son, the story concludes with her request for "permission" to remain as she is. Ascribing to Erickson the authority that goes with his being a healer, it matters to her that he gives her his permission *not* to change her appearance, but to accept her appearance as truly reflective of who she is. By giving her his blessing, he insures that this story of an apparent therapeutic failure is no less inspiring than any of the other stories that he tells.

Spreading Stories

I am well aware that the problems that brought patients to Erickson are not very representative of the problems that parishioners bring to their pastors. It is not very likely, for example, that a parishioner with a "weight problem" will immediately think of his pastor as the logical person to consult. At least, when I had a weight problem, I did not think of calling the pastor of the church I attended for a counseling session. My point, then, is not that Erickson's therapeutic stories are immediately transferable to pastoral counseling in the congregational context, but rather that Erickson's therapeutic work directs our attention to the inspirational story and to the art of the power of suggestion. Furthermore, it shows the effect of such stories on the lives not only of the persons he directly helped but also on many other persons who have heard these stories second- and third-hand.

We may think of the stories that he tells as "spreading stories," that is, as stories that go out from their original locus (his counseling office) and touch the lives of many other persons besides the one whom Erickson had helped. In the case of the "Walking a Mile" story, Erickson actually reports that the man who left his office in a rage subsequently talked to another man about what had transpired in Erickson's office, and this prompted the second man to go to see Erickson about *his* problem. This is a clear case of the spreading of a story. We can well imagine that others who also heard the retired policeman's story but did not actually come to see Erickson were also affected by the story and that their lives were also changed by it. Maybe they had exactly the same problem that he had and therefore simply took "the doctor's" advice as if it had been given directly to them. Or maybe they had a different problem but could see how the basic idea of the story—"I gave him the opportunity to walk"— could be applied to *their* problem, the "opportunity to walk" functioning more metaphorically and less literally for them. In either case, the doctor's advice proves both "free" and "freeing."

This property of stories—the fact that if they are inspirational they tend to spread—is, of course, reflected in the Gospels, where we are told that the stories about Jesus' healings spread throughout Galilee and actually preceded his own arrival in the towns he visited, so that crowds had already gathered to await his arrival. As the stories spread, they undoubtedly underwent considerable embellishment. But, equally likely, they underwent refinement, as what was important about the story—the inspirational point—was retained as other aspects of the story were deleted as being unessential to the primary idea of the story.[47] And, of course, the stories would elicit different responses. Some would respond with skepticism, doubting that they were true or that Jesus had the powers ascribed to him. Others would find the stories threatening, for the increase in Jesus' power would mean the diminishment of their own. Still others would find hope for themselves, a family member, or a friend in these stories, while yet others would find their own vocation or calling in the stories that they were hearing.

But how does this relate to pastoral counseling in the congregational context? I suggest that congregations where the pastor "inspires" individuals not only in preaching but also in the counseling role are thereby enhanced, and the congregations where the pastor does not so inspire through the counseling role are thereby impoverished. I do not mean to suggest that the pastor's counseling needs always to result in an individual's or couple's decision to make life-enhancing decisions, but I am suggesting that stories in which a pastor helped them to do so have a natural tendency to spread, and, in spreading, to affect the lives of many other persons who were not the direct recipient of the pastoral counseling.

As Erickson's "Cacti" story illustrates, not only the life of the newspaperman who came to Erickson but also the lives of his wife and his daughter were changed by what happened between Erickson and this man. The man's wife was inspired even though she did not come to Erickson herself but heard what he had advised her husband to do and acted accordingly. My point, then, is not that by inspiring one individual, the pastor's reputation will spread and many parishioners will begin seeking her out, eventually leading to the pastor being overwhelmed with an unmanageable counseling load. It *may* happen this way, but this is not what I am advocating here. Rather, my point is that when the pastor inspires one individual, many others are likely to hear about it and will be inspired as well by the spreading of the story. As the story spreads, it has a ripple effect that can neither be predicted nor programmed in advance. Erickson opens his office door one day and there stands the daughter of the man he talked with years earlier about how cacti get along without water. Or he opens his newspaper one morning and sees an obituary about the woman who, through his simple intervention, found her vocation in life. I believe that pastors can afford to be as intentional about being inspirational in the counseling setting as they are in their preaching, and this means developing the art of the power of suggestion in this context as well. And then they should trust the natural process of inspirational stories to spread on their own accord. If Erickson would say to his patients just before they went into a hypnotic trance that his voice would go with them, his reputation as an inspirational counselor has also spread in ways he could never have predicted, planned, or manipulated. As the scriptures attest, the spirit blows where it will, and where it blows, it makes its presence felt. It is not the number of persons the pastor counsels, or the number of hours the pastor spends in counseling that finally matters, but whether the pastor gives this spirit an opportunity to do its work. Thus, pastoral counseling is a wonderful setting in which to participate in the invention of stories that are inspirational, and a key element in the creation of such stories is the pastor's ability to use, with sensitivity and grace, the art of the power of suggestion.

Chapter 3

The Paradoxical Story

The Art of Untying Knots

From 1948 until his death in 1980, Milton Erickson lived and worked in Phoenix, Arizona. In 1953, Jay Haley was employed by Gregory Bateson, Director of the Mental Health Institute in Palo Alto, California, to work on Bateson's research project on human communication. John Weakland also joined the project, and Bateson, according to Haley, offered them "full freedom to investigate whatever we wished as long as we dealt somehow with the paradoxes that arise in the communicative process."[1] That year, Milton Erickson came to Palo Alto to offer a seminar on hypnosis, and Haley expressed interest to Bateson in attending it. As a result of his attendance at the seminar, Haley began to include the communicative aspects of the hypnotic relationship in his research investigation, and he and John Weakland began to make regular visits to Phoenix to talk with Erickson. Thus was born an informal but vital connection between the Bateson group and Milton Erickson.

In 1958, Don D. Jackson founded the Mental Research Institute in Palo Alto and several of Bateson's associates at the Mental Health Institute, including Haley and Weakland, joined its staff. This institute was one of the few places in the United States where family therapy was being done. They called their method "conjoint family psychotherapy." It involved

meeting with the members of a family at the same time and place rather than, for instance, treating family members individually and in separate sessions either by the same therapist or even by different therapists who may or may not communicate among themselves about their individual efforts.[2]

The Brief Therapy Center of the Mental Research Institute was established in 1966. It incorporated concepts of human communication, interactional therapy (both family and marital), the pathogenic and therapeutic effects of paradoxes (called double binds), and action rather than origin-oriented techniques of problem resolution. Paul Watzlawick came to the Mental Research Institute in 1960 and has been involved with the Brief Therapy Center since its beginnings. Jay Haley moved on to Washington, D.C., where he founded his own Family Therapy Institute.

In this chapter, I will give particular attention to the writings of Paul Watzlawick, mainly because he has been the Brief Therapy Center's most prolific writer. Many of the ideas he presents, however, were being promulgated at the Institute prior to his arrival there, and many of the Center's therapeutic ideas and concepts represent a joint effort, with Weakland an especially important contributor. While many of Watzlawick's books are quite theoretical, they are replete with stories, drawn primarily from obscure historical records and from contemporary counseling sessions.

Virtually all of these stories involve paradox. A paradox, according to *New World Dictionary*, "is a statement that seems contradictory, unbelievable, or absurd but that may actually be true in fact." As if to illustrate the paradox of even trying to define *paradox*, the dictionary also says that paradox "is a statement that is self-contradicting in fact and, hence, false."[3] Thus, a paradoxical statement may be true or it may be false. That it may be either, simultaneously, is also true. Obviously, it is an odd linguistic phenomenon, and is capable of creating a great deal of mischief in human communication.

Bateson's group focused on the behavioral effects of paradox in communication, and their work led to the postulation of the "double-bind" theory of schizophrenia, the theory that children become schizophrenic because one or both parents use paradox in communicating with their child. An example of "double-bind" communication is the well-known story of the mother who gave her son two new shirts for his birthday, a blue one and a brown one. When he appeared the next morning wearing the brown one, she asked, "What, didn't you like the blue one?"[4] We assume, of course, that had he decided to wear the *blue* one instead, she would have asked, "What, didn't you like the *brown* one?"

Another example is Watzlawick's story about the son who felt his mother was coddling him too much, and finally summoned the courage to say to her, "Mother, you treat me like a child!" to which she replied, "But, honey, you *are* my child." Whereas the son meant by "child" someone who is incapable of behaving like an "adult," his mother invoked the idea of "child" as "progeny," and thus "misunderstood" what her son was saying to her. Watzlawick points out:

> Such an answer can have a positively paralyzing effect. . . . In order to overcome the effect of this disqualification and get the conversation halfway back on the firm ground of logic, the son would have to undertake a not uncomplicated, meta-communicative explanation and point out that he used the word "child" in the sense of "immaturity," whereas his mother used it in the sense of "son." The son, especially if he is a so-called patient, might have great difficulties with this correction, while it would be easy for the mother to interpret his reaction as further proof of insanity and ignore it lovingly.[5]

Watzlawick continues with "a similar example from our own research," that of a mother whose psychotic son suddenly started shooting a gun in their apartment. When asked how she responded to this dangerous situation, she replied, "I told him for the hundredth time not to play *in* the house."[6]

While Bateson's group was initially interested in the role of double-bind communication in schizophrenia, subsequent work led to the conclusion that schizophrenia is only a special case of paradoxical language, and that paradox is often found in other types of disturbed communication, including nonpsychotic interaction. They also came to realize that the inadvertent creation of paradox is a typical way in which difficulties can be created and problems mishandled.[7] Systematic discussions of paradox appear in many of Watzlawick's writings. I will focus on the coauthored text, *Pragmatics of Human Communication*, which has two chapters on paradox; one concerned with paradoxical communication, the other with paradox in psychotherapy.[8]

In the first of these two chapters, Watzlawick et al. note that there is something in the nature of paradox that is

> of immediate pragmatic and even existential import for all of us; paradox not only can invade interaction and affect our behavior and our sanity, but also it challenges our belief in the consistency, and therefore the ultimate soundness, of our universe. Furthermore, we will try to show that deliberate paradox . . . has significant therapeutic potential. . . . We hope that from this treatment of paradox it will be seen that consideration of the concept of paradox is of central importance and by no means a retreat into an ivory tower.[9]

Watzlawick and his coauthors define paradox as "a contradiction that follows correct deduction from consistent premises." This definition is intended to exclude "false paradoxes" based on a concealed error in reasoning or a deliberate fallacy. They cite the familiar story about the six men who wanted six single rooms, while the innkeeper had only five rooms available. He "solved" the problem by taking the first man to room no. 1 and asking another man to wait there with the first man for a few minutes. Then he took the third man to room no. 2, the fourth man to room no. 3, and the fifth man to room no. 4. Then he returned to room no. 1, got the sixth gentleman who had been waiting there, and put him up in room no. 5. Problem solved! The fallacy here is in the fact that the second and sixth men are treated as one. The "fact" that six men can occupy five single rooms is only a seeming paradox.

The authors identify three types of real paradoxes, including logico-mathematical paradoxes, paradoxical definitions, and pragmatic paradoxes. Unlike the others, the third type occurs in the course of normal, nontechnical conversation. As they are writing a book on psychotherapy, the authors give most attention to it.

| Therapist: | What would you say, Mr. X, are the main problems in your family? |
| Mr. X: | My contribution to our problem is that I'm a habitual liar. A lot of people will use the expression—uhm—oh, falsehood or exaggeration or bull-slinger, many things—but actually it's lying. . . .[10] |

This response, while apparently forthright and honest, actually puts the therapist in a potentially immobilizing position. How will she know if and when the father is lying? How can therapy proceed in the face of such a paradoxical relationship message?

Since the dilemma in this case may not be immobilizing ("Surely a good therapist will be able to discern when Mr. X is lying and when he is telling the truth"), the following is a more instructive example of how pragmatic paradoxes place a person in a psychologically immobilizing position. This case involves a conversation between a mother and her schizophrenic daughter:

Mother:	I don't blame you for talking that way. I know you don't mean it.
Daughter:	But I do mean it.
Mother:	Now, dear, I know you don't, you can't help yourself.
Daughter:	I can help myself.
Mother:	Now, dear. I know you can't because you're ill. If I thought for a moment you weren't ill I would be furious with you.[11]

Here the mother introduces a paradox into the conversation: If you truly mean what you say, then you are bad, but since I won't believe that you are bad, you must be ill. There are only two possibilities, and the one is unthinkable. The daughter, of course, is placed in an untenable position, and becomes immobilized. Anything and everything she says will be held against her. Silence becomes her only safe recourse, yet it, too, is subject to her mother's paradoxical manipulations.

About such paradoxical communications, Watzlawick et al. cite the following finding by researchers on schizophrenia at the Mayo Clinic in Rochester, Minnesota:

When these children perceived the anger and hostility of a parent, as they did on many occasions, immediately the parent would deny that he was angry and would insist that the child deny it too, so that the child was faced with the dilemma of whether to believe the parent or his own senses. If he believed his senses he maintained a firm grasp on reality; if he believed the parent, he maintained the needed relationship, but distorted his perception of reality.[12]

A more subtle example of pragmatic paradox is this excerpt from the case of a family whose rather obese twenty-year-old son is allegedly mentally retarded. The family members are engaged in interpreting what the proverb, "A rolling stone gathers no moss," means to them.

Father:	Used as a proverb it means to us, to Mom and me, that if we are busy and active like a rolling stone, you know, moving, then, ah, we are not going to be too—fat, you're going to be more alert mentally. . . .
Son:	It does?
Mother:	Now do you understand?
Son:	I catch on.
Mother:	(overlapping): —do you understand?
Son:	(overlapping): Yeah, I *do.*
Father:	(overlapping): —that it would be *good* for—
Son:	(interrupting): *Mental retardation.*
Father:	(continuing): —keep busy—
Mother:	Ohh—does that seem like it means that to you, "a rolling stone gathers . . ."
Son:	(interrupting): *Well, getting over mental retardation, it does.*
Mother:	Well—
Father:	(interrupting): Well, keeping busy would *help,* that's— I think that's right.[13]

The authors ask: "How do his parents, or a therapist, deal with a 'mental retardate' who speaks about ways of overcoming his mental retardation, and even uses the term?" In their view, the son "jumps in and out of the frame set by the diagnosis" of mental retardation, thereby reducing the diagnosis itself to an absurdity, for his use of the term, especially his suggestion that he might "get over" mental retardation, excludes the condition which the term itself denotes. On the other hand, his paradoxical use of the term leads the therapist to be suspicious of the psychological tests showing his IQ to be 50–80. In the course of therapy, he was rediagnosed as schizophrenic, and his recovery proceeded well, his performance in many areas far exceeding the expectations of the IQ test results. The pragmatic paradox in this instance was that the speaker was using a term—mental retardation—in a way that falsified its truth, at least, as applied to him.

This case is reminiscent of Martin Luther's "fit in the choir," which Erik H. Erikson discusses in *Young Man Luther*.[14] Luther, a young monk, was attending Mass in the chapel of the monastery at Erfurt. The scripture lesson which was being read was the story of the man who brought his son to Jesus for healing, because the boy had a "dumb spirit" (Mark 9:14-29). Luther, deeply upset by the story, is reported to have fallen on the floor in the choir, raved like one possessed, roaring with the voice of a bull: "It isn't me! It isn't me!" The paradox here is that Luther's very behavior appeared to those present to falsify his claim that he *wasn't* the demon-possessed son in the biblical story. What could be better proof that he *was* the son in the story than his very denial of it? It is little wonder that the story of Luther's "fit in the choir" was circulated by those who sought to discredit him, and denied or discounted by his supporters and friends. It required someone with clinical sensibilities, like Erikson, to view this paradoxical performance by Luther as his bid to free himself from the "untenable position" in which he had been living for many years, as the son of a father who did not hesitate to suggest that his son was hallucinating when he thought he heard the protective voice of Saint Anne when he got caught in a violent, life-threatening thunderstorm.

As Luther's "fit in the choir" episode indicates, paradox has often been used throughout the history of humanity to accuse individuals of being mentally ill. In the following case, cited by Watzlawick et al., a patient writing in 1830–1832 tells how the voices he was hearing used paradox against him:[15]

> I was tormented by the commands of what I imagined was the Holy Spirit, to say other things, which as often as I attempted, I was fearfully rebuked for beginning in my own voice and not in a voice given to me. These contradictory commands were the cause, now as before, of the incoherency of my behavior, and these imaginations formed the chief causes of my ultimate total derangement. For I was commanded to speak, on pain of dreadful torments, of provoking the wrath of the Holy Spirit, and of incurring the guilt of the grossest ingratitude; and at the same time, whenever I attempted to speak, I was harshly rebuked for not using the utterance of a spirit sent to me; and when again I attempted, I still went wrong, and when I pleaded internally that I knew not what I was to do, I was accused of falsehood and deceit; and of being really unwilling to do what I was commanded. I then lost patience, and proceeded to say what I was desired pell-mell,

determined to show that it was not fear or want of will that prevented me. But when I did this, I felt as formerly the pain in the nerves of my palate and throat on speaking, which convinced me that I was not only rebelling against God, but against nature; and I relapsed into an agonizing sense of hopelessness and of ingratitude.

The authors explain that the patient, a schizophrenic, "is placed by his 'voices' into an untenable situation and is then accused of deceit or unwillingness when he finds himself unable to comply with their paradoxical injunctions."[16]

The foregoing examples focus mainly on paradoxical injunctions. There are also several examples in Watzlawick's writings of the paradoxical prediction, or what he later came to call the "self-fulfilling prophecy." In *The Invented Reality*, he uses the gas shortage problem as an example of how a paradoxical situation can get created and then become self-sustaining. In March 1979, when the newspapers in California began to publish sensational pronouncements of severe gasoline shortages, California motorists stormed the gas stations to fill up their tanks. This filling-up of twelve million gasoline tanks (which had been, on the average, 75 percent empty) depleted the enormous reserves and brought about the predicted shortage practically overnight. The public's effort to keep their fuel containers as full as possible instead of buying their gas when the tank was almost empty—the usual practice of the vast majority of motorists—resulted in endless lines and hours of waiting time at the gas stations, which in turn increased everyone's sense of panic. After the excitement died down, it turned out that the gasoline allotment for California had hardly been reduced at all.[17]

This is a paradoxical story. In their concern not to run out of gas, motorists caused the depletion of the gas supply. If you were to ask a motorist in the line to explain why he was there, he would say something like, "Because I want to make sure that I don't run out of gas." If you were to point out, "But the fact is that you and thousands of others are actually *causing* the gas shortage," he might, on reflection, accept this paradox to be true, but then say something like, "But what can I—one driver—do? I need gas for my car. If I act as if there isn't a gas shortage, I'll be the only one who is without gas." Thus, why people continue to behave in ways that are inherently paradoxical is because they believe they have no alternative. Even if they recognize the paradox inherent in the situation, they feel they have no practical way to extricate themselves from the situation. This is why pragmatic paradoxes are experienced as psychologically immobilizing.

Persons who seek counseling are often caught in a paradoxical situation, and are seeking some way to extricate themselves from it. For example, this case: "If I let my boyfriend move in with me so that he can help pay the rent, I'll be able to keep my apartment. But then he will assume that I am more open to marriage than before, which I am not." The action which is designed to solve the problem (that is, loss of apartment) threatens to create another problem (that is, boyfriend's false assumption that she is more open to marriage than previously). Hers is a paradoxical situation, as it is based on a fundamental contradiction. She is confronted with a situation that is not unlike that which schizophrenics experience time and time again. As Weakland and Jackson put it in an early paper on the interpersonal circumstances of a schizophrenic episode,

> In trying to make the right choice between two alternatives, schizophrenic patients encounter a typical dilemma: they cannot, in the nature of the communicational situation, make a *right* decision, because both alternatives are part and parcel of a double bind and the patient is, therefore, "Damned if he does and damned if he doesn't." There are no actual alternatives of which the "right" one "should" be chosen—the whole assumption that choice is possible and should be made is an illusion.[18]

The authors add that, in such cases, the solution lies in coming to the realization that there actually is an *absence* of choice, that one is not in fact being presented with any real alternatives. If real change is to occur, one will have to step outside the framework itself, and find a third alternative. The therapist who is presented with the client's dilemma—"If I get my boyfriend to share the rent he'll think I'm more interested in marriage"—will try to help her find or discern this third alternative.

Changing the Rules of the Game

In *Pragmatics of Human Communication*, Watzlawick et al. cite the case of a married couple who sought help because of the wife's excessive jealousy, which made life unbearable for both of them. Her husband was an extremely rigid, moralistic man who took great pride in his ascetic lifestyle and in his statement that "I've never, in all my life, given anybody reason to distrust my word." His wife, who came from a very different background, had accepted a subordinate position to him, except in one seemingly small area of her life. She was unwilling to forgo her predinner cocktail, a habit that to him, a teetotaler, was disgusting and the subject of endless quarrels throughout their married life. Two years ago, the husband, in a fit of anger, had said to her, "If you don't quit your vice, I'll start one of my own," adding that he just might begin to have an affair with another woman. This threat did not bring about any changes, however, so a few months later he decided to "allow" her to have a predinner drink for the sake of domestic peace. At precisely this point her jealousy flared up, its rationale being: He is absolutely trustworthy (he says so himself); therefore, if he has now accepted my drinking, he must be carrying out his threat to be unfaithful. He is now caught in the web of his paradoxical prediction, for he cannot convincingly reassure his wife that his threat was impulsive and ought not be taken seriously. The authors conclude: "They realize that they are caught in a self-made trap, but see no way out of it."[19]

The paradox in this case arises from two different meanings of the word *trustworthy*, even as, in a previous example, the paradox was imbedded in two different meanings of the word *child* (as "immature" and as "progeny"). The first meaning of *trustworthy* concerns the fact that all of the husband's actions, promises, and attitudes are exactly as he represents them to be, while the second links his threat of marital infidelity to his wife's habit of having a predinner drink. *Since* she continues to have a drink before dinner, and *since* he intimated that he would have an affair if she continued to drink, and *since* he has explicitly told her that she may continue to do so without any further objection from him, and *since* he is a man of his word, it *follows* from all this that he is having an affair. The paradox is that the more he pleads his innocence ("I am not having an affair") the more guilty he appears to be, because his trustworthiness now depends on his being untrustworthy (that is, going back on his threat to have an affair).

According to Watzlawick et al., what is needed here is a way to escape the dilemma created by the paradox, and this may be achieved by changing the rules of the game that the couple has been playing:

> The irreversibility of the situation lies in the fact that, like any other game without end, this one was governed by rules but lacked metarules for the change of its rules. One could say that the essence of psychotherapeutic intervention in such a case consists of the formation of a new, enlarged system (husband, wife, and therapist), in which it is not only possible to look at the old system (the marital dyad) from the outside, but for the therapist to use the power of paradox for amelioration; the therapist can impose on this new relationship game such rules as are appropriate for his therapeutic purposes.[20]

This statement, written in 1967, is reflective of the "systems language" of the period. In a footnote, the authors observe that the therapist's chances of achieving the desired change are much better at the *beginning* of therapy for "relatively soon the new system itself consolidates to the point where the therapist is almost inextricably caught in it and from then on is much less able to produce change than at the very start of treatment."[21] It is difficult to tell whether the authors are aware of the *paradoxical* nature of this very statement, as it suggests that therapy is effective *not* because it replaces the old system with a new system, but because it takes advantage of the opportunity afforded by the fact that there is not yet *any* system in place. This statement should alert us to the fact that it is not the "formation of a new, enlarged system" that produces the desired change, but what the therapist does with her or his knowledge of how paradox works. The key to the cure in this case is the therapist's use of "the power of paradox for amelioration."

How does the therapist go about doing this? In this case, the authors recommend the technique of "prescribing the symptom," which is paradoxical, but, unlike the paradoxes that get one *into* an untenable situation, this one is designed to get one *out* of it. They note that therapeutic communication needs to violate "common sense," as common sense counsel

> is customarily but ineffectually given by the protagonists themselves, as well as their friends and relatives. Prescriptions such as "Be nice to each other," "Don't get in trouble with the police," and the like can hardly qualify as therapeutic, although they naively define the desired change. These messages are based on the assumption that "with a little will

power things could be changed," and that it is, therefore, up to the person or persons concerned to choose between health and misery. Yet this assumption is nothing but an illusion of alternatives, at least insofar as the patient can at all times reject it by the unassailable retort: "I can't help it." Bona fide patients—by which we simply mean persons who are not deliberately simulating—usually have tried and failed in all kinds of self-discipline and exercises in will power long before they revealed their distress to others and were told to "pull themselves together." It is in the essence of a symptom that it is something unwilling and therefore autonomous. But this is simply another way of saying that a symptom is a piece of spontaneous behavior, so spontaneous indeed that even the patient himself experiences it as something uncontrollable. It is this oscillation between spontaneity and coercion that makes the symptom paradoxical, both in the patient's experience and in its effect on others.[22]

They suggest, therefore, that the therapist instruct the patient to do the very thing that he is trying no longer to do. By making an injunction to the patient to do what he has been doing, but to alter its timing, frequency, or degree, the patient "is put into an untenable situation with regard to his pathology. If he complies with the injunction, he no longer 'can't help doing it' but does it intentionally, and therefore has control over it, which is the purpose of therapy." On the other hand, if he resists the injunction, he can only do so by *not* behaving symptomatically, which is also the purpose of therapy: "If in a pathogenic double bind the patient is 'damned if he does and damned if he doesn't,' in a therapeutic double bind he is 'changed' if he does and changed if he doesn't."[23] Thus, in the case of the jealous wife and her absolutely trustworthy husband, the therapist will not attempt to talk her out of her jealousy by adding her own assurances to those of the husband that he is not having an affair, but will encourage her to remain suspicious of her husband, but, while doing so, varying her predinner drinking pattern so that he, in turn, will not be able to maintain absolute control over his philandering ways, but will be forced to modify them according to her drinking pattern, which she may modify at will. At no point will the therapist suggest or imply she considers his wife's jealousy to be without foundation. To do so would be to join those friends and relatives who have told her "it's all in your mind," to which she may justifiably have responded, "Of course, it's all in my mind, but just because it's all in my mind doesn't mean that it isn't true." There are many things in our minds that are *more* real to us than things outside of it. The woman's jealousy is undoubtedly one of those things.

Thus, in this case of the supposedly philandering husband, the therapist devises a therapeutic intervention that changes the rules of the game. This intervention offers a third alternative that effectively breaks through the double bind created by the assumption that there are only two possibilities involved (that is, her husband is lying when he says he is not having an affair or her husband is not having an affair but his attestations to this effect are unbelievable). By modifying her drinking pattern, she is able to take control of the situation. Any random pattern will do. She may, for example, have her drink on Monday, skip Tuesday and Wednesday, drink on Thursday, skip Friday, and so forth. Because the pattern is random, he will not "know" when he is having an affair and when he is not having an affair. The very idea that one can have an affair some days of the week and not others becomes an absurdity and the original interpretive frame is thereby broken.

An especially vexing example—but one that is not inherently therapeutic—of the control that a person may achieve by randomizing a previously predictable pattern of behavior is where a parishioner who previously came to church every Sunday is now coming on a much more random basis (for example, he comes two Sundays, misses the third, comes on the fourth, misses the next three). This behavior leaves the pastor in a quandary. What is going on? Does it have to do with dissatisfaction with my conduct of worship, or is something going on in his personal life? In either case, should I mention to him that I have noticed a change, and, if so, when should I do this? After all, he hasn't quit coming altogether. This parishioner may actually be in attendance more Sundays than one who comes the first Sunday of every month, but his behavior is far more vexing than that of the parishioner who attends less often but follows a predictable pattern. On the other hand, precisely because the taken-for-grantedness of the parishioner's previous behavior no longer obtains, the situation now has new potentialities that were previously impossible. By confessing that she has noticed the change but doesn't know what it means, the pastor may open the situation to these very potentialities, whatever they may happen to be. It may then have a "therapeutic" outcome. In the case of the allegedly philandering husband, the wife's *random* predinner drinking pattern makes her husband's notorious trustworthiness a moot point, thus breaking its tyranny over the couple and, it is hoped, creating the conditions for a very different, more intrinsic basis of trust between them.

Another story that illustrates the value of a third alternative for breaking an immobilizing interpretive frame is the following one that Watzlawick tells about a boy named Franzi Wokura, who lived in Steinhof, a small town in Austria.[24]

The Tale of Franzi Wokura

Franzi's trials and tribulations reached their peak when he was about thirteen years old. He was standing in the town's Beethoven Park, in front of a large flower bed, and there discovered a sign with the inscription "No trespassing." This brought back a problem that had been bothering Franzi more and more during recent years. Once again he found himself in a situation that seemed to present only two possibilities, and both were unacceptable. Either he exerted his freedom in the face of this oppressive prohibition and begin trampling on the flowers, at the same time risking arrest; or he stayed off the flower bed. But the mere thought of being such a coward, of obeying a stupid sign, made his blood boil. For a long time he stood there, undecided, at his wit's end, until suddenly, maybe because he had never looked at flowers long enough, something totally and completely different came to his mind: These flowers are beautiful.

Watzlawick asks, "Do you find this story trivial? Maybe so. But this is not how Franzi himself experienced it." On the contrary,

That realization ["These flowers are beautiful"] swept over him like a wave that lifts you up and swiftly, effortlessly carries you along. He was now aware that the world could perhaps be seen in a totally different, entirely new way. I want this flower bed just the way it is; I want this beauty; I am my own law, my own authority; he kept saying to himself over and over again. And suddenly that "No trespassing sign" had lost its importance, the pitfall of the Manichean opposites, "submission or rebellion and nothing else," had vanished.

Franzi was no longer caught in a hopeless double bind—to trample the flowers to assert his freedom from authority or to stay off the flower beds in deference to it. He had a third alternative, in which he neither trampled the flowers nor did he bow to external authority. Instead, he affirmed his own desire that the flower bed remain "just the way it is." Watzlawick continues:

> *Of course, Franzi's euphoria did not last, but something fundamental was changed; there now was a faint melody in him, often quite inaudible, but sometimes clear enough just when he seemed about to sink again into the morass of* either-or. *For instance, when he learned how to drive he always buckled up his seat belt, because* he *had decided that this was a reasonable thing to do. And when shortly afterwards the great public debate arose about the government's right to mandate the use of safety belts, he could not have cared less about all the hullabaloo.*[25]

Watzlawick imagines that Franzi had found a way to frustrate the efforts of the "diabolical witch" who had controlled his mind until the episode in Beethoven Park. She complains:

> *You spend a lot of time and energy constructing what seems like a fool-proof situation with only two possibilities, both ultra-solutions, and he somehow finds a third and walks away. I give him only the choice between cowardice and foolhardiness, and he chooses courage. I try to make him lust for something so that he may begin to dread the possibility of not attaining it, and he is indifferent to the one and to the other.*[26]

So, too, the boy whose mother gave him the two shirts may avoid the paradoxical dilemma she has created for him by deciding to wear *neither* of the two shirts: "They are both so nice, I wanted to save them for a special occasion." The woman who is faced with the choice of losing her apartment or inviting her boyfriend to live with her believes that she has no other alternatives, but this is true only within the framework of the current rules of the game. Many parents have subsidized their daughter's living expenses because they want their daughters to be able to avoid compromising themselves. Or, if she believes that the apartment would actually accommodate two persons (herself and her boyfriend), it would presumably accommodate herself and a *woman* friend, who would help to pay the rent. This alternative may not be as attractive as continuing to live in her apartment alone, but it enables her to avoid creating a serious misunderstanding between herself and her boyfriend regarding her feelings about marriage. Still another possibility, seemingly unthinkable, but not necessarily so, is that she may decide she has no lasting attachment either to the apartment or to her boyfriend, and that the prospect of his moving in with her helped her to see both things at once. In effect, her paradoxical dilemma has helped her to see that neither of them fit into her long-range plans.

In *Change*, Watzlawick and his coauthors tell the following story of an army officer who got himself out of an untenable situation by devising a third alternative. It appears in their chapter entitled "Second-Order Change":[27]

The Tale of the French Commander

During one of the many nineteenth-century riots in Paris the commander of an army detachment received orders to clear a city square by firing at the rabble. He commanded his soldiers to take up firing positions, their rifles leveled at the crowd, and as a ghastly silence descended he drew his sword and shouted at the top of his lungs: "I have orders to fire at the rabble. But as I see a great number of honest, respectable citizens before me, I request that they leave so that I can safely shoot at the rabble." The square was empty in a few minutes.

The commander seemed to be caught on the horns of a dilemma: Obey his orders and shoot into the crowd, causing an unspeakable tragedy, or disobey his orders, and be relieved of his post, replaced by someone else who would not hesitate to shoot the crowd. He found a third alternative by giving a literal interpretation to the word *rabble*. He was prepared to carry out his orders to shoot the rabble, but who, after all, constitute the rabble? Does it include the "honest, respectable citizens" assembled in the square? Surely not, as they do not fit the "rabble" description.

The operative assumption on which Watzlawick and his colleagues work is that paradox may be used therapeutically. If paradoxes may be used to bind and immobilize, they may also be used to free and release. This is done by out-paradoxing the paradox, giving the original paradox one final twist that effectively undoes it. This requires that the therapist be able to recognize a paradoxical situation when presented by the client, then help to figure out a way to untie the knot, so that the client may escape the hopeless bind in which she finds herself. This untying of knots may be done in a variety of ways, but chief among them is the "third alternative," which takes the paradox one step further and, in doing so, eliminates it altogether.

Sometimes the solution to the dilemma is remarkably simple. In *Uncommon Therapy*, Jay Haley tells the story of a husband and wife who own a restaurant. Their problem was that the wife felt that her husband was not assuming enough responsibility, that she had to do too much of the work. The husband said that he wanted to assume more responsibility but there wasn't much for him to do, as his wife was so efficient and capable. Milton Erickson, the therapist in this case, ascertained that they both arrived at the restaurant at 7 A.M. He "prescribed" the following minor change in their schedule. The wife was to see that her husband got to the restaurant on his own by 7 A.M. and she was to arrive thirty minutes later. The following week they came in and reported that the situation was much improved. By the time she arrived at 7:30 her husband had made the preparations that she would otherwise have made. As time went on, she felt she could arrive at 7:45, even 8:00.[28] What seemed a very small change in their schedule had a profound effect. Importantly, Erickson addressed the dilemma itself and did not attempt to probe the alleged "underlying dynamics" involved, such as the wife's "need" to dominate her husband or the husband's "need" to accept a subordinate role. On the other hand, Erickson felt it was quite important that he assigned the wife the task of seeing that her husband got to the restaurant at 7 A.M., as this gave her a role to play as she relinquished her "obligation" to get to the restaurant at 7 A.M. herself.

Sometimes, the solution to the dilemma involves challenging the unexamined assumptions behind the dilemma. Take the case of the parents who came to the therapist with the following dilemma: Both agreed that their children needed some form of discipline, but they each had a very different disciplining style. The mother was very firm with the children while the father was extremely flexible. They asked the therapist to help them find some sort of happy medium with which both parents could be reasonably comfortable. In this way, they reasoned, the two of them would present to their children a more "united front." The therapist indicated that she would help them achieve a happy medium if this was really what they wanted, but she wondered aloud why they felt this was so essential: "Your children will be confronted throughout their lives with persons who exercise authority with a great deal of firmness and others who are quite flexible in their exercise of authority. Why deprive them of the experience, as children, of learning to adapt to both styles?"

This line of reasoning took them by surprise, because they had simply assumed that the therapist would agree that parents need to present a "united front" to their children lest they be manipulated by their children. Yet, as they reflected on what she said, they found themselves agreeing with her, and responded, "Then, neither of us needs to change. We just need to let the children know that we respect each other's approach to disciplining them." The therapist indicated her agreement with this conclusion, and brought the counseling session to a close.

The following also illustrates how one may challenge the unexamined assumptions behind the dilemma. Once a student came to me to explain that he had been working on the paper for my course, which was due in a week, but had developed "writer's block." He went on to explain that he had been spending whole afternoons just sitting in front of a blank piece of paper, immobilized. I asked him, "How many hours do you think you should spend on this paper for my course?" He answered, "About twenty-five, but I've already spent that much time on it with nothing to show for it." I responded with genuine surprise, "But that's way too much. If you spend more than *seven* hours on the paper for my course, you're spending too much time on it." This response clearly piqued his interest. I doubt that he had ever heard a professor (at least, the professor for the course for which the paper was intended) say something like this. He responded, "Really? Then tell me how to get it down to seven hours." I replied, "I'm just guessing, but I think your problem may be that you believe you have to *think* as you write every single page, when, in fact, for a ten-page paper, you don't have to start thinking until page seven!" Note here that I am underscoring the number seven—*seven* hours, *seven* pages. I'm guessing that this repetition of the number seven will drive from his mind the double-digit numbers with which he came into my office.

He said, "What do you mean, 'not think' for seven pages?" I asked him what his topic was and what books and/or articles he was planning to use. He told me, and from this, I gathered that he had an idea for the paper. So I suggested that all he needed to do for seven pages was to pick out the major ideas from the literature he was using and basically write them down, putting them in a more or less coherent order so that they appeared to lead somewhere. "Just do a lot of quoting," I emphasized. "Then," I said, "after doing this for seven pages, spend the last three pages being analytical and critical. This is when you do some thinking of your own. *But not before.*" Then I added, "The paper is due next Wednesday. Let's you and I have lunch in the cafeteria on Wednesday. You bring in the paper when you come for lunch. If it takes you *more* than seven hours to write it, I pay for lunch. If it takes *less* than seven hours, you pay." On Wednesday he came with his completed paper and said that he had followed my advice. Seven pages, no thinking at all, then three pages, quite a lot of thinking. I asked him, "So how many hours did you spend on it?" "Ten," he said. "Really? Then I guess *I* pay for lunch." He grinned, "That's how I figure it."

I realize that this "therapeutic intervention" comes across as highly manipulative, a common criticism of Watzlawick's therapeutic method. Yet, I am quite certain that the student in this case "saw through" what I was trying to do and wittingly went along with it. In fact, over lunch, he said that it had been "a very interesting experiment," suggesting by this that he knew we were trying something rather unorthodox to see if we couldn't break his "writer's block." If we were to analyze my "therapeutic intervention," we would see that it involved (1) challenging the widely held assumption that it is better to spend *more* rather than *less* time on a paper; (2) challenging the widely held assumption that he had to *think* throughout the writing of the paper, a fallacy to which graduate students are especially susceptible; and (3) setting a time in advance for *celebrating* his success. In truth, he disproved my idea that he could write the paper in seven hours—it actually took him ten—but he also disproved his own idea that he needed to spend twenty-five hours on a ten-page paper. Over lunch, we didn't come up with any theories as to why the experiment worked. But, like previous examples, this story illustrates the third alternative, the possibility that is hidden within what has become an untenable situation, its untenability reflected in the double bind of, on the one hand, "I *must* write the paper," and, on the other hand, "I *cannot* write this paper." The third alternative does not involve giving the student more time to write (for instance, by extending the deadline), for this is precisely the problem. Whether *he* sees it this way or not, the student has *too much* time to write the paper. So the third alternative involves the paradoxical intervention of prescribing a much-reduced period of time spent in writing the paper, and then offering some advice as to how he might reasonably achieve his goal in this greatly reduced time period. The idea that he should think less rather than more is itself paradoxical, for our normal, common-sense assumption is that writing a paper requires a great deal of thought, and the more thought we devote to it, the better it will be. Yet, he had just testified to the fact that he had sat for several hours, deep in thought, and had come up empty. So my suggestion that he avoid "thinking" until he reached page eight was designed to undercut the idea that thinking and writing are commensurate activities. I offered the idea that he could write most of the paper without thinking, and he would only have to begin thinking when he was fairly close to finishing it.

A Strange, Disorienting World

To read Watzlawick's books is to enter a story world in which nothing is quite what it seems. In a world in which paradox reigns supreme, meanings are never stable or fixed. We feel as though we have entered a hall of mirrors that, in time, becomes dizzying. His world is a rather different one from Erickson's (in spite of their common interest in confused, and confusing, language), as Erickson's stories tend to emphasize "mind over matter," whereas Watzlawick's are concerned with "mind over mind." Erickson wants to motivate the mind so as to overcome the debilitating effects of matter—his own struggle against the effects of polio illustrates this—whereas Watzlawick, trained in methods designed for work with immobilizing communication patterns, wants to utilize the mind to "outwit" or "outsmart" another mind, or another part of one's own mind, which is all tied up in knots. If we are inclined to view Erickson's story world as more "graceful" and "benign" than Watzlawick's, since Watzlawick's story world is one in which one needs to outwit one's opponent, we should recall that demonic possession was among the pathologies that Jesus took upon himself to heal. If

Erickson's inspirational world puts us in mind of the more benign accounts of physical healings in the Gospels, Watzlawick's story world is more reminiscent of the darker Gospel stories of the demon-possessed. The demon-possessed are victims of paradoxical injunctions from which they cannot extricate themselves, and the cure involves out-demonizing the demons. Watzlawick's own example of the man who was hearing voices is a case in point.

We should not, therefore, make a categorical decision *not* to enter Watzlawick's strange story world, for there are situations in life—even everyday life—that call for the subversive measures that Watzlawick's therapeutic stories exemplify. Most of us prefer a world in which motivations are transparent, where we all say what we really mean, and what we do is entirely congruent with who we are. But Watzlawick's story world is one in which things are not as ideal as this, where we are confronted by powers that are not necessarily beneficent, where the good are not necessarily rewarded, and where the stakes are not necessarily low. In this kind of world, we need to learn how to be subversive as Jesus was subversive in his confrontations with the demons.

Demons:	What do you have to do with us?
Jesus:	[no reply]
Demons:	If we cast ourselves into the swine, will you then leave us alone?
Jesus:	[no reply]

So the demons entered the pigs, and the pigs, now demon-possessed, ran to their deaths (Mark 5:1-12). If Jesus knew when to be transparent about his motives and intentions and when to keep them hidden, so must we. Watzlawick's world of paradox is an uncomfortable one, as it appears to be without convictions, without secure foundations. But it is one from which we dare not hold ourselves aloof if we acknowledge that there are principalities and powers without, and resistances within, that are determined to break our wills and hearts.

The Aphoristic Sayings of Jesus

The stories of Jesus' healing of the demon possessed are not, however, the only instances of Jesus' association with the paradoxical story.

The story world we enter in the course of reading Watzlawick's texts also has significant parallels in the story world of Jesus' own sayings and parables. Watzlawick's discussion of "right hemispheric language patterns" in *The Language of Change* helps us to explore the connections between the paradoxical story and the aphoristic sayings of Jesus.[29]

Under the rubric of right-hemispheric language patterns, Watzlawick includes dream language, poetic language, figurative language, allusive language, humor, and puns. He also identifies aphorisms as belonging to the brain's right hemisphere, and quotes Webster's definition of an aphorism as "a short, pointed sentence expressing a wise or clever observation or a general truth."[30] In the aphorism, at least two concepts or thoughts are brought into an association that is unusual, startling, and therefore has impact. The saying, "Too little to live on, too much to starve from," is arresting because it states a kind of truth, though one that is technically illogical. If we assume two possibilities—life or death—then this aphorism violates that assumption and the logic that lies behind it. Yet, at the same time, it makes a qualitative observation: "It precludes death, but the life it affords is hardly worth living." What makes an aphorism effective, besides its paucity of words, is that it makes an unexpected association. If we normally associate "starving" with "little," and "living" with "much," this aphorism reverses the normal expectation and associates "little" with "living" and "much" with "starving."

For Watzlawick, the aphorism creates a third possibility where there seemed to be only two. If one assumes there are two possibilities, life or death, then this aphorism posits a third, a kind of living death or a deathlike life, a life that is not identical, yet tantamount, to death. Introducing the notion of first-order and second-order reality, he suggests that the aphorism locates us in second-order reality, where the usual black-and-white distinctions do not hold.[31] Oscar Wilde's aphorism—"The only difference between a saint and a sinner is that every saint has a past and every sinner a future"—demolishes, in one blow, what Watzlawick calls "the terrible simplification" of a typical black-and-white painting of human nature. Or this, also Wilde's: "The Lords Temporal say nothing, the Lords Spiritual have nothing to say, and the House of Commons has nothing to say and says it."[32]

Occasionally, aphorisms are the centerpieces of jokes, as in the following which Watzlawick borrows from Freud's *Jokes and Their Relation to the Unconscious*: "Mr. and Mrs. X live in fairly grand style. Some people think that the husband has earned a lot and so has been able to lay by a bit. Others again think that the wife has lain back a bit and so has been able to earn a lot."[33] The point, of course, is that Mrs. X has been sleeping with other men and being paid for doing so. This illustration, with an aphorism as its centerpiece, shows that a good aphorism—a saying—can be the genesis of a story, whether an anecdote, a joke, a parable, or even a full-fledged short story. The aphorism that begins "Too little to live on . . ." could be framed as a conversation between two prison inmates, or two monks, as they are handed their food ration for the day. It could also be told in reference to someone's sex life, or to a pastor's sermons. In that case, it is no longer just a clever saying, but has become the centerpiece of a story, a narrative. The basic requirement is that the saying is attributed to a speaker and the person or group to whom it was allegedly spoken is also identified. Other contextual elements may also be supplied:

> Mrs. Lindstrom was extolling the virtues of her church to a new neighbor of hers, Mrs. Petrie: "Our choir is wonderful, the youth group is the best in town, and the women's group is very active. We have a very nice pastor too." Mrs. Petrie replied, "One of the things I look for in a new church is good preaching. How would you rate your minister as a preacher?" "Well," Mrs. Lindstrom replied, "I'd have to say that his sermons are too little to live on and too much to starve from." Mrs. Petrie responded, "Oh, just like our minister back home."

This story, which I made up, proves how easy it is to create a story around an aphorism, with the aphorism as its centerpiece (or "punch line").

Biblical scholars agree that the historical Jesus spoke in "sayings." Sayings believed to reflect the thinking of the historical Jesus include:

1. "Don't judge, and you won't be judged. For the standard you use will be the standard used against you."
2. "Can the blind lead the blind? Won't they both fall into a pit?"
3. "A good tree does not bear rotten fruit; a rotten tree does not bear good fruit. Are figs gathered from thorns, or grapes from thistles? Every tree is known by its fruit."

4. "For the mouth speaks from a full heart."
5. "What father among you, if his son asks for a loaf of bread, will give him a stone, or if he asks for a fish, will give him a snake?"
6. "Don't be afraid of those who can kill the body, but can't kill the soul."
7. "For where your treasure is, there your heart will also be."
8. "When a man said, "Let me first go and bury my father," Jesus said, 'Leave the dead to bury the dead'."
9. "Whoever tries to protect his life will lose it; but whoever loses his life on account of me will preserve it."[34]

The last saying in this selected list—"Whoever tries to protect . . ."—fits the structure of the chiasm, a crosslike structure that owes its name to the Greek letter *chi* (X). In his discussion of right-hemispheric language patterns, Watzlawick calls the chiasm a "perplexing structure through which a complex state of affairs is apparently reduced to utter simplicity and clarity, and which belongs much more to our right- than our left-hemispheric 'syntax.'"[35] Small wonder, he adds, "that it is dear to the hearts of politicians, demagogues, and marketing experts." The *Communist Manifesto* contains this description of bourgeois society: "For those who work do not acquire anything, and those who acquire anything do not work." In 1809 Ferdinand Schill addressed his anti-Napoleonic volunteer corps with these words, "Rather an end with terror, than terror without end!" And we all know the National Rifle Association's "If guns are outlawed, only outlaws will have guns." Thus, the chiasm is an aphorism that precludes any third alternative (for instance, that honest citizens may have guns) and instructs the hearer to choose between the two available ones. To the one who might argue, "Can't I protect my life and thereby keep it?" Jesus responds, "No, your only alternatives are to protect your life and lose it, or lose your life and preserve it." It diagrams as follows:

The Chiastic Saying

Aphoristic vs. Proverbial Thinking

In *In Fragments: The Aphorisms of Jesus*, John Dominic Crossan focuses on the significance of Jesus' use of aphoristic sayings.[36] His opening chapter on the "Aphoristic Genre" underscores some of Watzlawick's points about the aphorism, and especially emphasizes the paradoxical nature of a good aphorism. He centers on the distinction between a proverb, which is not paradoxical, and the aphorism, which is. The proverb is a sentence or phrase that has been preserved by oral tradition, though it may be preserved and transmitted in written tradition as well. It expresses briefly and strikingly some recognized truth or shared observation about practical life. The emphasis here is upon "recognized truth" and "preserved by tradition." A proverb—"A stitch in time saves nine"—is expected to be received with an affirmative nod of the head, perhaps even a verbal, "How true." We do not expect to create an argument when using a proverb. The worst response we invite is "How trite" or "That's so obvious," but this, too, underscores the fact that the truth of a proverb is indisputable and uncontestable. We simply take it for granted.

The aphorism is something else entirely. At the heart of the aphorism is contradiction. Crossan quotes from Hermann Asemissen's treatise on the aphorism:

> Every effective aphorism is characterized by contradiction. To oppose is its passion. . . . The more perplexing the contradiction, the greater the tension, the greater the resulting attraction. Therefore the aphorism contradicts precisely all those things that appear unshakeable in their authority and that enjoy unquestioned general recognition.[37]

For Asemissen, even the form of an aphorism "is a spirited contradiction of the powerful tradition of systematic deductive thinking. And thus in its content it especially likes to contradict authoritative opinions, habits, customs, conventions, and traditions of all kinds."[38] The aphorism's passion for contradiction leads inevitably to paradox "as its ideal form of action," since "the paradoxical self-contradiction is the most astonishing of all contradictions and as such is the best suited to the purpose of the aphorism."[39] Paradox is also, however, the aphorism's greatest danger, its way of playing with fire, because paradox "imperils the insight which is the goal of the aphorism by threatening (permanently) to become absurd. But the special danger accords it a special charm. In the self-consciousness of its strength, it plays with danger." Aphorism especially "likes to make use of ready-made formulations, proverbial expressions for example, which it modifies in a surprising way for its purposes or brings into a paradoxical relationship."[40]

Crossan also cites the work of biblical scholar James G. Williams who distinguishes between the collective authority that stands behind the proverb and the individual authority implied in the aphorism. Williams believes that the major distinction between a proverb and an aphorism is in their function, a function that does not always show itself in formal literary signs:

> The proverb expresses the voice of the human subject as ancient, collective wisdom, whereas aphorism. . . . brings the subjectivity of the individual more to the fore. But both accord a significant role to the human origin of the word spoken, whatever the ultimate grounding of authority of the utterance.[41]

This distinction is reflected in the fact that aphorisms are often attributed to individuals, and seem to require such attribution, even if the attribution is erroneous. Persons to whom aphorisms are often attributed are Oscar Wilde, Gertrude Stein, Dorothy Parker, and, more recently, Yogi Berra. Frequently, the aphorism serves the individual speaker's intention of taking issue with ancient, collective wisdom, and represents her position of dissent. Mae West ("I was once pure as snow, but then I drifted") is never identified with traditional, proverbial wisdom, but always with aphoristic dissent.

On the other hand, Crossan notes that, in the course of time, the aphorism may be reduced to the level of the commonplace. He believes this has happened in the case of Jesus' aphorisms. "How fortunate the hungry; they will be fed" still has its aphoristic note of contradiction, but the usual translated form, "Blessed are you who hunger now, for you shall be satisfied," replaces the contradiction with a future promise. Thus, in the final analysis, it is not the literary form that distinguishes aphorism from proverb, but its function, especially its authoritative claim:

Both are short and pithy formulations. And both resolutely refuse to append any reason, argument, or explanation. But proverb gives no reason since none is necessary; it is the summation of the wisdom of the past. Aphorism, on the other hand, gives no reason because none is possible; it is the formulation of the wisdom of the future. Proverb is the last word, aphorism the first word. . . . Whether in form alone or content alone or form and content together, the aphorism appears as a voice from Eden, a dictum of dawn.[42]

On the other hand, Jesus' sayings are more than contradictory. "How fortunate the hungry; they will be fed" is contradictory if we focus only on the first half of the statement (How can the hungry be fortunate?), but, when taken as a whole, the statement shifts from mere contradiction into a profound paradox. Thus, for those who are unaccustomed to food, note how they experience its pleasures when they receive something to eat! As paradox, it carries an implied indictment: "There are some who are so accustomed to eating whenever and whatever they choose that they have long since forgotten the pleasures that eating affords."

The aphorism also differs from the proverb in its allusiveness. A proverb's relevance, sense, or applicability is usually self-evident. "A stitch in time saves nine" is easy to apply to many situations. But Jesus' saying, "Nothing is hidden that will not be made known, or secret that will not come to light," has a mystique about it that leaves us wondering. What exactly is he talking about? To what does it refer? Does it carry an implied threat? Thus, in cases where Jesus' aphorisms may not seem all that contradictory, or seem not to be playing with paradox, we do well to note their allusiveness, their inherent ambiguities, and to recognize that this, too, is a means by which aphorism appears as a voice from Eden, a dictum of dawn.

Furthermore, if aphorism reflects the authority of the individual who speaks, we associate it with a single voice, and not the chorus of voices with which we identify the proverb. The proverb is authoritative because we hear it from so many lips, and to try to recall who first spoke a given proverb to us is an exercise in futility. This, after all, is what we mean when we say it has the authority of the collective wisdom of the ages. I, personally, have no recollection of when, or from whom, I first heard that "a watched pot never boils." I do, however, have a vivid recollection of the time when I was mowing the lawn while my father was clipping the hedges and I noticed a dead robin in the grass. Afraid to pick it up, but aware that I couldn't just mow over it, I called to my father, who came over, looked down and saw the robin, then looked up into the sky, and said, "His eye is on the sparrow, but I see a dead robin." While he immediately solved the problem of the robin in the path where I was mowing, my father had thrown me a very large curve. I was shocked, amused, and impressed, all at once. And it made a very big difference that the speaker was my own father.

So, too, in the case of Jesus' aphoristic sayings. The voice of the speaker is inseparable from the words spoken: "What I tell you in the dark, speak in the light. And what you hear as a whisper, proclaim on the housetops." How could one who had heard this saying from the lips of Jesus not always associate it with his voice? There would be none of the equivocation we often hear: "Someone has said . . ."; "I don't know who said it, but . . ."; or even "Studies show . . ." Rather, the sayer and the saying are as a single image; word and voice are as one. When his followers went out from town to town, they would carry with them, as their most important possession, the sayings and the voice-image of the one who sent them. It was this voice-image that survived his death, and continued to give them the sense that he was with them. It was a voice that was capable of holding its own in public disputation ("Sir, who made *me* your judge and lawyer?") and could talk about tough choices ("Whoever does not hate his father and mother will not be able to learn from me. Whoever does not hate his son and daughter cannot belong to my school"), but was also known for its uncommon ability to reassure ("I am telling you, do not worry about your life, what you will eat, or about your body, what you will wear. Isn't life more than food, and body more than clothing?"). Yet, even here, it is a reassurance with a paradoxical edge, for the voice that goes with us does not tell us that we *will* be fed, that we *will* be clothed, but only tells us what we already know, that we have life and that we have a body, so we have no reason to worry. If this seems less than reassuring, we fail to see the paradox: It has nothing whatever to do with future contingencies (with whether or not we get food or clothes later today, tomorrow, or the day thereafter). Instead, it says, "When I look at you, I see that you have life. Can anything compare to that?"

I have discussed Jesus' penchant for the aphoristic saying so as to make a link between the good news of the Gospel and Watzlawick's search for the third alternative that breaks the bonds of a hopeless contradiction. The good news is rarely as we predicted or envisioned, because our predictions and envisionings were based on the either-or thinking that was keeping us trapped in the unresolvable dilemma. Instead, it comes from challenging the assumptions on which the dilemma itself is based. The son who receives two shirts from his mother for his birthday may decide to wear *neither* shirt the day thereafter. Franzi Wokura, caught in the dilemma of obeying external authority or exercising his personal freedoms, discovers that he wants the flowers to remain as they are because they are so beautiful. When a man comes to Jesus and asks him to enjoin his brother to share his inheritance with him, Jesus challenges the assumption on which the request is made, "Who made *me* judge over you and your brother?" Yet if in this case he refuses to take the bait, in other cases he responds to the challenge, as in the case of the adulterous woman who is about to be stoned by the very men who had enjoyed the pleasures of her company: "He who is without sin, let him throw the first stone." *They* thought this was a simple case of meting out punishment, but he turned it into a dilemma for them, immobilizing them from casting the stones they held in their guilty hands.

This story also illustrates Jesus' own method of untying knots by discerning the possibility of a third alternative. If he failed to condemn the woman, he would seem to violate Mosaic law, but if he did condemn her, he would violate Roman law, for in this period of Jewish–Roman relations it was believed that the Sanhedrin's power to levy a death sentence was removed by Roman decree. He evaded this carefully constructed double bind—his entrapment between two laws, one religious and one secular—but in a way that no one expected. By declaring to the crowd, "If there is one of you who has not sinned, let him be the first to throw a stone at her," he acted in much the same way, with a similar outcome, to the French Commander who was caught in the dilemma between obeying his orders and creating an unspeakable tragedy or disobeying his orders and being relieved of his post. By declaring, "He who is without sin, let him throw the first stone," Jesus replaces the proverbial either-or with the aphoristic third alternative, and, in so doing, he declared the good news of the Gospel, challenging the assumptions on which the dilemma of the either-or was based.

The Plot Thickens

I suggest that the stories Watzlawick tells help to account for the typical pastor's unease with pastoral counseling. Counseling a parishioner *does* feel very much like trying to untie knots, and the harder one tries, the "knottier" the problem becomes. A wife comes to tell her pastor about her husband's philandering ways (in this case, her allegations are well founded) and the pastor begins to get the sinking feeling that if he continues to listen, he will surely get in over his head. Or a parishioner comes to talk about her daughter who has become a disciplinary problem and complains that her husband is absolutely no help because he "encourages" the daughter to misbehave. Or a parishioner tells the pastor about his thirteen-year-old son who was arrested for trampling the flowers at the local park where he was hanging out with a bunch of his friends, and when asked why he did this, responded, "I don't know. I just felt like it." These stories, too, create a sinking feeling in the pastor, the sense that, if she is not already in over her head, that moment is fast approaching.

If Erickson's stories reflect the natural tendency of stories to spread, Watzlawick's stories reflect another property of stories, which is that their plots tend to thicken, and, when they do, the listener begins to get nervous and anxious. When we read a novel or watch a film, this thickening of plot is precisely what we bargained for, and we are disappointed if no such thickening occurs. Watch a group of children listening to a story during "circle time" and note the disappointment on their faces when the plot *fails* to thicken: "That was a pretty dumb story" or "Nothing much happened" or even "Did you leave something out?" are all predictable responses to a story whose plot fails to thicken. But when we are in a pastoral counseling situation where we are expected to respond helpfully to the story being told, we are likely to react to the thickening of the plot with alarm, if not panic. The story is *more* than we bargained for. In spite of our genuine desire to be helpful, we don't really want to hear a story that has the storyteller all tied up in knots and that threatens to tie us up in knots as well. Little wonder, then, that as the story begins to unfold and the plot begins to thicken, *we* begin to think of ways to extricate *ourselves* from the story by making a "good referral."

Before we act on our impulse to extricate ourselves from the story, however, we should recall that in the story of the woman taken into adultery, Jesus is the very one who thickens the plot. Before he came upon the scene, the story was a rather simple, uncomplicated story about a woman who had sinned and was about to be punished for doing so. But when Jesus made his seemingly disingenuous statement—"If there is one of you who has not sinned, let him be the first to throw a stone at her"—he thickened the plot of the story. The listener knows that a situation that had seemed cut and dried has now become unpredictable, ominously so. The potential for violence is still there, and, in fact, this potential has been heightened, not lessened. A routine, systematic stoning by a collective group has been replaced by a situation in which each individual searches his own conscience and behaves according to what he concludes from such searching. As this is an individualistic and internal process, not a well-organized and carefully orchestrated social drama, heaven knows what may happen next. In the meantime, Jesus writes something on the ground, and the fact that the storyteller does not tell us what he wrote (he probably doesn't know himself) only enhances the listener's anxiety and tension. Enormous relief comes as the plot "de-thickens" and one after another of her accusers, "beginning with the eldest," leaves the scene of confrontation.[43]

In spite of our natural, understandable desire to avoid the thickening of plots, pastors need to devote some of their time and attention to hearing and responding to stories with plots that thicken. The major reason they need to do so is that God acts in and through the thickening of plots. As Paul Ricoeur pointed out in a sermon on "Listening to the Parables of Jesus," "the Kingdom of God is not compared to the man who . . . to the woman who . . . to the yeast which . . . but to *what happens* in the story." Consequently, he suggests that we ought not stick too closely to the situations described in the parables, situations of agricultural activity and of rural life, but that we should center our attention more on the *plot*, "the structure of the drama, its composition, its culmination, its denouement."[44] This also implies that God is not merely a *character* in the story (the parable of the prodigal son notwithstanding) but is disclosed through what *happens* in the story, that is, God is in the way the plot thickens and develops from there. Especially relevant to the personal stories that parishioners tell the pastor is John Dominic Crossan's observation that, unlike myths, parables do not always end in reconciliation. For parables, "reconciliation is no more fundamental a principle than irreconciliation. You have built a lovely home, myth assures us; but, whispers parable, you are right above an earthquake fault."[45] This means that we may not assume that God is always on the side of satisfying endings. A story with an ambiguous ending, leaving the listener in suspense, may be precisely what God intended. We should not impose our own story values on God.

On the other hand, if we do not attend to this property of stories—the tendency of plots to thicken—we will have no clue as to how God *is* acting in parishioners' lives, and we will not be able to help them to perceive that God has not abandoned them, but is actively involved in the realization of "the third alternative" that has yet to unfold itself. I suggest that the pastor intuitively knows that a pastoral care situation has become a pastoral *counseling* situation when the plot begins to thicken. Furthermore, it is the thickening of the plot rather than the location (for instance, pastor's study) or other situational factors (for instance, a prearranged time to meet) that makes it a pastoral counseling situation. Thus, if a pastor goes to the hospital to see a parishioner who has just suffered a heart attack, and, in the course of her conversation with the parishioner, is informed that his heart attack was "brought on by worries about [his] daughter's failing marriage," what began as an act of pastoral care has become a pastoral counseling situation. With the parishioner's surmise (allegation?) that his daughter's marital problems are responsible for his health problems, the plot has thickened, and the pastor has no choice but to recognize that this is so.

While congregations, like pastors, tend to prefer to live as though their collective life story is simple and uncomplicated ("We're just your normal, friendly congregation"), the indulgence of such preferences is counterproductive in the long run because it is contrary to fact. In my article, "The Pursuit of Unhappiness in American Congregational Life,"[46] I used Watzlawick's book, *The Situation Is Hopeless but Not Serious*, subtitled "The Pursuit of Unhappiness,"[47] to analyze congregational stories. I will not replicate this whole analysis here, but instead simply note Watzlawick's suggestion that individuals have a knack for plunging themselves into unhappiness and misery just when they seem to be on the verge of achieving happiness in their lives. He identifies the various games that individuals play in their relentless pursuit of unhappiness, several of which involve invoking the past, others of which involve future projections. In my article, I show that congregations use these same games, and I conclude that the pastor who is aware that such games are being played (and that *she* is frequently their intended victim) has a better chance not only of surviving but also of helping to improve the congregational ethos. Congregational plots are never simple. They are always thick (often, several plots are thickening at once), and this means that the pastor who devotes some of her time to listening and responding to the plot-thickened stories of individual parishioners will be more attuned to the fact that the congregation's own story has a thick plot, and she will therefore be able to respond more effectively to this reality as well.

As such, plot-thickening is neither a good thing nor a bad thing. It is simply a property of any story worthy of the name. But how we *respond* to plot-thickening is never a neutral matter or one of indifference. We can respond self-protectively and put down the book or leave the theater when the plot begins to thicken, or we can grit our teeth, hold onto our seats, and prepare for the roller-coaster ride that is sure to follow. The paradoxical story type testifies to the fact that we will be the better for having stuck with the story, for even should it come to some unfortunate ending, as many real-life stories do, we will have seen how God enters into the stories of our lives as the one who dispels the fog that accompanies the thickening of plots and prepares for us some sort of clearing. I suggest that just such a clearing occurs, in the story of the woman taken in adultery, when the men who are her accusers leave the scene, and Jesus looks up.

Jesus:	Woman, where are they? Has no one condemned you?
Woman:	No one, Lord.
Jesus:	Neither do I condemn you; go and do not sin again.

If we had put down our book or left the theater when the plot began to thicken, we would not have been witness to this scene, where everything became clear, and the color returned to her face and his.[48] A truly living story.

Chapter 4

The Miracle Story

The Art of Identifying Exceptions

S teve de Shazer is cofounder and senior research associate of the Brief Family Therapy Center in Milwaukee, Wisconsin. He received his training as a family therapist at the Brief Therapy Center in Palo Alto, and counts John Weakland as a major influence on his work. Equally important is his colleague, Insoo Kim Berg, who is also a therapist at the Brief Family Therapy Center in Milwaukee. What distinguishes de Shazer from Erickson, but reflects Watzlawick, is his desire to ground his work in philosophical thinking. Like Watzlawick, he has had a strong interest throughout his career in the philosophical ideas of Ludwig Wittgenstein, and quotes him frequently throughout his work. He has also been interested in French philosophical thought, especially as it interfaces with psychology, so he frequently quotes Foucault, Derrida, and Lacan.

One of his major philosophical concerns is the facile use that others have made of the term *system* to characterize what they consider family therapy to be about. He is concerned that "system," originally an "explanatory metaphor," has become reified:

> It is, of course, altogether too easy to reify concepts and explanatory metaphors. The little phrase "as if" is most easily ignored and even lost by accident or deliberately discarded. It is but a simple step from "The family can be seen as if it were a system" to "The family is a system," from saying "The rules of general system theory help us make sense of our observations of families" to saying that "The family does what it does because it is a system." This sort of misreading reifies

concepts and moves the entire discourse into speculations about causation similar in kind to an explanation for behavior that attributes the behavior to "poor ego strength." Like the ego, the system is nowhere because it does not exist.[1]

He is also concerned that "In the family therapy discourse (reflected in the literature), the terms family and system are often set together (i.e., 'the family system') as a symbiotic or mutually defining pair."[2] The usual rationale for this symbiotic pairing of "family" and "system" is that it becomes a way to mark the distinction between family therapy and other kinds of therapy, and especially to make the point that the pathology in question is defined not only by the behavior of one family member but also by the interrelationships of all the family members. In this way, "the family, as equated with 'system,' is the patient and therefore the target of family therapy's intervention."[3]

But what troubles him about this habit of setting "family" and "system" together as a symbiotic or mutually defining pair is that it creates an "imaginary opposition" between the family and what the therapist and client are doing together in the therapy situation. The methodological boundary around the family as system denies the relationship between therapist and client by placing the therapist outside the system. To illustrate the problems this creates, he cites the view of one team of therapists that the family typically engages in "dirty games" and it is the therapist's task therefore to pursue the family "like a hunter whose intervention is somewhat like a harpoon." He contends that such metaphors "tear the interactive system (the therapeutic situation, a whole) apart, and the resulting imaginary differences lead to a power-oriented relationship involving a certain kind of violence."[4] At this violent extreme, "the concept developed from the methodological boundary around the family-seen-as-a-system has outlived its usefulness and needs to be gotten rid of because, once reified, it can never again be a useful metaphor."[5]

Thus, the "system" that interests de Shazer is that which obtains between client and therapist; and, because he utilizes a see-through mirror that allows other members of the team to observe the session and make recommendations, the system includes them as well. This does not mean that he will not see and treat families—he *is*, after all, a family therapist—but it does mean that the presence of all or even most family members is unnecessary for him to do his work. If one wants to talk about a "system" comprised of several individuals, de Shazer prefers to employ the term in reference to the therapeutic system itself. He also, however, uses the word *system* to apply to language. When this application is made, emphasis shifts from the interactions of persons in the social system (whether the "family system" as traditionally defined or the "therapeutic system" as de Shazer prefers) to the language systems used in the therapeutic conversation itself.

This is where Wittgenstein comes in. De Shazer suggests that one way of conceptualizing and describing the system involved in doing therapy is to use a framework developed by Wittgenstein, and to look at doing therapy "as an example of an activity involving a set of related, but distinct 'language games.'" According to Wittgenstein, the term "language game" is meant to bring into prominence the fact that the speaking of language is part of an activity, or of a form of life. Thus,

> A language game is an activity seen as a language complete in itself, a complete system of human communication. Language games are complete in the sense that, you've got what you've got and that's all there is. There is no need to look behind or beneath since everything you need is readily available and open to view. Nothing is hidden.[6]

In de Shazer's view, language games are more fundamental than social systems (like the family) because they are "activities through which social realities and relationships are constructed and maintained. The signs (or moves) during the game consist of sentences (or signs), which are made up of words, gestures, facial expressions, postures, thoughts, etc."[7] Since this is a system complete in itself, "any particular sign can only be understood within the context of the pattern of the activities involved. Thus, the meaning of any one word depends entirely on how the participants in the language game use that word."[8] He concludes that

> The therapeutic relationship is a negotiated, consensual, and cooperative endeavor in which the solution-focused therapist and client jointly produce various language games focused on (a) exceptions, (b) goals, and (c) solutions. All of these are negotiated and produced as therapists and clients misunderstand together, make sense of, and give meaning to otherwise ambiguous events, feelings, and relationships. In

doing so, therapists and clients jointly assign meaning to aspects of clients' lives and justify actions intended to develop a solution.[9]

This definition of the therapeutic relationship locates the system in the *conversation* that occurs between therapist and client, in their mutual misunderstandings and partial understandings of otherwise ambiguous events, feelings, and relationships. This language system, not the "family system" or even the "therapist-client system," is the center of attention and the locus of change.

To illustrate how this focus on language systems works, de Shazer cites the case of a woman and her husband who came for therapy because, six weeks earlier, she, in her words, had become a "nympho-maniac," a condition that she attributed to "a problem in her infancy that would require deep therapy."[10] Prior to this session, she had been able to restrain herself from forcing herself on her husband for two nights in a row by sleeping, fully clothed, on top of the blanket. The therapist, Insoo Kim Berg, first tried to use these two "exceptional nights" to sow some doubt in the woman's mind about her self-diag-nosis. That is, instead of "accepting" these successful self-restraints as illustrative of how insatiable her need for sex had become, Berg took the approach of "misunderstanding" these two "sexless nights" as genuine exceptions to her complaint, and thus encouraged her to think this may be a viable solution to her problem. But she would have none of this: "If her [only] choice was to coercively restrain herself from sex, then, to her this meant that her marriage was no good."[11]

Berg continued to search for some element of the client's com-plaint—either in its behavioral elements or in the meanings involved—that might be used as a focal point, a point where the complaint included some undecidable element which could be used to begin constructing a solution. But nothing presented itself. The woman's description of the problem simply went from bad to worse. She wanted normal sex, uncontaminated by compulsion, and she wanted to be able to go to sleep without having to have sexual inter-course first. The conversation shifted to her husband who described her agony about her nymphomania and his tiredness. As he saw it, he was being robbed of the opportunity to be romantic with her. He was just there for her to get her daily "fix" of sex, without which she was unable to get to sleep. Then he added:

Husband:	But, for me, it's more of a sleep problem for us.
Therapist:	I wonder about that. Maybe we've been looking at this the wrong way.
Wife:	Do you have any cures for insomnia?
Therapist:	I don't know. We've been looking at this as a sex disturbance, but it's beginning to look more like a sleep disturbance.[12]

De Shazer suggests that the husband's viewpoint was a "misunderstanding," as it amounted to a failure to "understand" the situation in the terms in which his wife understood it. But his "misunderstanding" created doubt in everyone's mind that the situation had to be understood in the way it was originally understood. As de Shazer puts it, "Now the complaint itself has become undecidable: The behaviors have at least two sets of possible meanings."[13] One is that there is a sexual disturbance (with sleep disturbance attached), while the other is that there is a sleep disturbance (with sexual disturbance attached). It is also possible that there might be some other sort of utterly different disturbance (with sexual and sleep disturbances attached).

As they continued to talk about the "sleep problem," the woman realized that both problems had begun at the time she began to have scheduled and structured exercise for one hour a day every day of the week. Could this, then, be an "exercise problem"? "At this point in the session, the meaning(s) of what was going on was set adrift in a sea of possible meanings."[14] Berg began asking questions about sleep and nonsleep, looking for times when the woman went to sleep normally and naturally without first having sex (exceptions). Her rationale for asking these questions was that if such exceptions could be identified, a model for getting to sleep normally could be found within the woman's recent experience. There were some rare and unclear exceptions but both the woman and her husband dismissed these as flukes. As the conversation about sleep continued, however, it became clear that the "sleep problem" label for her complaint did not have the highly pathological meanings that the "sex problem" had. Since she accepted this new name for her complaint, Berg focused the conversation around her difficulties with getting to sleep and emphasized that occasional sleep disturbances are quite normal. As de Shazer notes, "It is, of course, easier to develop a solution to a 'normal difficulty' than it is to develop a solution to a 'very pathological problem that has roots deep in one's infancy."[15]

In the remaining minutes of the session, Berg kept the conversation "strictly on a behavioral level" and avoided any further discussion of thoughts, feelings, and meanings. The woman's "sleep disturbance" problem became a behavioral or technical difficulty to be resolved through technical means. After consulting with the team behind the see-through mirror, Berg suggested the following options: One would be to quit exercising for now to see if her sleep problem would go away on its own. The other would be to use a traditional brief therapy intervention for insomnia complaints (that is, if awake after one hour of going to bed, she might either get up and do hateful household chores or lie in bed with her eyes wide open, concentrating on keeping her tongue from touching the roof of her mouth).

Two weeks after this session, the woman sent a note thanking the therapist for seeing that her "insatiable need for sex" was only "a symptom of her insomnia." She added that "immediately my sleep patterns and my libido returned to normal." She did not say whether she ever tried the team's suggestions that she give up exercising for awhile or use a technique for insomnia. As de Shazer concludes, "Perhaps the new name, with its attached meanings, was enough to solve the client's problem and the suggestions were unnecessary."[16]

In discussing the solution in this case, de Shazer notes that *insomnia* is a much less emotionally freighted word than *nymphomania*. Dictionary definitions make this point:

> *nymphomania*, excessive and uncontrollable sexual desire in the female, from the Greek, *nymphe*, bride, and *mania*, madness.
> *insomnia*, prolonged or abnormal inability to sleep, from the Latin, *in*, not, and *somnis*, sleep.[17]

In the one case, there is excessive and uncontrollable desire; in the other, an inability. Of the two complaints, the second is much easier to "treat," and is therefore much to be preferred. De Shazer cautions, "Of course the therapist cannot just pick a new meaning or a new label at random. The new meaning must fit within the context, within the pattern of conversation." But, in this case, "Fit was a simple matter because the new name for the complaint simply gave precedence to what was seen as secondary (the sleep disturbance) over what had been seen as primary (the sexual disturbance.)"[18] He adds that words like *nymphomania* are like freight trains which are pulling boxcars behind them filled with all their previous meanings. Everyone involved in the conversation—the woman, her husband, the therapist—bring to this new specific context all the previous meanings that this word has had for them. Because we do not know what all of these meanings may be for each of them, misunderstanding is more likely than understanding.

The issue, therefore, is not whether the therapist will achieve full or approximate "understanding" of the client, but whether she will "misunderstand" in a constructive way, in a way that helps the client toward a solution to her complaint. De Shazer concludes:

> The therapy system can be seen as a set of "language games," a self-contained linguistic system that creates meanings through negotiation between therapist and client. What a therapist and client do during the interview is akin to writing or coauthoring and reading a text. What the rest of the team behind the see-through mirror does is akin to reading a text. . . . Thus, a therapeutic interview is a putting together of various misunderstandings (misreadings) and whatever is meant is a result of how therapist and client agree to misunderstand (or misread) what is said: "Nymphomania" becomes misunderstood as "Insomnia." The secondary becomes the primary and the primary becomes secondary, and the misreading becomes useful to the client.[19]

De Shazer suggests that this misreading is consistent with Wittgenstein's view that "we can only know what a word means by how the participants in the conversation use it." But it takes this a step further:

> In the therapy situation, metaphorically following the second law of thermodynamics, misunderstanding (chaos) is much more likely than understanding (order), and perhaps the best that therapists can do is creatively misunderstand what clients say so that the more useful, more beneficial meanings of their words are the ones chosen. Thus, creative misunderstanding allows the therapist and the client to together construct a reality that is more satisfactory to the client.[20]

While de Shazer does not explore this fact, we may note that the "language game" used by the client in this case is actually more "psychologically" freighted than that of the therapist. The woman brings in a self-diagnosis of "nymphomania" and suggests that it must be related to a problem rooted in her infancy which will require "deep therapy." In her note of thanks to the therapist, she expresses her appreciation to her for seeing that her "insatiable need for sex" was only "a symptom of her insomnia." Immediately, her "libido" returned to normal. Nymphomania, symptom, libido—these are the words that she derives from the psychological culture in which we live. We might have expected that these would be the words that the *therapist* would use to "explain" her problem. Instead, the therapist's "misunderstanding" involves setting aside the woman's psychological language because it was likely to impede, rather than to aid, the discernment of a satisfactory solution to her dilemma.

Therapy as the Writing and Rewriting of Stories

As quoted above, de Shazer describes the "therapy system" as a "negotiation" between therapist and client which is "akin to writing and coauthoring and reading a text." It is a short step from the view of therapy as "language games" to the view that therapeutic conversations are stories. He writes:

> The conversations that therapists and clients have can be seen as stories, as narratives. Like any story, each case or each session of each case has a beginning, a middle, and an ending, or at least a sense of an ending. Like any story, the conversation is held together by the patterns involved, by the plot. Like many stories, therapy conversations deal with human predicaments, troubles, resolutions, and attempted resolutions.[21]

Change becomes a central interest when we begin to think of the therapeutic conversation as story. He continues:

> Viewed as stories, the conversations between therapists and clients are subject to change within and across situations as they negotiate and deal with the issues emergent in their conversations. Indeed, the discontinuities and transformations in meaning may be understood as changes in therapists' and clients' storytelling activities. Such changes partly involve the development of new "plots". . . . That is, new depictions of events are linked together to produce new patterns and meanings. It is through their depictions of unexpected events and exceptions as aspects of larger patterns of

solution development that therapists and clients construct clients' lives. Further, in developing new plots, therapists and clients recast the predicaments of clients' lives and their attempts to manage them.[22]

Thus, the possibility for change lies in the abilities of therapist and client, together, to develop a new plot. The raw materials are the same, as the fact that such-and-such events have occurred cannot be denied or ignored. But events derive their meanings from the context in which they are located, and *plot* is the word we use for this meaning-context. Thus the same events may be replotted, and thereby given an entirely new meaning. They may be emplotted as "the case of the nymphomaniac" or as "the case of the insomniac." The latter is not as lurid, and perhaps lacks something of the sense of danger and mystery of the former, but, from the therapeutic perspective, it produces a more satisfying solution. As Paul Watzlawick points out, "any reality testing is bound to lead to disappointing anticlimaxes."[23] While the woman may be secretly disappointed to "discover" that she is not a nymphomaniac, she is relieved that her problem could be solved so effortlessly. Moreover, the "fact" that her problem was not nymphomania but insomnia doesn't take away the "fact" that she has "libido" (her own "misunderstanding" of what had taken place).

De Shazer cites Kenneth Gergen and Mary Gergen's effort to identify the "narrative types" available to people for describing and evaluating their own and other people's lives. These include:

1. *Progressive narratives* that justify the conclusion that people and situations are progressing towards their goals.
2. *Stability narratives* that justify the conclusion that life is unchanging.
3. *Digressive narratives* that justify the conclusion that life is moving away from their goals.[24]

For de Shazer, analysis of therapeutic conversations as progressive, stable, and digressive narratives is useful for assessing whether the desired change is actually taking place:

Clearly, stability narratives are problematic for therapists and clients because they signal and are sources for perceived lack of change in clients' problems and lives. Although both progressive and digressive narratives involve some sort of change, they have very different implications for therapy conversations. Progressive narratives are sources for producing desired changes, whereas digressive narratives involve undesired changes. Indeed, as Gergen and Gergen note, digressive or regressive narrative structure is central to the telling of tragic stories which focus on people's movement away from their desired life circumstances.[25]

He also notes that therapists' concerns and responsibilities vary depending on the types of narratives that dominate in their interactions with clients. With stability and digressive narratives, their concern is to help clients construct new stories that signal and are sources for desired change. With progressive stories, the therapist points to ways in which clients are attaining their goals and helps them develop new and related goals that involve further change. He concludes:

> These stories and narratives take on the attributes of a system. That is, it is the whole of the story, or at least the whole of a narrative told jointly by the client and the therapist in a session, that is different from the sum of its parts, which include both the client's depiction of the situation and the therapist's description from a different perspective. This is the most readily available interactional behavior.[26]

It is certainly more available than the interaction between the client and the family member (or members) that brings the client to therapy.

A Novel Experience: Reading Cases as Stories

In *Words Were Originally Magic*, de Shazer is concerned to distance himself from a structuralist understanding of psychotherapeutic discourse and to adopt a narrative understanding instead.[27] Within contemporary therapeutic discourse, Richard Bandler and John Grinder are clearly heirs to the structuralist tradition, and this means, according to de Shazer, that, for them, what the client actually says (called the "Surface Structure") is not necessarily what she means, or at least all that she means, since, according to them, "in the case of a Surface Structure, its source and fullest representation is the Deep Structure."[28] Thus, for Bandler and Grinder, to get at what the client

really means (that is, the pieces that are missing in the surface structure), the therapist may choose to interpret or guess, and such interpretation "can be seen as the search for a truth that is missing in the
Surface Structure and is hidden in the Deep Structure and, therefore,
being kept a secret."[29]

De Shazer, once a structuralist himself but no longer, thinks there
is a fatal flaw in this structuralist model of language, with its distinction between the surface and depth structures of language. This
is the problem that even as the surface structure may have missing
pieces, so may the deep structure. As Bandler and Grinder themselves
acknowledge, the deep structure is sometimes incomplete, requiring
the interpreter to introduce realities from outside the structure.
Furthermore, the deep structure functions much like a deep black
hole, for there is no way to determine whether there might not be
another secret hidden beneath the one just uncovered:

> One result of this way of looking at structuralism is that the certainty
> built into the relationship between the Deep Structure and the Surface
> Structure simultaneously includes uncertainty, because the Deep
> Structure, which is the full representation of the meaning of the
> Surface Structure, may turn out not to be full enough. . . . We can have
> no certainty whatsoever, no matter where we look, that we can find
> the missing pieces.[30]

Thus, for de Shazer, the structuralist theory that there is a surface
and a depth structure in language is, literally, full of holes. An additional critique, one prefigured by his earlier criticism of "family systems" language, is that Bandler and Grinder allow a certain kind of
violence to invade the therapeutic relationship itself. By adopting the
structuralist view that clients are unaware of the underlying system
or logic of the language they use, an "imaginary boundary" is created between the therapist and client, for this view implies that only
the therapist—the one who takes a "reflective" view of how the language works—is able to discern the "deep structure" of which the
client is more-or-less unaware.

De Shazer admits that when he first began thinking about the
doing of therapy, he too, was searching for its essence, "an essence
that provides a fixed stable center or foundation . . . a 'scientific,'
'structuralist' set of assumptions."[31] He began this search by reading

and rereading the writings of Milton Erickson: "The quest, as I saw it, was to look for an underlying, fundamental theory upon which Erickson built his approach. Of course, once you start reading Erickson's many papers, it becomes obvious that this is not a simple task."[32] The more he tried to distill the essence of Erickson's work, the more frustrated he became. What kept him going was Erickson's own assertion that "I know what I do, but to explain how I do it is much too difficult for me."[33] This implied that Erickson had an underlying theory, and that with effort, de Shazer could articulate it. Yet, what he kept running up against were "the odd-ball, miscellaneous cases that did not fit."[34] No matter what approach to theory construction he tried, he was confronted with the exceptional cases that did not fit neatly, or even unneatly, into the theory.

This experience taught him that the exceptional cases are at least as important as the ruling cases, if not more so:

> Even if these exceptions are accidents (and of course accidents are always possible), then these exceptions need to be included within the theory. It was no longer possible to view the cases in . . . the miscellaneous pile as flukes: These cases involving seemingly arbitrary therapist activity (activities outside the rules) *must* be included within the theory, within the rules, and not left outside as examples of Erickson's idiosyncratic genius. That is, this apparent arbitrariness must necessarily be covered by the rules of a theory for doing therapy that includes and is based, in part, on Erickson's approach. To me, this whole damned project now seemed hopeless.[35]

But this, in turn, led to a further insight: What if he had been missing the point all along? What if the secret was that there is nothing hidden away, "and that variety and diversity were the 'essence' of Erickson's approach?" If so, this would mean that

> just accepting things as they are would be the only option available to me. This would mean that my theory of Erickson's approach had many branches but no center whatsoever. Furthermore, this would mean that there was no Theory, no grand design, but instead, just local, rather idiosyncratic, activities that were primarily situationally dependent.[36]

He concluded that his only recourse was to follow Wittgenstein's advice and renounce all theory, and, as Wittgenstein said, "to put all this indefiniteness, correctly and unfalsified, into words."[37] This led him to abandon structuralism as a way of understanding what goes on in therapy, and to reread all of Erickson's case examples as though for the first time, but this time without his structuralist assumptions:

> Somehow I had to take the words at face value, to keep my reading on the surface, to avoid any and all reading between the lines, and to somehow overcome the urge to look behind and beneath. This is not an easy job; the structural urge can be overwhelming.[38]

To assist him in his rereading, he decided to interpret these case examples "as stories—not as exemplary lessons, but pure stories":

> That is, to read them as if they were fiction, which meant that I was no longer taking the distinction between "literature" and "science" very seriously at all. It was no longer feasible for me to search for the author's intention or what he really meant while ignoring my role as reader. That is, the unit of investigation switched from (1) Erickson and his papers to (2) Erickson, his papers, and me.[39]

What he discovered on this rereading was that Erickson's cases "are good stories with plots and subplots, beginnings, middles, and endings, strong characterizations, frequent unexpected twists and turns . . . everything a reader [at least, one stripped of former theoretical interests] could want."[40] As he continued reading, he came to see Erickson-the-therapist in these stories as the persona developed by Erickson-the-author. This persona he came to call "Erickson-the-clever." He also found himself viewing Erickson as a kind of Sherlock Holmes, with Jay Haley as his Doctor Watson. He was especially struck by his discovery that the Erickson-the-clever stories, like the Sherlock Holmes stories, actually underdevelop or underrealize all the other characters in the stories, especially the clients. Clients are like cardboard cutouts, and, furthermore, "We have little or no idea about their contributions to the therapeutic endeavor."[41]

As he began to reread his own cases from the story perspective, he discovered that, by contrast, his *clients* were the clever ones: "Most of the ideas for 'unusual interventions' in the miscellaneous pile in fact came from the clients themselves!"[42] This was also the case with his colleagues. For example, he recalls one of Insoo Kim Berg's cases in which the client devised a homework scenario very similar to one that his mentor, John Weakland, had once formulated for a client. Also, the case of the nymphomaniac-turned-insomniac has the woman's husband coming up with the "answer," even though the woman, in her thank-you note, attributes this insight to the therapist. The conclusion was inescapable:

> To re-read my own cases using the persona of clever-clients unfortunately forces the therapist-in-the-story to appear to be incredibly stupid. Undoubtedly we therapists could not learn as much from de Shazer-the-stupid as we did from Erickson-the-clever. Maybe we all need to remember the dialogic or conversational nature of doing therapy and re-read all these stories with an interactional focus which would lead us to the idea that clever therapy depends on having clients and therapists cleverly working together in clever ways.[43]

De Shazer now believes that a more useful construct than structuralism, with its distinction between surface and deep structure, is one between "text-focused" and "reader-focused" reading. He thinks that anyone who comes to the session with a theory will be reader focused, whereas someone who comes to it without a theory will be text focused. In a chapter of *Words Were Originally Magic* in which he contrasts a family therapy session by Nathan Ackerman with one by John Weakland, he shows that Ackerman is "reader focused" whereas Weakland is "text focused." Ackerman reads a client's sigh as a signifier of something being wrong, revealing of a deeper structure, whereas the client himself believes it is merely a plain, simple sigh indicating that he has had a tough day at work. In de Shazer's view, Ackerman is thus "reader focused," especially in his view that "Nothing is what it appears to be."[44] In contrast, Weakland "makes every effort to 'just read the lines,' to stay focused on the text itself, to take nothing for granted, and not to make any assumptions."[45] He sees the Ackerman approach as an effort to get to the "bottom" of the problem: "In Ackerman's case, the therapist is constructed as a powerful interpreter of obscure signs, which suggests that only he and not the client knows what is really going on. The therapist is constructed as an expert and the client is someone who is ignorant about what she is doing." In Weakland's case,

> While the therapist is constructed as having special knowledge (about how problems are maintained), the client is constructed as having all of the information/knowledge necessary for resolving the problem. . . .

Thus the client's construction is privileged and taken seriously, in contrast to the situation in Ackerman's case where the client's construction is disqualified and the therapist's privileged.[46]

Identifying Exceptions

De Shazer does not disguise his clear preference for the text-focused reading. This preference is already prefigured in his criticism of structuralism, with its distinction between surface and depth. But he wants to bring to his reading of these texts several strategies—not theories as such—to assist the client in telling a story with a more positive outcome than might otherwise be the case. These strategies are the result of his discovery that many of Erickson's stories would fall outside the theory, or set of rules, that he himself had tentatively constructed. What is the significance of the fact that there were so many exceptional cases? From a reader-focused perspective, these exceptions would be attributed to the therapist, to the fact that she did something this time that she does not normally do. From the text-focused perspective, exceptions are already there, in the client's own "text," and the therapist does well to take notice of them. Supposing, for example, that a client complains of being depressed. Much of the conversation between the client and therapist is likely to center on how she talks about her depression. If the therapist contributes to the story, this is by asking her questions: What typically precipitates a depressive episode? How do you manage to come out of it? How severe is the pain that accompanies it? and so forth. All of this may be very valuable. But if the therapist were to ask about occasions when the depression is *not* there, when it is "in remission," they may together hit upon a strategy for solving her depression by maximizing the instances when the depressive state is absent. What are the conditions that account for its absence? When it is *not* there, what has the client done that she has not done when it *is* there? Here, the idea is not that the exception proves the rule, but that *the exception proves the exception*.

De Shazer illustrates the strategy of identifying exceptions by exploring the hypothetical case of a depressed client further: Suppose you came to de Shazer for counseling for depression. You know that you are depressed because this view of yourself fits in with what happens to you in real-life situations and has real predictive value. For example, you know how you will respond to efforts to cheer you up and you also know what will be other people's predictable response to your being down. De Shazer does not dispute the fact that you *know* that you are depressed, but *he* doesn't *know* from your statement that you are depressed. To say that you are depressed is not the same as *being* depressed, any more than saying "I am a nymphomaniac" is the same as actually being one. So he will ask, "How do you know you are depressed?" He asks this question not because he wants to challenge your claim, but because this is the only way he will come to know what it means for you to be depressed. In response, you might say, "Because I've been depressed all my life." This, however, won't do, as there is the possibility that you have been mistaken all your life. So he asks again, "How do you know?" This time, you provide concrete evidence: "I never get anything done. I either sleep too much or have difficulty sleeping and I either gorge myself or starve myself." This is progress because now you and de Shazer both know how you are using the word *depressed*. The two of you may agree or disagree about your use of this word, you may agree to use some other words, or you may continue to call it "depression" while de Shazer (knowingly misunderstanding) calls it something else. But you both know that when you use the word, you are referring to those situations in which you never get anything done, or you sleep too much or have difficulty sleeping, or you either gorge yourself or starve yourself.

De Shazer will then ask the "exception" question: "When was the most recent time when you were not aware that you were depressed?" You will search your memory for awhile, as you were probably unprepared for this type of question, and then reply, "Oh, last Tuesday." He will ask, "What did you do last Tuesday?" and you will answer, "I got up early and played golf for the first time in eight months." He may say, "What else was different last Tuesday?" and you will answer, "I went out for pizza and beer, danced with a couple of women, and fell asleep on the couch before I went to bed." Now, both de Shazer and you have a meaning for your use of the word *depressed* that includes *not* playing golf, *not* going out for pizza and beer, *not* dancing with women, and *not* spontaneously falling asleep on the couch before you are ready for bed. He concludes, "This definition, what we have agreed you mean by your use of the word 'depressed,' may or may not have been part of the meaning you brought with you into the session, and it may or may not have been part of the meaning I brought into the session."[47] By asking the "exception" questions, however, he has elicited important information both about what you mean by "depression" and what you do *not* mean by "depression." On a day when you play golf, go out for pizza and beer, dance with a couple of women, and fall asleep on the couch, you are *not* experiencing depression. You have also provided counterevidence to the claim that you are always depressed, or never not depressed. Last Tuesday, at least, your depression was in remission.

De Shazer notes that clients will often come for a counseling session complaining that they are no better than the previous week. But when he asks about specific days—"What about the day after we last met? Or Thursday? Or Friday?"—the client will usually recall that there were days that went better than others. How, then, to account for this? What happened on the better days that did not happen on the other days?

Constructing Miracles

Building on the idea that exceptions prove the exceptions (not the rule), de Shazer takes the next logical step and asks, "Would it not follow from the fact that exceptions are more real than rules that miracles might happen routinely?" After all, if a miracle is defined as "an event or action that apparently contradicts known scientific laws," and if there is no such lawfulness or regularity in the universe, miracles must be happening all the time.[48] We just haven't been using the word *miracle* in connection with such events. This sort of reasoning leads him to ask clients this question:

> Suppose that tonight after you go to sleep a miracle happens and the problems that brought you to therapy are solved immediately. But since you were sleeping at the time you cannot know that this miracle has happened. Once you wake tomorrow morning, how will you discover that a miracle has happened? Without your telling them, how will other people know that a miracle has happened?[49]

He freely admits that such a miracle seems "unrealistic and impossible," and that "most people do not believe in miracles." Moreover, even for those who do believe in them, "such occurrences are very rare indeed." We would therefore expect that a client would find this question nonsensical, unproductive, or, at the least, to respond, "I don't know." Yet, in de Shazer's experience, the "I don't know" response is very rare. Instead, clients make an effort to answer this question and their answers are usually very telling:

> The "miracle question" is a way to begin constructing a bridge between therapist and client built around the (future) success of the therapy. The phrasing of the question includes a radical distinction between problem and solution, which is a result of our noticing that the development of a solution is not necessarily related to the problems and complaints in any way.[50]

In other words, the absence of the complaint or problem is a given and the client is being asked to describe an effect, that is, the morning after the miracle or the day after success that is either without a cause or at least without a known or knowable cause: "The client's answers to this question, the descriptions of the day after the miracle, give both client and therapist some sense of what it is that the client wants out of therapy."[51]

Because a "miracle" intervenes, the solution is not necessarily predictable from the preceding exploration of the problem. The client whose depression went into remission the day he played golf, had pizza and beer, danced, and fell asleep spontaneously, will not necessarily describe the day after the miracle as one in which he repeated the exceptional day. Instead, he might describe it as one in which he slept in (but wasn't bothered by this), spent the day unproductively (but didn't feel guilty about this), and had a big meal (and enjoyed every bite of it). In other words, he had his usual "depressed" day but actually enjoyed it. Or it could be something entirely different (for instance, he takes a pleasant ride into the country, goes to the art museum, calls up an old friend, and browses in a local bookstore).

An important element in de Shazer's framing of the "miracle question" is the confirmation of the "miracle" by others: "Without your telling them, how will other people know that a miracle has happened?" This way of putting the questions suggests that miracles need to be recognized by others, especially the significant others in our life, for otherwise our claims will be subject to doubt, challenge, or even extinction. In the following case, the frustrated parents of a misbehaving fifteen-year-old boy were unable to imagine the day after the miracle. The son, however, gave the following response to the miracle question, supporting de Shazer's observation that "clients frequently are able to construct answers to this 'miracle question' quite concretely and specifically":[52]

Son: I will get up at 7:30 without anybody calling me, I
                will take a shower and put the towel into the hamper,
                get dressed, go downstairs and eat breakfast—remem-
                bering to put my dirty dishes into the dishwasher.
                Then I will catch the first bus to school, get to school
                on time, and go to all my classes—and maybe even
                learn something. Then I will catch the first bus home,
                do my homework, set the table for supper, eat supper
                with the family, put the dirty dishes in the dishwasher,
                and then go out with my friends, getting home by
                10:30.
Father: That *would* be a miracle!

Since the son had described the day after the miracle in such con-crete and specific terms, the therapist, Insoo Kim Berg, asked him to pick two days, one in each of the coming two weeks, on which he would act *as if* the miracle had happened, and to observe how his parents, his peers, and his teachers react. His parents' task was to see if separately they could figure out which two days he picked. Two weeks later, the father said that the son had pretended on Tuesday of the first week and Wednesday of the second. Mother disagreed, say-ing that it had been Thursday of the first week and Tuesday of the second. The son said they were both wrong, as it had been Wednesday of the first week and Monday of the second. The father responded, "Regardless. It was the best two weeks in the entire his-tory of our family."[53]

In the course of seven sessions spread out over the next six months, the parents' doubts about the solution diminished as addi-tional, specific desired goals were met. De Shazer acknowledges that, of course, things were not perfect. The boy still misbehaves now and then. But he is doing better in school, coming closer to the school's and his parents' expectations for him in his course grades. The parents still sometimes think that his misbehavior is a symptom of some deeper problem, yet for over six months they have not felt the need for additional therapy. As for the son, de Shazer thinks that pretending that there has been a miracle allows him to save face:

> Pretending is only make-believe. That is, he can change without having to admit that his parents had been right about there having been a problem. He can change without changing because he is only pretending. When the therapist, parents, peers, and school personnel respond in a favorable manner, then he can forget to pretend.[54]

De Shazer does not attempt to account for the son's occasional misbehavior, but in noting that he only does so "now and then" indicates that misbehavior is now the exception. Conceivably, the boy wants to prove to himself that he hasn't *lost* the ability to misbehave!

On a Scale of One to Ten, Where Are You?

A third strategy that de Shazer employs is the "scaling question." If the exception and miracle questions use *words* to build a bridge between therapist and client, the scaling question uses *numbers* for the same purpose. He credits his clients with having inspired the scaling question: "As in our usual practice, we took a cue from some of our clients' spontaneous use of scales and developed ways to use scales as a simple therapeutic tool."[55] But, "Unlike most scales used to measure something based on normative standards (i.e., a scale that measures and compares the client's functioning with that of the general population along the Bell curve), our scales are designed primarily to facilitate treatment."[56] They are used not only to "measure" the client's own perception but also to motivate and encourage, and to elucidate goals, solutions, and anything else that is important to each individual client. De Shazer quotes John Weakland's comment on the scaling device:

> When there's something that's not concrete, you concretize it in a way that, from a distance, looks very strange: You invent one of these scales. By inventing one of these scales, you can take a whole, amorphous thing and reduce it to a number; now it's real and concrete. In a logical sense, that's an impossible task. But you do it, and now it's

real. . . . [Thus] when it's global, general, amorphous, and vague—you give it a number.[57]

Normally, the scale used is from 1 to 10, with 10 standing for the desired outcome. On such a scale, 6 is clearly better than 5. But none of the numbers has a fixed or absolute meaning. They mean whatever the client intends them to mean: "Scaling questions were first developed to help both therapist and clients talk about nonspecific, vague topics involving feeling states such as 'depression' and obscure topics such as 'communication.' All too frequently people talk about topics like these as if the experiences depicted by these terms were controlled by an on-off switch; one is either depressed or not and couples communicate or they do not." But, fortunately, it is not that clear-cut: "Even people who say that they have been depressed for years will usually be able to describe times (minutes, hours, days) when they were less depressed. By developing a scale, the range of depressed feelings, as well as both the complaint and progress, is broken down into more or less discrete steps."[58] Thus, if 0 stands for the most depressed a client has felt recently, or for how the client felt at the time of the original phone call seeking therapy, and 10 stands for the day after the miracle (for instance, not being aware of any depressed feelings and therefore being able to do something that the client has been unable to do), then any rating above 0 says not only that the complaint is less bothersome but also that things are already better and progress is being made toward the solution. The great majority of the scales used by de Shazer and his colleagues go from 0 to 10, with 10 standing for the desired outcome. This enables the client to envision discernible progress being made, something that a scale from 0 to 100 is likely to discourage. The scales are "content free," since only the client knows what she means by a certain number, but the therapist *can* discuss with the client how life will be different when she moves from 5 to 7, and what the client feels would need to happen in order to get from 5 to 7.

The scaling questions work well with small children and developmentally disabled adults. For example, a little eight-year-old child was brought to therapy in the aftermath of having been molested by a stranger in a shopping mall. During the fourth session the therapist drew an arrow between a 0 and 10 on the blackboard, with 10 standing for the time when therapy was finished. The therapist asked the child to indicate how far she had come in therapy by drawing an X on this line. She placed her X at about the 7 mark. She was next asked what she thought it would take to go from X to 10. After several minutes, she replied in a rather somber voice, "We will burn the clothes I was wearing when it happened!" The therapist said, "That's a wonderful idea!" and soon after this session the child and her parents had a ritual burning and then went out to dinner in a fancy restaurant to mark the end of therapy.[59] Note that in this case it was the girl herself who came up with the solution. The therapist "merely" asked the questions that elicited her creative response.

Each of the cases that de Shazer reports in *Words Were Originally Magic* follows the same basic formula, moving from the exception question to the miracle question to the scaling question, giving the impression that the therapist is very much in control, giving directions and manipulating the whole process. Yet, interestingly enough, reading a typical de Shazer case from beginning to end leaves one with the impression that the process fits his description of the text-focused approach, where "the therapist is constructed as having special knowledge (about how problems are maintained)" while "the client is constructed as having all of the information/knowledge necessary for resolving the problem."[60] Furthermore, both the "exception question" and the "miracle question" invite the client to tell a story, and the counselor's role in each instance is to encourage an "expanding" story. In one case, this leads de Shazer to use several headings for the exception question, "Constructing an Exception," "Constructing Another Exception," and "Another Exception." In another case, there are two headings for the miracle question, "Constructing the Morning After the Miracle" and "Broadening the Scope of the Day After the Miracle." These headings, with their accompanying dialogue between therapist and client, illustrate how the storytelling remains with the client, and how the therapist encourages the client to tell a story that gets better as it goes along.

Here is a story elicited by the miracle question told by a male client who had a drinking problem after we remove the therapist's interjections and retain only the client's own statements.[61]

The Morning After the Miracle

I probably wouldn't feel like I'm leaving something behind. Because, you know, in your dreams sometimes you never have a chance to complete it, so you therefore feel like you left something. Way it is with all the other crap that kinda lingers on me. If it was gone, I probably feel like I'm high, a natural high. The good feeling of joy. The first time I felt, the first time I realized what Santa Claus and a big Christmas was. With the snow and the presents. That feeling. When you wake up early in the morning you got your presents and Santa Claus there. That kind of feeling. I have those days. And I get up in a good mood singing to myself and just do something I hardly ever do, just get up and clean the whole house and mop the floors. I guess my self-esteem is so low right now too. I really don't feel like it's worth trying, only thing important to me is search around for a can of beer tomorrow. And going to sleep.

This is a good story about the day after the miracle. It is vivid, dramatic, expressive. It begins slowly and builds up steam. But then, in the last few sentences, the reader can feel the energy going out of it, as the client becomes self-critical, even despairing. The story begins with an observation about how dreams are, and ends with his taking refuge in sleep.

And yet, as de Shazer notes, the reading of his cases reveals "what clever clients" he has. Or, rather, how good they are at storytelling. Unlike Erickson's *My Voice Will Go with You*, de Shazer's *Words Were Originally Magic* does not convey *his* storytelling abilities. Instead, it communicates his and Insoo Kim Berg's ability to evoke the storytelling abilities of those who come to them for therapy. The clients themselves tell the stories as they respond to the therapist's seemingly simple, innocuous question about the day after the miracle.

It might be asked, however, What value is this? Does it actually make any difference? Does it do anything besides making a client feel good for having imagined what a day after a miracle would be like? De Shazer's own response in the epilogue to *Words Were Originally Magic* is helpful, as it indicates what he believes is and is not achieved by the way he goes about doing therapy. The following quotation from Wittgenstein serves as an epigraph: "A problem has the form: 'I don't know my way about.'"[62] De Shazer comments: "Frequently by the end of a session clients are beginning to know their way about or at least are starting to have some confidence that they can find their way about." He then notes that he no longer, or only rarely, creates the kinds of elaborate "tasks" for the client to carry out which he learned to construct under the tutelage of the staff at the Brief Therapy Center in Palo Alto: "In the great majority of cases these clever tasks seem to be no more, perhaps even less effective than simpler ones based principally on what the clients have already said they know how to do."[63]

But what about the miracle question? Does it create false expectations? To believe that the miracle question actually "creates" miracles would be terribly naive:

> In fact, no matter what the method, therapy never creates anything whatsoever. The miracles clients describe do not even happen [in therapy] and they cannot be expected to happen [there]. All the miracle question is designed to do is to allow clients to describe what it is they want out of therapy without having to concern themselves with the problem and the traditional assumption that the solution is somehow connected with understanding and eliminating the problem.[64]

He is also wary of the constraints that the "day after the miracle" story may place on the counseling process itself:

> The details and specifics of where the clients want to go and what they wish for frequently change in the course of therapy, much to the surprise of both clients and therapist. That is, even though we depend on the clients' answers to the miracle question to give us some sense of direction, actually, whether clients can know what they wish for before their wish is fulfilled cannot be known. . . . For therapists to expect clients to know at the beginning of therapy exactly where they want to go is unrealistic; if they did, they probably would not need therapy.[65]

For this reason, he doesn't consider it necessary to contract with clients for a specific number of sessions, for specific goals, or to measure progress on specific goals: "To do so would again constrain and limit the possibilities for change and limit the possibilities for the clients to invent or discover something that satisfies them as much as or more than what they imagined or wished for when they described their ideas about the morning after the miracle."[66] Which is to say that the "10" they assigned the story they told is not an absolute number, but relative to where the client is at the moment. It does not, or, at least, should not impose a ceiling. It was long believed that the Dow-Jones stock average would never exceed 2,000 points. Then it was believed it would never exceed 3,000 points, then 4,000. If a miracle story may sometimes seem grandiose, it may, at other times, be too constrained. For de Shazer, the scale is a sliding scale. Thus, paradoxically, the miracle never happens, yet, also paradoxically, there are often better things in store for us than the miracles we envision.

It Takes Only One to Make a Problem

One of the easily overlooked features of de Shazer's approach is that the therapist typically works within a particular constraint that, if it were not present, would make therapy extremely easy. In most cases, the therapist is confronted with the problem that two or more individuals are in disagreement about what the problem is, or even whether a problem exists. The parents who brought their fifteen-year-old son for counseling were certain that there *was* a problem while their son was equally convinced that there *wasn't* a problem. The problem that this presents is that the therapist needs somehow to respect both: "Yes, you are right that there is a problem," and "Yes, you are right that there is *not* a problem." In other words, the therapist is presented with a seemingly insoluble dilemma. If she sides with the parents ("Young man, there's a problem here alright"), she relinquishes all leverage she may have to get the son to recognize that as long as his parents believe there is a problem, a problem exists. If she sides with the son ("You and I know how parents are, they see problems where there aren't any"), she ignores the fact that as long as the parents believe there is a problem, there *is* one.

De Shazer's "exception" and "miracle" questions are actually quite clever devices to get the therapist off the horns of this dilemma. Together, they enable the therapist to agree with both parties at the same time, even though they are saying diametrically opposite things. The "exception" question tells the one who believes that there *is* a problem that *sometimes* the problem isn't there. The "miracle" question gets the one who *doesn't* believe there is a problem to envision better circumstances than currently exist, and to do so without accepting the premise that the so-called "problem" has anything to do with why his life may not be what he can readily envision it to be.

Thus, these two questions enable de Shazer to address the fact that as long as *someone* believes there is a problem, there *is* a problem, even if the other disagrees.

His account of his efforts to find the "essence" of Erickson's work is a case in point. His problem was that he believed that Erickson's work had an underlying essence, but that, so far, he hadn't been able to figure out what it was. This problem was exacerbated by Erickson's seeming implication that there *was* an essence to his work, but that he himself had found it too difficult to figure out what it was. This was enough to set a bright young therapist like de Shazer on the quest: "I'll be the one who figures it out." Thus, on the one hand, we have Erickson saying (*a*) there is an essence to my work; (*b*) I don't know what it is; and (*c*) but the fact that I don't know what it is isn't a problem for me. On the other hand, we have de Shazer saying (*a*) there is an essence to Erickson's work; (*b*) I don't know what it is; and (*c*) the fact that I don't know what it is *is* a problem for me. This means that it only requires *one* of the persons (de Shazer) to perceive that there is a problem, while it takes both (Erickson *and* de Shazer) to perceive that there is *not* a problem. The problem in this case vanishes when de Shazer comes to the view that (*a*) there is no essence to Erickson's work; and (*b*) this is not a problem for him, even as it was not a problem for Erickson.

This means that a problem will continue to "exist" until both persons are satisfied that it no longer exists. In the case of the fifteen-year-old boy, the therapy is declared a success when the parents no longer believe there is a problem. Since the boy occasionally misbehaves, the parents have some lingering doubts, sometimes believing that his misbehavior is "symptomatic" of some underlying problem that they are unable to put their finger on, but they are willing to downplay these doubts because their son's behavior has markedly improved. In *Change*, Watzlawick et al. quote the following aphorism of Wittgenstein: "The solution of the problem of life is seen in the vanishing of the problem."[67] De Shazer would not disagree with this, but his therapy cases tell us that all who have a stake in the matter need to agree that the problem is no more. When this occurs, therapy has achieved a real-life miracle. The therapeutic key to this ultimate goal of having everyone agree that the problem has vanished is the exception question, as it has it both ways: Yes, there *is* a problem here, but there are times when it is *not* here. For the person who believes there *is* no problem, the therapist's suggestion that there are times when there is no problem is an important concession to his position, while the therapist's acceptance of the other person's claim that a problem exists and needs to be taken seriously is an important concession to *her* position. The "exception question" plants the seed for the eventual mutual declaration that the problem itself has vanished. This can be an especially important therapeutic intervention in marital counseling, where it is sometimes the case that one of the two believes there are "real problems with our marriage" while the other believes "our marriage is just fine." The exception question enables the therapist to avoid the dilemma of choosing between the who who believes her spouse is "in denial" and the other who believes his spouse is "making a mountain out of a molehill."

Recovering the Language of Self

In chapter 1 I discussed how family therapists give relatively less attention to what Hudson and O'Hanlon call "experience" than some other therapeutic traditions do, and I introduced Carl Rogers's concept of the self in order to identify and explore the process of experiencing that underlies and undergirds the stories that clients tell. I want to return here to this matter of the self because it has direct relevance to de Shazer's way of approaching the stories that clients tell. As we have seen, he rejects the structuralist idea that a deep structure lies beneath the language that the client uses, and thus also challenges the idea that the therapist's task is to identify the deep structure of which the client is more-or-less unaware. On the other hand, he recognizes that a client has experiences that are difficult to articulate, such as the experience of "depression," and has developed the exception question to enable the therapist and the client to agree on when, or under what set of circumstances, this experience is present and when it is not. While the client ascribes a given "experience" a name ("depression"), de Shazer does not give the "experiencing" phenomenon itself a generic name for, as we saw from his discussion of the term *system* as used by family therapists, he is strongly opposed to words that reify or make "things" or "entities" out of metaphorical ways of speaking, or that give definitive names to ambiguous events, feelings, and relationships. He does not oppose the use of working names or titles because these are needed in order for therapists and clients to communicate (actually, to miscommunicate), but he opposes the use of definitive names because their use introduces a metalanguage into the therapeutic process. When this happens, therapist and client become engaged in a game of words that has only a tangential connection to what is the client's actual experience.

While de Shazer's understanding of experience is very close, if not identical, to Carl Rogers's, there is one major difference between them: Rogers believed that a client could develop the capacity to communicate her experiencing with increasing accuracy and that the therapist could understand her experiencing. For Rogers, empathy is the critical factor here, for genuine empathy involves not merely responding to the client's words but internalizing her experiences as if they are the therapist's own. Rogers had great confidence in the capacity of empathy to effect genuine understanding. In contrast, de Shazer takes the view that the conversation between therapist and client is one of misunderstanding, though he seems to believe that there are degrees of misunderstanding, that some misunderstandings are closer than others to the reality of the client's experience.

Another important difference is that Rogers assigned the term *self* to this process of experiencing. In doing so, he followed in the footsteps of William James who, in his *The Principles of Psychology*, uses the term *self* in a way similar to how Rogers uses it. James noted that "What we experience, what *comes before us*, is a chaos of fragmentary impressions interrupting each other." Clearly, what we experience "out there" cannot easily be identified or defined.[68] James also took interest in our experience of ourselves, the experience of being aware of ourselves and of what is happening to or within us. Like de Shazer, who points out that the "ego" does not exist in fact, he was reluctant to talk about the "essence" of this experience, and he rejected the idea of calling it "the soul," but he was also opposed to the idea that the experience of being aware of oneself is "nothing but a fiction, the imaginary being denoted by the pronoun I."[69] He notes that, whether one views it as "a spiritual substance or only a delusive work," the fact of the matter is that the self is "felt." Just as the body is "felt," so the self is "felt" in the sense that we are aware of its presence, and we are further aware that the "central nucleus" of this self is the "palpitating inward life" that is within us.[70]

Thus, James avoids an "essential" understanding of the self, but, precisely because he does so, he provides a basis for introducing "self" language into de Shazer's approach to therapy without doing violence to it. The client who complains of feeling "depressed" is communicating his self-experience. It is not that he "gets" depressed but that his experience of himself is that of depression. The exceptional question is designed to elicit whether there are moments in his life when his self-experience is *not* that of depression but of something else. In those moments or on those occasions, his felt sense of himself is something different. De Shazer's therapeutic intervention will not be designed to eliminate the "depression," as though the goal of therapy is a state of nonbeing, of self-evacuation, but to identify what the client experiences in the place of his experience of depression and to see if there are ways to make these other experiences occur more often, on a more regular basis.

My point here is that there is much to be gained from recovering the concept of the self if we do it in such a way that we avoid assigning the self fixed characteristics or properties. When we mean "self" in the sense of "felt awareness" or even the "palpitating inward life," we are able to see that the "exceptions" which de Shazer wants to identify and make more prominent in the life of the client are already present in the client's self-experiencing, but she is unaware of them because there are felt senses that are much more dominant. The experience that is identified as "the miracle" is not one that is alien or foreign to the client's self, for it is already there. The therapist's task is to enable this already-present experiential process to occur more regularly and not merely by happenstance or chance.

For this to occur, the client is encouraged to take a more intentional view of the self. Here again, James is very helpful because he does not take an activist view of intention. Intention is not a matter of exercising willpower, of forcing oneself to do what one is reluctant to do. James notes, for example, that a person may have the intention of saying something before he actually says it. James asks, "Of what does this intention consist?" Does it consist "of definite sensorial images, either of words or of things?" James says no, there is nothing that specific or definite involved. As these words or things to say begin to come to mind, however, the "anticipatory intention welcomes them successively."[71] Thus, to say, after the fact, that one "intended" to say what one has just said is not really true. Rather, one had the intention to speak, but how this intention actually manifested itself was determined by what came *after* the intention itself. This is also the sense in which de Shazer's "miracle question" needs to be understood. If this question elicits in the client an "intention," it is not that it "motivates" her to change her behavior in any predetermined way, but that it introduces to the self-experiencing process a state of anticipation, a sense that something different may begin to happen. It was precisely this way with the miracles of Jesus. The "patient" or "client" was neither active nor passive but "intentional." Jesus' question, "Do you want to be healed?" evokes this very intentionality. He does not go on to say, "How do you want it done?" or "Have you given some thought to how the healing would be accomplished?" All that is required is an "intentionality" as understood by James. In his article entitled "The Mitigated Self," James E. Dittes describes this as a kind of "yielding," of allowing oneself to be acted upon instead of always being the actor, the doer, the one who does the exerting.[72] James took a great deal of interest in "automatisms," such as in the familiar phenomenon that forgotten names "come to" a person precisely when she has given up trying to recall them.[73] The "A Lazy Way to Diet" case presented in chapter 2 illustrates this understanding of "intention," as does Erickson's use of hypnotic suggestion in his therapeutic work. This is precisely the kind of intending that enables the miracles that de Shazer invites to occur.

There is another issue that needs to be addressed in this context, which is the fact that the self is shaped by previous experiences and is thus associated with what has transpired in the past. The woman who asked Erickson if he would mind if she quit fooling herself and gave up on the idea that she would lose weight experienced her "self" as having a history, and she felt this history and its influence upon her in the present moment. This does not take away from the fact that she made an important breakthrough in discovering that she did not have the intention to lose weight and that she accepted this fact about herself. Still, this story, like Erickson's "Cacti" story, indicates that when patients come to see a therapist about a problem, they bring a sense of their own history with them. If, as James asserts, the self is not a reified entity but a form of awareness, this *is* an awareness that includes memory, specifically of past experiences that are considered to have some influence on one's present self-experiencing.

In *The Self in the System*, Michael P. Nichols tells the story of his work with the Templetons, a couple who were at their wits' end because their son, Raymond, had confided in his school guidance counselor that he wanted to die. The counselor considered this a serious threat and arranged for Mr. and Mrs. Templeton and their son to see Nichols for more intensive treatment. In the course of the treatment, Nichols took the rather standard systemic approach of trying to change the quality of the family's relationships. He especially focused on the father–son relationship, and encouraged the mother to pull back and give the father and son a chance to develop such a relationship. He also taught Raymond how to befriend his father by fitting in with his habits and moods. Over the course of therapy, the problem of Raymond's threatened suicide began to subside, but Mr. Templeton was unable to move toward any greater intimacy with his son. At the time, Nichols found this somewhat perplexing. He realized that he did not know very much about this man even though he had seen a great deal of him in therapy.[74]

But several months later, after Nichols had terminated therapy with the family, Mr. Templeton came to see Nichols by himself because he perceived that the pattern which had prevailed in the family prior to Raymond's threat to kill himself had returned, and he felt personally responsible for this. As he and Nichols talked together, he began to tell his own story about how, as a young man, he worked out a life pattern of serious purpose and hard work that helped him to achieve his professional goals while at the same time compensating for his shyness and masking his anxiety. He organized his life so that nothing got in the way of success and he controlled his schedule the way he controlled his emotions. He experienced the births of his children as an intrusion into his carefully constructed life and the children quickly discovered that their mother was more responsive and available than their father. Nichols notes that "a pattern, familiar to family therapists, emerged; the enmeshed mother and disengaged father." It was this pattern to which his earlier therapeutic efforts had been devoted. But now, in listening to Mr. Templeton tell his story, he was hearing for the first time about the one "self" in the "system" who could make an enormous difference in the family as currently patterned if only he were "free" to do so. This, however, was a self who, in spite of his feelings of guilt, could not terminate his endless isolation from the rest of the family.

Nichols does not go on to chronicle his work with Mr. Templeton, and, in any event, my purpose in introducing this story here is to illustrate the point that an integral part of one's self-awareness is the sense of having a personal history, and this history cannot be disregarded as one envisions or intends a new and different future. If it is true that I *am* my experiencing, then this experiencing extends back into the past and while, literally speaking, the past no longer exists, it has a "presentness" about it that can neither be denied nor ignored.

The following story, which is about myself, illustrates the problem that this history poses. Even more importantly, it enables us to explore the value of de Shazer's "exception" and "miracle" questions for creating a context for change to occur even if, in this case, the problem has proven quite resistant to any lasting solution.

The Confessions of a Telephobic

The story concerns a particular phobia of mine, one of several that have become an enduring aspect of my self-experiencing. This particular phobia centers around the telephone. I tend to recoil from talking on the phone, and much prefer communicating through letters, even when this takes considerably more time, and, in some cases, is self-defeating, because the time delay adversely affects the outcome of the matter about which I am corresponding. When others view the telephone as a convenience (and nuisance), I view it with phobic apprehension, as though it has threatening—even demonic—powers far outweighing its weight, size, and seeming innocence. Obviously, it is not its technological complexity which I find so threatening for, among the various electronic instruments available today, the telephone is surely the most "user-friendly." Strike a few buttons, wait a brief moment, and, presto, either a voice answers "hello" or a few easily identifiable sounds indicate either that the other line is busy or there is no one to take the call, but I can leave a message.

Since the telephone is one of the few technologies that I experienced as a child growing up, I have often wondered if the causes of
my "telephobia" may be traced to childhood. My efforts to trace it
recall an incident when I was ten or eleven years old. A neighborhood friend and I had in common the fact that our fathers worked
for the same company in downtown Omaha. Occasionally, he and I
would board the bus after school and go downtown to meet and ride
home with our fathers. These jaunts afforded us a look into the
world of business and gave each of us some undivided time with our
fathers. As both of our fathers had managerial positions, we were
allowed to enter the building (with its impressive lobby) and take the
elevator up to their respective offices. Our fathers usually remained
a few minutes after the other employees left, so we would sit in their
offices while we waited for them to finish their work. One afternoon
when I was sitting near my father's desk the phone rang. My father
was out of his office looking for some files and since it was after
hours, I decided to answer, thinking it might be my mother calling
my father, perhaps to ask him to stop at the grocery store on our way
home. Instead, it was my friend Tom, calling from his father's office
several floors above. We talked briefly, then he said, "Hang up and
call me back." I waited a few moments and then called him back.
The voice on the other line said in a low, official tone, "Peters here."
I thought it was Tom pretending to be his father, so I said, "You can't
fool me." But the voice persisted, "This is Peters. What is it?" Then
I realized to my utter dismay that I was in fact speaking to Tom's
father, and, not knowing what to do, I put the phone down on the
hook and felt myself shaking. How could I have mistaken the two
voices? How could I have spoken so rudely to a man in his position?
This was, of course, a deeply shaming experience. Moreover, as I tell
the story now, much of the original shame returns and I "feel" this
shame in the present. To the degree that I *am* my shame, even as de
Shazer's client *is* her depression, an experience that happened many
years ago has a "living presence" that many other childhood experiences do not and could never have.

Another, more recent experience that I associate with my "telephobia" is still far back in the past. I was in my early twenties and
had placed a long-distance call to the woman I had been dating for
several years. We had been geographically separated for two or three

months, and our relationship had had its ups and downs, but I had been working hard during these months of separation to resolve a particular matter that had been a major sticking point between us. When she answered the phone, I began to relate to her these efforts, believing that she would be very happy to hear of them. But, before I could get it all out, she interrupted and said, "There's someone else in my life now, and, in fact, he's with me now." Then, to this "someone" she said, laughing, "Stop it, John, you're tickling me." I mumbled an apology for the interruption, and hung up the phone. I stood immobilized for several minutes, physically shaking. Again, there was the devastation of having totally misconstrued the situation and the shame and humiliation of having been literally laughed off the phone and, I might ruefully add, out of her life.

These two experiences loom large in my efforts to understand why I have had a phobic reaction to telephones throughout my adult life. But these two experiences are only the tip of the iceberg, in that while they may help to "explain" my phobia, they do not begin to register its ubiquity and omnipresence. For example, I am unusually sensitized to the role that phones play in other person's lives. I had a friend in my graduate school days with whom I shared several evenings of animated conversation, but the single thing I recall from these talks is his telling me that his wife's parents always called her "person-to-person" so they would not have to talk to him. He told me other things about his in-laws that were equally rejecting and that, to him, were even more despicable, yet this is the story that fixed my attention, and is now the only thing I still remember about our conversations.

Let us suppose that I am the client, and that I have told the therapist the above story of my telephobia. The therapist, working from the de Shazerian perspective, asks me the miracle question: Suppose a miracle were to happen one night and you woke up in the morning and your problem had suddenly vanished. How would you describe yourself now? How would others know that the miracle occurred? I would say something like this: "The day after the miracle, I would no longer view the telephone as an instrument that has an inexplicable power over my life, but as a useful form of technology that I could use more effectively to make certain aspects of my life less complicated. I would be able to pick up the phone at will and call anyone that I happened to want to talk with and I would be able to pick up a ringing telephone and respond to the incoming message without feeling any anticipatory anxiety. Others would know the miracle had occurred because I would be the *initiator* of a phone contact and not only its reluctant or delinquent receiver. *They* would pick up *their* phones and hear me say, 'Hello, just thought I would call because we haven't talked for awhile and I was thinking about you.' They would also notice the difference because, as my phone calls *increased*, my letters to them would probably *decrease*."

If the therapist were then to ask, "Are there exceptions to what you call your 'phobic' relationship to the telephone?" my answer would go something like this: "This is an especially good question because I often ask it of *myself* in order to see if I can somehow solve the problem. Unfortunately, this question is difficult to answer, possibly because the phone has so many methods for inflicting pain. As the Gerasene's demons exulted, 'We are legion!' For example, there are occasional exceptional days when I will go to work, look at the list of calls I have received and duly noted on my scratch pad but which have thus far gone unanswered, and I decide to do something heroic about it. So I call one number after the other in quick succession, and then, finding some at their phones, others not, with a great sense of satisfaction and a sigh of relief ('Now that didn't kill you, did it?'), I throw the list of previously unanswered calls into my wastebasket. Success! The problem is that another phone call is lurking out there on the horizon somewhere so I know that my satisfaction is short-lived."

Another way of addressing the exception question has been to ask myself, Under what conditions do I experience a phone conversation as pleasant and welcome? Phone calls from my wife and son are never threatening because they seem like they are just a part of an ongoing conversation between us. This is also true of phone calls from a few close friends and former students, persons with whom I have also had many face-to-face conversations. Another exception is when the caller is exceptionally tongue-tied and confused, or leaves an extremely garbled and incomprehensible message on my answering machine—obviously, a kindred soul. Yet, interestingly enough, even in the case of close friends, it may take me several days to "get around" to returning their calls, and, while I enjoy hearing their

voices, I know deep down that I would have enjoyed receiving a letter, however brief, a good deal more.

In other words, the exception question tends to elicit from me the
response that while there are, indeed, exceptions, the exceptions tend
to reinforce for me the power and intractability of the phobia itself.
I agree with de Shazer that the exceptions prove the exceptions, and
I even agree in principle that it should be possible to find ways to
maximize these exceptions—more days in which I reel off a series of
phone calls with amazing dispatch, or more self-initiated calls to
close friends solely for the purpose of "staying in touch." Yet, in an
odd sort of way, the exceptions do seem to "prove" that the phone
is "in reality" a continual, ever-present threat to my personal well-
being, as it has *so many ways* that it can elicit anxiety. That is, its
powers *are* legion, and I am no match for all of them put together.

This fact has led me to "choose," as it were, to "believe in" my
phobia, much as one might believe in a ghost that one's rational
mind tells him is not "really there." This way, at least, I feel that I
gain a small margin of freedom from its all-pervasive power. If I act
as though it does not exist, that it is a stupid illusion, it seems then
to have greater power to get the upper hand. Thus, paradoxically, the
more that I believe that I am beginning to defeat the phobia, to send
it packing, so to speak, this is precisely when it seems to strike back
with a vengeance. The "miracle" would be nice if this would be the
end of it, but I fear its inevitable backlash, and therefore choose to
believe in my phobia, embracing it as my very own. I find myself con-
troverting President Roosevelt's famous dictum, "The only thing we
have to fear is fear itself," offering in its stead, "I know that my fear
is all in my head, but my head is a mansion with many rooms, and
I've no reason to expect that every room will be sunny and delight-
ful." I don't especially like having my "phobia" as a permanent res-
ident in my "home," but I have come to accept that "he" has no
plans to leave, and that there isn't much point in my trying to evict
him, that it is better to try to work around "him."

Here, the story ends on a certain note of irony: In explaining his
scaling question, de Shazer suggests that 0 may stand for how the
client felt at the time *of the original phone call* seeking therapy,
while 10 stands for the day after the miracle. For the person who
has "telephobia," however, the "original phone call" *is* the day after

the miracle. How might others know that the miracle has occurred? Because the telephobic would be able to call the therapist's office for an appointment![75] This very anomaly makes "telephobia" appear to be an unusually odd form of phobia, but it is perhaps no different, fundamentally, than the story that Watzlawick et al. tell about a man who suffered from agoraphobia:

> A middle-aged, unmarried man [was] leading a rather isolated life compounded by an agoraphobia; his anxiety-free territory was progressively diminishing. Eventually this not only prevented him from going to work, but threatened to cut him off even from visiting the neighborhood stores upon which he depended for the purchase of his food and other basic necessities. In his desperation he decided to commit suicide. He planned to get into his car and drive in the direction of a mountaintop about fifty miles from his home, convinced that after driving a few city blocks his anxiety or a heart attack would put him out of his misery. The reader can guess the rest of the story: He not only arrived safely at his destination, but for the first time in many years he found himself free from anxiety.[76]

Watzlawick et al. describe this as a case of "spontaneous remission" of the phobia in question. In de Shazer's terms, it is truly a miracle story.

If I find myself demurring, even a little skeptical, this is because, in my own experience, the problem appears to be connected with past experiences that insinuate themselves into my present self-experiencing, and there doesn't seem to be much that I can do to keep this from happening, given the ubiquity of the telephone in my life. (If my phobia were of snakes, it would be more easily relegated to the periphery of my life.) Gershen Kaufman and Lev Raphael's explanation in *Coming Out of Shame* that "shame binds become stored in memory in the form of scenes" and that through "a process of psychological magnification, a family of related scenes emerges"[77] has helped me to understand what is happening here. Still, the only "solution" I have found to the problem itself has been to embrace the phobia as my own, "welcoming" it, as it were, into my overall sense of who I am. It is potentially inspiring to read the case of the Gerasene demoniac, to experience the terrified "Legion" taking refuge inside the pigs, freeing the man from the powers which had gotten the better of him. But this story may also be demoralizing for those who do *not* experience a "spontaneous remission," for whom it is more a matter of noting an occasional success followed perhaps by a relapse of sorts, and observing this self-same process day in and day out, year in and year out. To me, this is the real genius—and lesson—of de Shazer's scaling question, as it indicates that there are in fact no zeros and there are in fact no tens. That is, *there are no absolutes*. Yet, we can measure our progress (and regress) in terms of movements from 3 to 4, or 7 to 6. We do not even demand of ourselves that we make permanent gains that are secure from subsequent erosion. We content ourselves with an occasional small miracle and with the fact that we are at least *somewhere* on the scale—a scale which is, after all, an important part, but only one part, of the self that we are.

The Pastor as Minor Miracle Worker

To draw the implications of de Shazer's therapeutic approach for pastoral counseling in the congregational context, I want to begin by focusing on the role of the pastor as a "minor miracle worker" and then return to the self issue that our excursion into the views of William James made possible.

In his chapter "Seeing Through Expectations to Find Ministry," in *When the People Say No*, James E. Dittes considers the miracle performed by Peter at the "Beautiful Gate" (Acts 3:1-10).[78] Dittes notes that in his request for alms, the crippled man was saying no to Peter and John's life of prayer (the purpose for their going to the temple), and that Peter, in observing that he had no silver or gold to give, said no to the man's request for alms. But the text says that "Peter fixed his eyes" on the man, and that the man, expecting a gift, "was all attention to Peter." Peter did not look away from him, the customary reaction when one does not give a beggar what he asks for, but instead looked into his eyes, thus discerning the "you" to whom he offered the gift that he *could* give. As Dittes puts it, Peter and John "saw through" the beggar's expectations in order to find ministry. He adds:

Ministry lies precisely in seeing through the facades, in exposing and exploring and changing questions more than in giving answers, in enlarging quest and demand more than in fulfilling settled and conventional role expectations. Ministry is in seeing through what others see as a matter of course, what others accept blindly, and this is never more true than with the expectations of ministry that others hold routinely.[79]

In addition to fixing his eyes on the man, Peter reached out and took him by the hand: "In that sudden touching of yearnings each risked an unfamiliar and unlikely act of ministry. In sacrificing their habituated expectations of ministry, they found, together—it could not have been otherwise than together, it could not have been otherwise than in sacrifice of expectations—a surprising meeting of their yearnings in a new wholeness."[80]

When does a pastor become a minor miracle worker? When the pastor "sees through" her own expectations and those of the other and, in consequence, something quite wonderful occurs. It is wonderful precisely because it *is* unexpected, precisely because it goes against all expectations, prompting each to wonder at and wonder about what has—and is—taking place. A miracle need not be understood as an event that "goes against" known scientific laws. It is enough that it "goes against" expectations, as when the fifteen-year-old boy's father, on hearing his son describe the day after the miracle, remarks, "Now, that *would* be a miracle."

That pastors will in fact perform miracles is one of the expectations (usually unstated and implicit) that congregations have of them. Pastors often note that their congregations expect them to work miracles, to be "able to walk on water." The pastor *may* respond to such expectations by pointing out how unrealistic they are—"After all, I'm just as human as the rest of you"—but de Shazer's approach suggests that there may be a better way, one that involves the pastor in *not* refusing to claim the identity of a *minor* miracle worker, basing this willingness to claim what appears to be an impossible role and a formula for certain failure on the fact that in a world where the exceptions prove the exceptions, miracles are a lot more common than we think. We just haven't been trained to think of them as such.

De Shazer notes in *Putting Difference to Work* that both clinical experience and research indicate that "workable goals" tend to have the following characteristics:

1. They are *small* rather than *large*.
2. They are *relevant* to clients.
3. They are described in *specific, concrete behavioral terms*.
4. They are *achievable* within the practical contexts of clients' lives.
5. They are perceived by clients to involve their own "*hard work*."
6. They are described as the "*start of something*" and not as the "end of something."
7. They are treated as involving *new behaviors* rather than the absence or cessation of something.[81]

Since de Shazer presents his "miracle question" immediately after providing this list of the characteristics of workable goals, the obvious implication is that the "miracle stories" that clients tell usually have these very characteristics. This means that miracle stories are not wild fantasies, the work of an imagination gone berserk. They are actually quite practical, albeit unorthodox, like an Erickson helping a man navigate on glare ice by closing his eyes, or Franzi Wokura getting distracted from his authority issues by observing that the flowers in the park are indeed very beautiful. Especially, they take personal and contextual factors into account, and they emphasize the beginning of something new, not just resolving *not* to do what one has always done (Erickson's "Walk a Mile" is a case in point.)

De Shazer's list of "workable goals" suggests that miracles are more likely when our goals are small, when they are relevant, when they are specific and concrete, when they are achievable within the practical context of our lives, when they involve hard work, when they are the start of something new and not the end of something old, and when they involve new behaviors rather than the cessation of existing ones. Of course, on the basis of my own minor miracle of losing a great deal of weight by sleeping, I may want to qualify the idea that miracles involve hard work, for miracles often occur when we quit exerting ourselves and yield. One could perhaps argue, however, that for someone accustomed to trying to master his problems, such yielding might be viewed as hard work, not unlike a general being confronted with the hard work of taking a dip in the River Jordan. I would also note that new behaviors may be behaviors that are already a part of one's behavioral repertoire, but not yet employed in the problematic situation. Thus, I had slept virtually every day of my life, so sleeping did not constitute a "new behavior." *How* I slept *was*, however, a new behavior.

The miracle stories in the Gospels have most if not all of these characteristics. An especially good example is the story of the friends who made a hole in the roof of the house where Jesus was staying and lowered the paralytic man, strapped in his own bed, into an interior room. Jesus, himself a frequent disturber of domestic tranquility, was most impressed by their ingenuity and their concern for their friend, and commended their faith. By the time he entered the picture, the healing process was already under way (Luke 5:17-26). Their actions were on a small scale, relevant, specific, achievable, involved some effort, were the start of something new, and initiated new behaviors. Cutting a hole in the roof was an unorthodox but effective way to get something started. "Cutting a hole in the roof" may, in fact, be viewed as a valuable metaphor for how miracles get intended; it certainly went against normal expectations.

So, if it is not true that pastors can walk on water, it does not follow that they are not involved in minor miracles more often than we realize. If a fifteen-year-old boy can go about his daily life in a sufficiently different manner that leads his father to exclaim, "Now that is truly a miracle," we have every reason to believe that pastors are already performing miracles. I suggest that my assistance of the student in overcoming his "writer's block" qualifies as a minor miracle. Even if it wasn't one, the two of us celebrated as if it were! What de Shazer cautions against, however, is our claim to know in advance what would constitute a miracle for someone else, which is why he asks the client to tell *him* what would he consider to be a miracle in *his* life. Furthermore, the wise pastor knows that primary credit must be given to the parishioner, the one who did the "hard work" to make it happen. In all of the "day after the miracle" stories that de Shazer reports, the clients assume that they must do something, or, at least, be receptive to being acted upon by someone or something else, in order to make it happen. This is in spite of the fact that de Shazer has just told them that the miracle has already happened, that it happened while they were asleep, and that all he is asking them to do is to describe it so as to explain how the rest of us would know that the miracle has already taken place. This indicates that few of us really believe that miracles occur without some intentionality on our part, without our contributing or acquiescing to something new.

Typically, this means relinquishing some old assumptions or settled convictions about how the situation that has become problematic ought to be "handled." Maybe these assumptions or convictions worked before or maybe they worked for someone else, but they are not working now, if, indeed, they ever really did. On the one hand, one has to admire the persistence of the man at the pool at Bethzatha who devoted thirty-eight years to a method that was apparently working for others. But this story also illustrates Watzlawick's point in *The Situation is Hopeless but Not Serious* that we often assume that a method which is not working needs only to be applied more forcefully.[82] Meanwhile, this method acquires a monopoly on our thinking and acting, forcing other possible methods to wait in the wings until we finally acknowledge that the original method is not working and never will.

This discussion of the pastor as a minor miracle worker may seem to imply that all difficulties faced in life have a solution. In fact, the healing stories in the Gospels tend to give this impression, and, as a consequence, while they have been inspirational stories for many, they have also been the occasion for disillusionment when a hoped-for healing did not take place, when the desired wholeness in body or spirit proved elusive, leading to disappointed hopes, even to despair. The well-attested dangers inherent in miracle stories, whether those in the Gospels or those conceived by clients of therapists like de Shazer, lead us back to the issue of the self, and especially to the fact that the self is comprised of its remembered past as well as of its anticipated future. Like it or not, this remembered past plays a significant role in our efforts to solve our problems in the present. We bring a lot of baggage to our current problem-solving efforts, the baggage of previous experience. And this is one reason that I do not believe that all difficulties faced in life have a solution, no matter how "faith-ful" we may happen to be.

The Self in the Language System

Is de Shazer sufficiently attentive to the "self" that the client brings to the language system and to how it functions within this system?

Like Erickson and Watzlawick, de Shazer gives little attention to the self. As I have noted, however, his appreciation for the difficulties involved in communicating one's own experience to another invites reflection on the self, and it is for this reason that I have raised this issue specifically in my discussion of de Shazer. Moreover, the idea of the self that his approach invites is the one that I consider the most tenable, the most defensible, precisely because it does not fall into either of the extremes that James identifies (that is, of positing a self that has certain essential characteristics or of judging that "I" is merely a convenient fiction). Because he, like Watzlawick, places great emphasis on the claim that we "construct" or "invent" our own worlds, we might have expected that de Shazer would argue that the self is nothing but a construct, created in the narrative process itself.[83] That he does not make this familiar postmodernist argument is not primarily because he does not have a theory of the self, but is due, instead, to his belief that there are personal experiences that cannot *be* constructed, as they do not lend themselves to any kind of verbal or written expression. This does not mean that he believes in the structuralist distinction between surface and depth, for, as we have seen, he no longer accepts this formulation. What it does mean is that we all have things about ourselves for which we have not yet found the words and perhaps never will. These are not depths that we have yet to plumb, or secrets that remain hidden, even from ourselves, but experiencings that so far remain incommunicable because they are unclear and amorphous.

The scaling question, as trivial as it may appear, is actually his way of acknowledging that we all have self-experiencings that others—and even we ourselves—cannot directly know. We have a "feeling" of depression, and the therapist accepts our claim to having such a feeling, but how it feels can only be inadequately communicated, and, however we communicate it, it will be misread, misunderstood. The scaling question works precisely because it is based on the admission that there is something about my experience that another cannot know. If the scaling question were simply used as an easy substitute for seeking to understand another person's experience, it would be a cheap gimmick. But, as de Shazer indicates, he began to use it in therapy because clients themselves used it to try to get across to him that for which they could not find the words.

Thus, the miracle question elicits the story of the self that can be told, a story that tells the therapist, "This is how I envision myself," whereas the scaling question accepts the fact that there will always be something that cannot be told, that cannot be expressed in the story that I tell about myself. If the scaling question elicits our intentions, the miracle question invites us to construct a fictional self— "This is me after the miracle"—and this fictional self proves an invaluable construct for effecting therapeutic change, for making the fictional more real and true.

To Embrace the Self That One Would Rather Not

I am concerned, however, that the miracle question may give such emphasis to the new, realized self that it virtually erases the remembered self. In the description given by the fifteen-year-old boy of his "day after the miracle," the remembered self was the reality that the miracle story stood over against, the self who would not get up in the morning without being prodded, the self who refused to take a shower, the self who left his dirty dishes on the table, and so forth. The miracle story envisions this remembered self being somehow erased so that the realized self can be written into the space that the remembered self has occupied. Yet, the very fact that the father and mother could not agree on which days the son had intended the new self indicates just how easily and naturally the remembered self insinuates itself into our experience, even when we are making a conscious, deliberate effort to leave it behind.

As I consider my own efforts to be cured of my phobia, which I know is based on groundless fears, I become more, not less, aware of the power of the remembered self and of the relative helplessness of the realized self to break its power. The male client of de Shazer who has a drinking problem puts it well when he describes his morning after the miracle: "I probably wouldn't feel like I'm leaving something behind. Because, you know, in your dreams—sometimes you never have a chance to complete it, so you therefore feel like you left something. Way it is with all the other crap that kinda lingers on me. . . ." Does anyone—this man, the therapist, de Shazer, or the reader of this story—really believe that he will be able to divest himself completely of "all the other crap that kinda lingers on me"? I think we know, and we know that *he* knows, that this will never be the case. In fact, if de Shazer really believed that it would be this way, he would not have adopted the "scaling question," which measures progresses (and regresses) and actually exhibits rather little faith in miracles, at least in miracles where the individual's remembered self is rendered powerless.

I would therefore nominate Jesus' story of the prodigal son (Luke 15:11-32) as the relevant text for the situation in which the remembered self exhibits marked survival skills, the ability to persist against all efforts to erase it. We *may* think of this story in terms of "family systems," as the story of a rather dysfunctional family, an approach that always, eventually, raises the question of "the missing mother." But we may also view it as a story about the self, with each of the brothers symbolizing an aspect of one individual's (perhaps even the storyteller's?) self-awareness. There is the self who envisions a better, more open future for himself (the younger brother) and there is the self who is oriented toward the predictable past and prefers it to the unpredictable future (the older brother). As the story continues, the self that envisioned a new life comes home, demoralized and defeated, his dreams of a bright future as much in tatters as the clothes he is wearing, while the self that was suspicious of the dreams of the other assumes a superior and ungenerous attitude: "Let him suffer the consequences of his dreams, or the lies he told himself." As handed down to us, this is not a miracle story. True, the father anticipates his son's return and welcomes him back, and the fact that it is the father (not the mother) who welcomes him is certainly a minor miracle. But what about the brothers? The miracle would be their intention to live together in peace, to relinquish their mutual suspicions and resentments, to take one another by the hand and gaze into each other's eyes, each embracing the self that they would rather not. In this way, the self would be unified, its duality overcome. Who but the living God, who heals our divided selves and restores them to wholeness, would be the one who enabled this miracle to happen? Who but the living God plants within us the intention to reconcile our competing, distrustful selves? But it was not to be.

Still, by introducing into de Shazer's approach a concern for the self in the language system, we are able to see that, sometimes, the miracle does not involve the "cure" of the disability that cripples us, but takes the form of an embracing of the self that we wish we could magically erase from our lives. In this sense, the healing stories in the Gospels are *not* deceptive, for they do not present Jesus as a magician, but as one whose ability to heal did not involve cheap gimmicks but a mutual intentionality between two selves. A similar mutual intentionality may occur within an individual, and when we find it within ourselves to embrace the self that we experience as deficient, inferior, fearful, delinquent, vulnerable, shameful, or ugly, we should know that God, having already embraced this self, wonders what has taken us so long to come around and to make peace with ourselves?

The Self in the Congregational Language System

What, then, does pastoral counseling contribute to the life of the congregation? In addition to those contributions noted in our discussion of Erickson and Watzlawick, it prompts us to bring the self into the language system—the discourse—of the congregation. As we all know, there is a great prejudice against the "self" in much of the discourse that occurs in the church, a prejudice that is fueled by much of the theological thinking of our day, which uses the word *self* pejoratively. When we inveigh against the "self-centeredness" of our day (as our predecessors inveighed against "self-importance," "self-indulgence," and even "self-pity" in theirs), we may score some moral points and may even, on occasion, say something that is true. But the larger effect of these condemnations (where even "self-reliance," formerly viewed as a signal virtue, comes in for attack) is that we communicate to our parishioners that we have something against the self as such, as though the "self" is the devil incarnate. As used in this book, the word *self* has none of these inherently negative connotations, but merely applies to the fact that we are all conscious of our experience, that, in a real sense, we *are* our experience. This sense of ourselves is itself a precious gift whose importance to us may not be recognized until it is threatened. As Erik H. Erikson puts it, "No one who has worked with autistic children will ever forget the horror of observing how desperately they struggle to grasp the meaning of saying 'I' and 'you' and how impossible it is for them, for language presupposes the experience of a coherent 'I.'"[84] The confusion that we witness in a person who suffers from Alzheimer's disease is another case in point. But, even more importantly, if we think of the self in only negative terms, we may find that we are unable to speak knowingly of God as well. In explaining why he wrote an account of his own life, Saint Augustine explained that if he had hidden himself from God, he "would be hiding [God] from *myself.*"[85] Or, as Meister Eckhart, the German mystic, put it, "The eye with which we see God is the same as the eye with which God sees us."[86] This means that there is a complementarity between our self and the living self of God.

If we use self language in mainly pejorative ways, we will also lose touch with a vital aspect of our religious tradition that traces back to the biblical psalms: the tendency of our predecessors to speak of the self in metaphorical ways. In an earlier article, I noted that the Book of Psalms has over one hundred references to the heart, which may roughly be divided into those that speak of the "desires" of the heart, those that concern the "intentions" of the heart, those that view the heart as the place or locus of "discernment," and those that refer to the various "emotions" of the heart. Clearly, the heart functions here as a metaphor for the self, and its use enables the psalmists to identify and to explore the meanings and functions of the self.[87]

In his major work on Christian heart language and its complex relationship to theological, psychological, and philosophical language of the self, Troels Nørager notes that in the traditional Danish hymnal, "heart" is the single most frequently used noun, and it stands for "the inner core and center of a person." He also notes that the heart is credited with being the "organ" of a special kind of knowledge, both in relation to its quality and to our relation to God (which is predominantly one of love): "The epistemic verbs employed by the hymns (feel, perceive, sense, taste, understand) all connote a way of knowing whose evidential force seems to be beyond dispute."[88] He notes further that his analysis of the recently published appendix to the Danish hymnal consisting of 150 hymns written in our own time reveals that the prominence of heart language has declined, both qualitatively and quantitatively. While a positive development is the tendency in the contemporary hymns to view "religious inwardness" as clearly related to our experience of the vitality of our body, it is, nonetheless, "disturbing to realize that what used to be fundamental elements in describing [our] relation to God seems now to have disappeared."[89] Of course, "heart" is only

one metaphor for the self. Current efforts to view the brain as a
metaphor for the self, thus shifting the locus of the remembered self
from the heart to the brain, provide another fruitful avenue for
metaphorizing the self.[90] My point, however, is that we lose contact
with our own religious traditions when we indulge this prejudice
against the self, treating it as though it were the nemesis of a communal vision, when, in fact, the self has so much to tell us about the
communing that occurs in the community of faith.

Against those who argue that the self is a construct, nothing
more—or less—than a narrative, I think it is just the reverse: When
the self carries through on its intention to speak about itself, to give
voice to one's awareness of being an "I," it tends to tell a story. In
this sense, many of the psalms are self-narratives and are revealing of
the writer's self-experiencings. The wonder of this story is its uniqueness. It is a story that only "I" can tell, one that no one else can tell
in my behalf. Thus, pastoral counseling begins autobiographically.

In the epilogue to *Words Were Originally Magic*, de Shazer
acknowledges that the "character" of his book

> depends a lot on the authors cited that help to make my solo voice into
> a sort of chorus. A lot of voices, living, dead, and fictional have had
> their say along with mine. I hope that my use has in no circumstance
> been abuse. When they had something to say that I thought they said
> well, I let them speak for themselves. Perhaps sometimes they spoke
> too long or too often, but I find paraphrase too difficult.[91]

Besides being difficult, paraphrase is a special kind of misreading,
an especially pernicious form of it, as it misreads while pretending
not to do so. As the dictionary defines it, paraphrase is "a rewording
of the thought or meaning expressed in something that has been said
or written before." It implies that the one who paraphrases can say
it better—or, at least, more succinctly—than the one who originally
said it. But for me to say in my words what you have said in yours
is to put your story in another context, and to create a false, imaginary boundary between the story and the self whose story it is. The
better way is to allow the original self to speak where it can, and to
be silent where it cannot, and to accept the fact that, in either case,
it neither requires nor invites our mediation.

Chapter 5

Social Gossip and Pastoral Counseling

Throughout this book, I have been contending that pastoral counseling has an essential place in congregational life because it exemplifies storytelling within a constructive context. In the pastoral counseling context, the stories that parishioners tell are treated respectfully, are handled responsibly, and receive a helpful response. I have also suggested that the pastor who is aware of the different types of story that are generated and favored by important representatives of the brief therapy movement (Erickson, Watzlawick, de Shazer) will find this to be a valuable resource for responding helpfully to the stories that parishioners tell.

An issue that I briefly mentioned in the introduction but did not develop in detail is the problem of gossip, which is usually judged to be detrimental to the life of the congregation because it involves storytelling that does *not* occur with a constructive framework. Now, however, I would like to explore the matter of gossip further, not only because it is such a common form of communication within the life of any social group, including the congregation, but also because it sometimes, perhaps often, plays the same constructive role in the life of a social group that I am ascribing to pastoral counseling. By identifying the ways in which it is not destructive but constructive, we gain a better idea of what it is that makes pastoral counseling a constructive form of communication, and we also gain valuable insights into the dangers that are also inherent in pastoral counseling. As we will see, gossip is a much more complex form of social interaction than we realize, and not all gossip is a bad thing. The problem is that we usually decry it as an unmitigated evil (in spite of the fact that we all engage in it!) and because we indict it in such broad and general strokes, we are not in a very good position to judge when it is a destructive element in the life of a congregation and when it may be serving the better interests of the congregation as a social body. The need to make these more discriminating judgments about gossip as a form of storytelling is already implied in my earlier discussion of the spreading of stories in my earlier chapter on Erickson. Such spreading of stories about how a pastor was genuinely helpful to a parishioner in the context of pastoral counseling is one way in which gossip can have a positive influence in the life of the congregation.

In this chapter, I will take up recent discussions of gossip in the social sciences and in literary studies, and will relate these studies to the social context in which Jesus carried out his ministry. This exploration leads to conclusions about how pastoral counseling provides a model for communication within the congregation, and thus has influence outside and beyond the more limited context in which it occurs.

The issue of gossip arises in the Gospels in the context of a debate about Jesus' rejection of traditional dietary laws and restrictions. Matthew tells us that the disciples of John the Baptist were critical of Jesus because, unlike them and the Pharisees, Jesus' disciples did not fast (Matt. 9:14-17). Their criticism, however, seems mild in comparison to that of the Pharisees and scribes who, according to Matthew, came to Jesus from Jerusalem, complaining to him that his disciples transgressed the tradition of the elders for failing to wash their hands when they ate (Matt. 15:1-2). Matthew indicates that Jesus responded not by defending his disciples' actions but by lambasting his critics who, in his judgment, had a lot of explaining to do for *saying things* that directly violate the commandments of God. For instance, "God said, 'Honor your father and your mother,' and 'Whoever speaks evil of father or mother, must surely die.' But you say that whoever tells father or mother, 'Whatever support you might have had from me is given to God,' then that person need not honor the father'" (Matt. 15:4-5). Then he called the people to him and said to them, "Listen and understand: it is not what goes into the mouth defiles a person, but it is what comes out of the mouth that defiles." (Matt. 15:10-11). In other words, it is what we say, not what we eat, that condemns us.

Matthew tells us that the disciples came to him and said, "Do you know that the Pharisees took offense when they heard what you said" (that is, that it is not what one eats but what one says that defiles a person). Perceiving that his disciples were not convinced that he was right, Jesus said, "Do you not see that whatever goes into the mouth enters the stomach, and goes out into the sewer? But what comes out of the mouth proceeds from the heart, and this is what defiles. For out of the heart come evil intentions, murder, adultery, fornication, theft, false witness, slander. These are what defile a person; but to eat with unwashed hands does not defile" (Matt. 15:17-20). Another example of the claim that he was particularly disturbed by the destructive effects of "evil talk" is Matt. 12:34-37: "You brood of vipers! How can you speak good things, when you are evil? For out of the abundance of the heart the mouth speaks. The good person brings good things out of a good treasure, and the evil person brings evil things out of an evil treasure. I tell you, on the day of judgment you will have to give an account for every careless word you utter, for by your words you will be justified, and by your words you will be condemned."

These citations from the Gospel of Matthew indicate that gossip was at least as common in Matthew's time as in our own time. It is also evident that Jesus, as presented by Matthew, considered careless and malicious talk—false witness and slander—a more serious offense against God than what and how one eats. In effect, one can do a great deal more harm in one's community by saying things about someone else that are not true or by divulging secrets to those who are in a position to do harm than by failing to follow traditional ways of eating one's food. These warnings against careless and malicious talk were necessary because Upper Palestine was a largely rural society that relied almost exclusively on oral transmission of information as a means of communication from village to village. In his book on the historical Jesus, John Dominic Crossan calls it "the peasant grapevine."[1] Like the contemporary congregation, there was not much of a written tradition that could challenge assertions and allegations made orally.

If the Gospels themselves reveal the role that gossip played in the
social life in rural Palestine, we need to turn to other sources for
insight into the role that gossip plays in social interaction. The
Gospels, Matthew especially, represent Jesus as warning against careless and malicious talk, but they do not help us very much to understand the role that gossip plays in social groups like the congregations. Contemporary *social-scientific* studies on gossip can be very
helpful in this regard. Before we discuss these, however, we should
consider the word itself. What does "gossip" mean? Etymologically,
it actually means "god-related" (it was originally "god-sib"). As a
noun, it originally designated a godparent of either gender.[2] Then its
meaning enlarged to include any close friend, that is, someone
belonging to the group from which godparents would naturally be
chosen. These would be persons to whom one could reveal one's personal secrets, trusting them to keep these secrets to themselves. But,
in time, the word underwent a process of degradation, perhaps
because the trust that was placed in god-sibs proved misplaced. In
the eighteenth century, Samuel Johnson's dictionary added a second
meaning—"tippling companion"—and a third meaning connecting
gossip with women (that is, "One who runs about tattling like
women at a lying-in"). The second meaning would apply only to
men, as a tippling companion would be a friend with whom one
drinks together in a tavern, something that women would not do.
The third meaning adds the word *tattling*, implying that private matters which one ought to keep to oneself are being told to others who
should not be privy to this information. With this meaning, women
are being identified as gossips in the negative sense. With a "tippling
companion," the talk is "just between us," and therefore not considered harmful to whoever might be the subject of conversation. But
much harm can be done when one "runs about tattling as women at
a lying-in," for this implies that no discretion or circumspection is
being exercised in what is being communicated.

In Webster's dictionary, first published in 1811, gossip is defined as
"idle talk, trifling or groundless rumor, tittle-tattle." By the late twen-
tieth century, gossip has acquired a mostly negative connotation. Its
"god-relatedness" is no longer recognized. The "just-between-us"
quality of gossip, as in the case of "tippling companions," is not taken
very seriously either, probably because there is little confidence that

what has been communicated will, in fact, remain "just between us." Thus, the third meaning of gossip, as "tattling," is the prevailing one today, and the only real distinction now being made is between "idle" and "malicious" gossip, with the gossip engaged in by women more likely to be considered "malicious," while men's is considered merely "idle" and thus harmless, in spite of the fact that men are more likely to hold positions of power and influence, and their gossip may therefore be unusually damaging to another.

In her book on gossip, Patricia Meyer Spacks offers as a minimal definition of gossip that it is "idle talk about other persons not present." The word *idle* implies absence of announced purpose. Thus, talk in a personnel committee about an employee who is being considered for promotion is not considered gossip.[3] This definition shifts the emphasis from persons who engage in gossip to gossip as a kind of talk in which anyone might engage. Also, the fact that gossip is about persons not present leads to the natural assumption that it is mainly derogatory and unkind. In a study conducted by Jack Levin and Arnold Arluke, however, in which a student would sit in the student lounge and overhear the conversations of other students, it was found that 27 percent of all student gossip was clearly positive, 27 percent was clearly negative, and the rest was mixed. Levin and Arluke suggest that "There is probably far less negative gossip than most people might have predicted, as gossip is so often associated with nasty talk only."[4]

Recent books on gossip by social psychologists, sociologists and anthropologists take the position that, while seemingly trivial, gossip is actually an important form of social exchange. This does not mean that it is a uniformly good thing, but it does mean that it is not as trivial as it may appear. In discussing gossip as a form of social exchange, the social anthropologist Max Gluckman suggests that gossip is primarily used by groups for the purpose of maintaining exclusivity or an established social hierarchy. He identifies three such groups. One is the professional group (for instance, lawyers, educators, physicians) in which gossip is interwoven with technical terms and is practically indecipherable to the outsider. A second type is social groups that seek to preserve their exclusiveness by closing the doors to newcomers: "To be a true insider, one must know and be able to gossip about the present membership as well as their forebears."[5] The third group is one that has exclusiveness thrust upon it, as, for example, an ethnic or minority group. Here, gossip helps to preserve the unity of the group vis-à-vis the wider society, and it may also support a class system within the group in that it keeps individuals in their assigned places in the social order, especially in instances where those assigned to the lower positions have come into possessions which, in an earlier generation, would have qualified them for a higher social position. An insider's knowledge about the lives of others in the group is a source of power.

In their study of gossip, Ralph L. Rosnow and Gary Alan Fine note that each social group has its own etiquette for gossiping, and

> one who doesn't follow the rules is seen and treated as a deviant. In the medical community there is gossip that is considered proper and gossip that is considered improper; proper gossip is that indulged in by all M.D.s, which preserves the status of the profession; improper gossip aims at raising the teller's self-esteem at the expense of his professional peers. Thus again we observe that gossip is not merely *idle* talk, but talk with a social purpose. Like gamesmanship, the art of winning games without actually cheating, the etiquette of what is proper and improper in gossiping is rigidly controlled.[6]

Noting that gossip walks a fine line between impressions and reality, these authors contend that "this kind of gossiping can be a potent force for wreaking vengeance. Talk about someone's drinking or sexual habits can strip away his respectability."[7]

Yet, not all gossip, as social exchange, is negative or degrading of another. As Rosnow and Fine also point out, gossip offers a means of passing time, and, as chitchat, helps to maintain the fluidity of communication patterns. It is also the repository of folklore within a given community, as stories about members of the community, living and dead, are often recounted, and the very fact that a story is told about another person, even one in which the subject is satirized, is often taken to be a sign of affection and respect. They also note that gossip serves the desire of the gossipers to reaffirm their shared values, for talking about someone else who behaves in a manner judged to be offensive or wrong enables us to reaffirm our commitment to values that the person portrayed has violated.

Levin and Arluke also point out that gossip serves an initiatory function. For some social groups, gossip is used to exclude. But, in others, it is used to welcome new members. In a study of high-tech organizations in California's Silicon Valley, gossip was found to be helpful to newly hired employees in "learning the ropes" by providing information about what to expect from the boss. For example, "Will he come on to female employees?" or "Will he chew you out if you make a mistake?" The newcomer also learned "which co-workers should be avoided because their personalities were obnoxious or because they never paid back loans. Conversely, newcomers heard who was good to talk with when they had personal problems or who would stick up for them when work fell behind schedule."[8] The study also found that employees exchanged stories about people which communicated, correctly or incorrectly, the likelihood of being promoted or fired. Thus, gossip "reflects basic survival issues faced by employees. This kind of informal 'on-the-job training' is every bit as essential as the formal training in classrooms and apprenticeships."[9]

The same authors note that gossip has entertainment and relaxation value. Informal gatherings "convened for the purpose of playing cards, welcoming newcomers to the neighborhood, taking a break on the job, or eating dinner with friends often provide an excuse to gossip." Typically, the manifest purpose for meeting takes a backseat to conversation:

> Individuals become so engrossed in gossip that they may decide to modify their original plans for the evening so as to accommodate their need for gossip; a card game is transformed into a lively talk over drinks; several employees take their coffee breaks together to swap information about their new boss; over the dinner table, the members of a family discuss the sexual activities of a neighbor.[10]

Yet, the same authors acknowledge that, even if gossip is shared with a new employee or a new neighbor, it is likely to serve the purposes of exclusivity more than inclusivity. Even the very act of sharing gossip with a new employee is not from a motive of being more inclusive, but to present this individual with an opportunity to become a part of the in-group. If he responds to this implied invitation in a noncommittal manner, failing to express appropriate interest in or gratitude for the inside tips that have been offered to him, he risks affronting the group, and may well become the object of its ire, not to mention a new target for their gossip sessions. Thus, as Levin and Arluke point out,

Gossip is used to maintain the dividing line between those who are part of the "in group" and those who are not. To gossip is to indicate that the teller and the recipient share a degree of closeness or intimacy not necessarily shared with others. Thus, gossip can be a sign of trust between people which can create and maintain boundaries around "in-group" members.[11]

Furthermore, gossipers need to share a common set of values: "Most important, in order to gossip together, people must share the same set of values and must know a third person in common whose behavior either upholds or violates those values."[12]

If social scientists recognize that gossip is not a trivial thing, that it plays an important role in social exchange, they do not, however, consider it a very high form of social exchange. This is partly because many of them include gossip in a larger study of rumor, and, for them, rumor, especially in periods of national crisis, has much greater social impact than gossip. A false rumor can create enormous havoc in a town, a city, or a nation, whereas the social effects of gossip occur within the family, the church, or the workplace, and are therefore of lesser social importance, even though they may be just as devastating for the persons involved. Furthermore, of the many forms of social exchange involving language, gossip is considered among the least valuable, precisely because the functions it serves in social interaction are not considered by most social scientists to be among the most important. Even where gossip is not malicious or degrading of another person, the fact that it supports exclusivity, favors in-groupism, and is entertaining, implies that it is more to be tolerated than valued in an egalitarian society. Also, if gossip has an effect outside the in-group (that is, actually becomes a rumor and/or actually hurts the person it is about), it is then considered malicious. But if it has none of these effects, it is considered trivial. Its potential for malice or triviality outweighs its positive effects, such as its role in supporting and confirming the shared values of those who engage in it. Social scientific studies have therefore avoided much of the pejorative tone of moralists who merely inveigh against gossip, but they have also, for the most part, considered it to be a rather trivial form of communication (not nearly as "important," for example, as their own writings on the subject).

Gossip As Expression of Freedom

One needs to turn to Patricia Meyer Spacks, a professor of literature, to find a strong and persuasive defense of gossip. Spacks is primarily concerned in her book on gossip with the relationship between gossip as it occurs in real life and gossip as it functions in literature, particularly biography and novels. In discussing her views on gossip, I will not be concerned with her interpretations of various literary texts as this would take us far afield from our primary interest in gossip as it occurs in congregational life. On the other hand, it is obvious that she has come to her appreciative view of gossip through her reading of literature, for literature reveals, in ways that social science does not, that gossip plays a vital, even essential, role in human interaction, and that this role is not always negative. Also, in writing as a woman, Spacks has an agenda that she readily acknowledges, that of contesting the devaluation of women that has been an integral part of the attribution of gossip to women. If gossip can be revalorized, then, in her view, the degradation of women as "gossip mongers" may also be challenged.

Spacks reports that the inspiration for her book originated in two personal experiences. One, sustained over some years, involved a close friend, a woman colleague:

> Beleaguered though we both felt, trying to sustain families and careers, we met early every morning for half an hour of coffee and reinvigorating conversation. Sometimes a male colleague would come in, his expression conveying—or so we fancied—contempt at our verbal trivialities as our talk moved from details of our own lives to speculation about others, or from discussion of novels to contemplation of friends' love affairs. Our husbands couldn't understand why, considering our frequently proclaimed, desperate need for more time, we counted those morning minutes sacred: only dire emergency interfered with them. Both married to unusually sensitive, understanding men, we felt shocked to discover their incomprehension of this essential part of our lives. But we couldn't explain to them; nor did we ever fully explain to ourselves.[13]

The other experience was when she went to China with a group of professional women, several of them social workers or psychiatrists with a special interest in adolescence. The group met with

Chinese mental health workers and asked questions. One question they would ask concerned teenage pregnancy, and, over and over again, they would be told that it simply does not exist. Skeptical, they kept asking until someone provided an explanation. China has little adolescent pregnancy because a neighborhood of voluntary spies prevents it. Chinese men retire at age fifty-five and women at fifty. Life expectancy has risen to seventy-five: "The huge resultant population without paid work found various socially acceptable occupations; among them, watching and discussing individual activities of neighbors, to forestall as well as to criticize impermissible deviation."[14]

This experience demonstrated the uses of gossip as an instrument of social control: "I thought of the Salem witchcraft trials." But, then, Spacks wondered, what of those treasured daily conversations, which, in self-condemning moments, she and her friend referred to as gossip?

> If gossip could have useful public functions, it also appeared to have useful private ones. Yet the very word, to my ear, implied severe derogation. I looked it up in the dictionary, to discover that official definitions suggest triviality as a concomitant of gossip, but nothing worse. How had the word acquired such negative overtones? Why did my friend and I feel faint guilt about what we did every morning? Why were we so addicted to it? What was the relation between gossip as public and as private instrument? Such questions inspired my investigation. I started giving public lectures about gossip, and found that the subject elicited general interest. But almost every time I held forth, someone in the audience would suggest, helpfully, that I find another word to designate the kind of talk that preoccupied me—a term without such bad connotations. My mission began to define itself as a rescue operation: to restore positive meaning to a word that had once held it, and to celebrate a set of values and assumptions particularly associated with women, as well as with gossip.[15]

Spacks readily acknowledges that much of gossip's narrative—the stories told—generates itself out of trivia. But, quoting Reinhold Niebuhr, who was reported to have said that "surfaces are not superficial," she observes that "Much gossip delights by an aesthetic of surfaces. It dwells on specific personal particulars. People and their concerns preoccupy gossipers, by definition, but the special way in which they matter evolves from belief in the importance of the small particular." If, then, the assumed triviality of gossip has constituted a major basis for attacking this activity, it might equally well supply a ground for defense: "To make something out of nothing is gossip's 'special creativity.'"[16] (Could it be that gossip was originally viewed as "God- related" because this is how God also created the world, that is, *ex nihilo*?)

Spacks calls this feature of gossip its "self-containment." That is, gossip creates its own territory, using materials from the world at large to construct a new oral artifact, and its special value as a resource for the oppressed or dispossessed partly derives from this fact: "The remaking that takes place as gossipers pool and interpret their observations expresses a world view." Yet, because gossip deals in small particulars, in local knowledge, the worldview it expresses is not that of the dominant culture, but rather "the beliefs of quiet sub-cultures." As gossip "inhabits a space or intimacy, it builds on and implicitly articulates shared values of intimates."[17]

But what of the longstanding view that gossip is frivolous and/or malicious? Using Heidegger's and Kierkegaard's condemnations of "idle talk" as foils, Spacks argues that they "inadvertently clarify the possibility of claiming for gossip a special kind of moral penetration." In Heidegger's view, the trivial can never achieve intelligibility because its articulation occurs at a distance from the true ground of being. Lack of struggle is the work of gossip, whereas "authentic discourse" wrenches meaning from profound sources. Put another way, "Gossip's assertions exist for their own sake, referring to nothing beneath the apparent. Anyone can gossip. People like to do so because they thus achieve an effortless illusion of understanding."[18] Kierkegaard's objections to gossip, more passionately expressed than Heidegger's, focus even more emphatically on its subject matter. Kierkegaard opposes gossip to "real talk" and identifies it with "talkativeness" which is "afraid of the silence which reveals its emptiness." He claims that gossip obliterates the "vital distinction between what is private and what is public" and centers its attention on things that are of only passing interest. According to him,

> It always consists of some trivial fact such as that Mr. Marsden is engaged and has given his fiancee a Persian shawl; that Petersen, the poet, is going to write some new poems, or that Marcussen, the actor, mispronounced a certain word last night. If we could suppose for a

moment that there was a law which did not forbid people talking, but simply ordered that everything that was spoken about should be treated as though it had happened fifty years ago, the gossips would be done for, they would be in despair. On the other hand, it would not really interfere with any one who could really talk.[19]

Spacks suggests that, for Kierkegaard, "real talk" concerns "the inner life," and specifically the inner *religious* life, meaning the spiritual as opposed to the merely intellectual. Thus, like Heidegger, he also objects to the triviality of gossip: "He knows the nature of the important: Mr. Marsden's fiancee's shawl does not qualify."[20]

But, says Spacks, what Kierkegaard does here is to suggest the superiority of *ideas* to *happenings* as matters for reflection, and he privileges *thought* to *emotion* as a means both to self-knowledge and engagement with others. Furthermore, "Heidegger's distaste for gossip, and Kierkegaard's, deny the moral possibilities of trivia." Gossip depends for its existence on the assumed importance of "the concrete personal particular in all its revelatory power." Thus, these men's "sweeping judgments of the triviality and inauthenticity of gossip suggest their deafness to the possible moral overtones of dialogue and of attention to personal detail." The shawl that Mr. Marsden gave his fiancee possesses untold narrative possibilities. In the giving of this gift "lie all the moral intricacies of exchange."[21]

Thus, as the social scientists' recognize, gossip is a mode of social exchange, and herein lie its moral possibilities. But Spacks goes further, and argues that it is a particular form of social exchange: "More insistently than other forms of conversation, gossip involves exchange not merely, not even mainly, of information, and not solely of understanding, but of point of view." When two or more persons gossip together, they give voice to a point of view that is mutually shared, and one that reflects their location in a subculture that is different from if not antagonistic to the dominant culture: "Gossip may involve a torrent of talk, yet its most vital claims remain silent. Seldom does anyone articulate the bonding that it generates or intensifies." Also, noting that social scientists explain how gossip consolidates and uses social power to influence status and opinion in a community, Spack suggests that, on the more personal level, "gossip gets its power by the illusion of mastery gained through taking imaginative possession or another's experience."[22] By speculating on what another is doing in privacy, the gossip enters imaginatively into the other person's private world, and thereby gains a kind of power over him. This mastery, she readily acknowledges, is "pseudo-mastery," for it changes nothing in the real world of social power and status. Yet, it can be used for any number of purposes: to generate feelings of superiority, to provide evidence for argument, and even to manipulate the subject's reputation.

Gossip's manipulation of another's reputation gets the most attention from moralists, who are concerned about gossip's power to destroy an innocent person's reputation. But, without minimizing its power to destroy an innocent person, Spacks also wants to draw attention to the fact that gossip, traditionally engaged in by those who lack power and influence in a given society, is a form of dissent, a refusal to be dominated by those who hold the power. It can be helpful when the two (or more) persons engaged in gossip have a common enemy, such as an abusive boss or a mean-spirited co-worker. As a psychoanalyst friend commented to Spacks, gossip is "healing talk," for healing comes from sharing: "Indeed, in the most common paradigm of gossip—two people talking about a third—aggression becomes in effect a function of sharing. The gossiping pair establish their alliance at the expense of another, displacing hostility onto the absent third. Reduced to means rather than ends, aggression serves alliance."[23]

Spacks also draws on the writings of psychoanalysts Erik Erikson and D. W. Winnicott to explore the playful nature of gossip. As creative play, it enables those who engage in it to feel a sense of freedom, the freedom that comes from involvement in "the socially and the psychically impermissible." Like all expressions of freedom, however, gossip creates potential problems: "Whether or not gossip actually does harm, it unleashes potentially explosive forces. Gossipers may know the guilt of toying with such forces, the guilt of possessing great resources for aggression. Or they may experience the guilt of intimacy: two consciousnesses united by using happenings from other people's lives to engender the pleasure of shared response, jointly achieved judgment."[24] In short:

> Gossip feels good: a form of closeness, a mode of power. And gossip feels bad: devious and treacherous power, potentially threatening attachment. In literature and in life, it signifies ambivalence. The

metaphor of play, in its multiple senses, summarizes gossip's complexities of emotional meaning. Play as dramatic performance: a shadow-theater in which absent actors play their parts at the behest of talkers who direct or even dramatize the production. Play as musical performance: theme and variation, rhythms of interchange, patterns of improvisation. Play as game: partnership in the service of competition, competition in the service of partnership. As recreation: an alternative to the utilitarian, free, "licentious," responsible to no pre-ordained program. As parody or imitation of work: subversive commentary on or faithful support of established mores, like the child's "playing house," which may suddenly expose bourgeois convention from the underside even as the player tries to act just like Daddy. . . . Like other forms of play, gossip expresses both aggression and intimacy, sometimes simultaneously, sometimes in bewildering shifts.[25]

Spacks also argues that, while gossip is inherently subversive, it may, nonetheless, be in the service of the larger community, whether the dominant culture realizes this fact or not. It may transcend its exclusive character as well. Thus, gossip may not just *feel* good but *is* good, as it expresses "a community's principles of continuity" and helps to "generate its sense of continuity." It is true that words set down on paper provide permanence, but the more fluid permanence of oral tradition may possess equal or greater power as happenings are told and retold: "Heightening the felt significance of detail through repeated tellings, those who speculate about the small happenings of their group create its legends, solidify its values, in speech."[26] In support of this view that gossip serves the community's best interests, she cites the following comment by anthropologists Melville J. Herskovits and Frances S. Herskovits in their book *Trinidad Village*:

> Old and young delight in telling, and hearing told, all the little incidents that go on in the village. To the outsider the speed with which news spreads never ceased to be a source of amazement. Equally amazing was the celerity with which the story acquired a texture that made of the commonplace a thing of meaningful or ironic sequences, often going back to relatives long dead, or at the very least recalling to memory some comparable happening that led to the unforeseen climaxes. No story was too trivial to stir an active response from the community, and to set in motion the weaving backwards and forwards in time of tales of supernatural deeds, and of retribution. Repudiating the meagerness of his everyday world, the Tocoan [resident of a settlement in

northeastern Trinidad] draws on tradition and wit to fill a canvas with more than life-size figures—and always there is the humorous detail, the grotesque situation, the incisive comment.[27]

Spacks adds that "Most groups demonstrate the same collective capacity to lend 'texture' to the commonplace by placing it in a context of past happenings literal or imagined—or literal touched by imagination."[28]

Such gossip, which depends on a relatively stable group of talkers who feel themselves members of a larger collectivity, interprets a community to itself. In this interpretive use, the force of gossip is relatively benign: unifying, reassuring, more often inclusive than exclusive, sometimes defensive but rarely aggressive. This is not to say that, even in this form, it may not have negative consequences, but the benefits of "good gossip" far outweigh the negative as "the talk itself, as well as its results in lasting legend, unites its participants." Such gossip serves individual as well as communal ends as it incorporates individuals into the communal myth, and individual psyches need myths to locate themselves in their social environment. To be sure, as Trinidad small talk reveals, gossip about "the half-surmised activities of other people often attributes petty motives." But it may also, "especially through often repeated stories and slowly elaborated speculation, enlarge its characters' stature."[29]

As studies of rumor transmission conducted during World War II have shown, ignorance or difficulty in recall leads to the loss of many significant features of the original happening but, at the same time, speculation or imagination gives the surviving material a narrative coherence.[30] Drawing on her knowledge of literature, Spacks makes a similar point: "Individual human beings tell ostensibly true stories about other individuals; the compulsion toward meaning subtly shapes anecdotes into comprehensible forms. Dramas of actuality shaped by fantasy develop in the telling. Persons loom larger than in everyday life, their sexual or financial escapades removed from personal emotional consequence, converted into matter of social import."[31] Thus, to be the subject of gossip is not necessarily a fate to be deplored. Just as gossip can affect one's reputation negatively, it can also transform an individual into an exemplar of the community's most deeply felt values and convictions about itself.

Spacks concludes that gossip, as a kind of myth-making, differs from tradition in the temporal emphases of their material. Gossip deals with the present, while tradition concerns the past. Yet, "Both involve the working of imagination on the material of experience; both embody verbal freedom."[32] For some, especially those who have little control over the allocation and distribution of the community's resources, such verbal freedom may be all the freedom that they enjoy in life. But this is not a specious form of freedom. It is real freedom, and one that the powerful in a community can do little about, for where two or three gather for talk, gossip is always possible. This is why those who are insecure in their power employ informants on the speech of others and impose heavy sanctions against gossip. Spacks emphasizes that gossip in these circumstances, however, while subversive of those in power, may conserve the deeper values of the community, values that the powerful are flaunting for their own selfish ends.

The Importance of the Trivial

When Spacks announced that she was working on a book proclaiming her belief that "gossip is good for you," she received a letter from a woman who assured her that she would sell more books if she alleged that gossip is *bad* for you. (In this way, gossip would, paradoxically, be *good* for Spacks!). Realizing that she was taking an unpopular position, she notes, however, that "even the popular press registers uneasy awareness of gossip's positive energies." Various publishers, including *Time, Newsweek, McCall's* and *Family Weekly*, "have printed articles suggesting, with comic exaggeration or irony or careful qualification by way of protection, that gossip is fun, that it purveys useful information, that it helps avoid embarrassment (if you know your boss is sleeping with his secretary, you don't complain about her to him), that it enables people to help one another, that it offers opportunities to test moral courage." These articles suggest, however, that it is possible to separate destructive from useful gossip. On this point, Spacks is not so sure, for this denies "gossip's essential ambiguity, its mixed and often unconscious motives." Still, she is intrigued by these recent published justifications of gossip and speculates as to why they have begun to appear at just this moment in our history. The answer, she feels, lies in the fact that the articles claim the "importance of the trivial, the value and the pleasure of talk. They assume that people naturally interest themselves in other people. They say that one can find out things that matter by speculation about others."[33]

From Gossip to Gospel

As we have seen, Matthew presents Jesus as vehemently opposed to "careless talk." Even if this says more about Matthew and his position in the early Christian community than about Jesus, it certainly places the early church against certain forms of gossip. On the other hand, in noting the importance of "the peasant grapevine," John Dominic Crossan recognizes the positive role played by gossip in spreading word about the early Jesus movement. While much of this gossip was undoubtedly detrimental, the spreading of Jesus' reputation as a teacher and healer is unimaginable apart from the role played by the gossiping community. What is also significant about the Gospels themselves is that they give such great importance to the seemingly trivial events and conversations that presumably occurred in the daily life of Galilee's peasantry. In the Gospels, we are presented one story after another of what, in comparison to the political events of the times, seems rather trivial and parochial. To say that the Gospels are filled with trivialities is not, however, to disparage them. It all depends on our point of view. To talk about trivial matters when others would have us discuss weighty, important matters is itself a subversive act. To others, the villagers in Jesus' time should be talking about national politics and important philosophical ideas. The Gospels suggest that these villagers had other things on their minds, such as a Greek woman's witty retort to a visiting healer: "Yes, Lord, but even the dogs under the table eat the children's crumbs," a retort that, far from offending him, wins this admiring response, "For saying that you may go—the demon has left your daughter" (Mark 7:24-30). Stories such as these say to those who are in power, and those who are struggling to gain power, that what *they* have to say about the so-called big issues of the day is not worth thinking and talking about too much, and that, in any case, *we* and not *they* will decide what constitutes "real" versus "empty" talk. It says that *we* will choose those topics about which it is worth our while to speculate, for imagination, and the freedom to use it, is a power we have, and the dominant culture cannot force us not to use it.

We are so used to thinking of the Gospels from the perspective of those who privilege ideas over happenings that we have become desensitized to the fact that the Gospels are the product of gossip. Without gossip, no Gospels. We can open any Gospel at any page and begin reading, and what we find ourselves reading is a series of happenings—all local—and loosely connected. Mark 2 begins, "When he returned to Capernaum after some days, it was reported that he was at home." A happening is then described and then we read (v. 13), "Jesus went out again beside the sea." Another happening is described and then v. 15 begins, "And as he sat at dinner . . ." Another happening, then (v. 23), "One sabbath he was going through the grainfields." This is both the form and subject matter of gossip. Happenings are far more important than ideas, and the narrative is a string of happenings, in no particular order, with only the semblance of connectedness. But the narrator achieves something very important in telling "this and that" about an imagined day in the life of Jesus.

In the first place, he establishes that "surfaces are not superficial," and that, as Spacks puts it, "Much gossip delights by an aesthetic of surfaces. It dwells on specific personal particulars. People and their concerns preoccupy gossipers, by definition, but the special way in which they matter evolves from belief in the importance of the small particular."[34] We err, I believe, in trying to make these stories about Jesus deeper and more profound than they are, or when we try to generalize from two or three such stories to make a larger point. Gossip works because it does not share the dominant culture's desire to assimilate the small particulars into a larger schema of meaning, for, when this happens, the particulars are no longer entertaining in their own right, and we lose the pleasure of *pretending* that the story *I* am about to tell has a connection to the one *you* just related. The dominant culture despises non sequiturs. Gossip thrives on them.

Second, like gossip, the Gospel "gets its power by the illusion of mastery gained through taking possession of another's experience." By speculating on what another is doing in privacy, the gossip enters imaginatively into the other's private world, and thereby gains a kind of power over the other. In this case, the other is Jesus, and the private world that the Gospel writer enters is the one that Jesus inhabited but the Gospel writer did not, because the writer was not actually there. By adding various local touches about which only someone who was there could have known, the writer presents himself as an intimate of Jesus, as an insider, and thus as one of Jesus' own. An especially noteworthy example of the storyteller making himself an intimate of Jesus by telling it as though he were actually there is the story (Luke 7:44-50) of the woman who anointed Jesus with expensive oil. We have already discussed this story as an example of an inspirational story. What contributes to its ability to inspire is that, in telling it as one who was present, the storyteller draws us into the story as well, and makes us feel as though we, too, are inside the house where this event is taking place. The storyteller is able to tell us *exactly* what the householder, Simon, was thinking when Jesus allowed the woman into the house: "If this man were a prophet, he would have known who and what kind of woman this is who is touching him—that she is a sinner." He also tells us *precisely* what Jesus said to Simon in rebuke for thinking what Jesus perceived Simon to have been thinking: "Do you see this woman? I entered your house; you gave me no water for my feet, but she has bathed my feet with her tears and dried them with her hair. You gave me no kiss, but from the time I came in she has not stopped kissing my feet. You did not anoint my head with oil, but she has anointed my feet with ointment. Therefore, I tell you, her sins, which were many, have been forgiven, hence she has shown great love. But the one to whom little is forgiven, loves little."

There is power in this freedom to enter imaginatively into the life of another, to take possession of the very experience of Jesus, to make oneself an intimate of his. The Gospel stories of Jesus entering the house of a villager for a meal are especially significant in this regard, as they present him in intimate surroundings and create a more conversational Jesus. In doing so, they express the storyteller's longing, his intense desire to be among Jesus' intimates, to be at table with him, to know him as a personal friend and confidante. To take possession of his experience is not for the purpose of cutting Jesus down to size, but to experience the empowerment that comes with being an intimate of his. The reader can virtually feel the storyteller's pride in Jesus as Jesus deftly counters Simon's "If this man were a prophet . . ." with his withering comments about Simon's failure to accord his guest the hospitality that the woman offered so simply and beautifully. The line between gossip and Gospel is a very fine one. To say this is not to disparage the Gospel, but to elevate gossip, especially its belief that intimacy may happen on the very surfaces of life.

Pastoral Counseling as a Higher Form of Gossip

Patricia Meyer Spacks's effort to rehabilitate gossip provides valuable insights into what pastoral counseling can model in the life of the congregation. Because pastoral counseling is a more intentional form of conversation than gossip, I suggest that it can reflect the positive features of gossip while minimizing (if never completely eliminating) the negative ones. Or, to put it another way, it can more closely approximate the original meaning of the word, when it meant "god-sib," or persons who could be expected to keep confidences and never take advantage of the trust that the other person has placed in them. Thus, while we may appear to demean pastoral counseling by identifying it as a type of gossip, thinking of it in these very terms may actually have the opposite effect of showing how pastoral counseling attempts to model a higher or purer form of gossip, and holds this model up to the congregation as the standard by which all of its conversations may be measured. The very fact that pastoral counseling has the potential to serve as such a standard—and often does—makes the abuses of power that sometimes occur in the context of pastoral counseling all the more unfortunate and tragic.

Like gossip, the "subject matter" of pastoral counseling is the "trivia" that often gets demeaned by those who, like Martin Heidegger and Søren Kierkegaard, value only "important" subject matter, whether complex "intellectual matters" on the one hand or "deep spiritual matters" on the other. Unlike so-called higher forms of intellectual discourse, the subject matter of pastoral counseling is, indeed, as Kierkegaard puts it, "some trivial fact such as that Mr. Marsden is engaged and has given his fiancee a Persian shawl." The pastor, engaged in counseling a parishioner, does not make a prejudgment that the Persian shawl is unimportant and not worth talking about. As Spacks points out, in the giving of this gift "lie all the moral intricacies of exchange." Furthermore, the fact that pastoral counseling concerns itself with events and happenings in everyday life does not make it any less intellectually demanding than, say, a graduate seminar in theology. While some people believe that it is more difficult to think through a theological issue such as a doctrine of revelation or election, this belief merely reflects the bias of a particular discursive community (that is, theological scholars). In point of fact, some of the "knottiest" problems, and thus most intellectually demanding, are those that occur in the context of counseling.

If a major similarity between pastoral counseling and gossip is their "trivial" subject matter, another is that, precisely because it deals in "small particulars," the worldview that pastoral counseling expresses is not that of "the dominant culture" but "the beliefs of quiet sub-cultures." Thus, like gossip, pastoral counseling "inhabits a space of intimacy, and builds on and implicitly articulates shared values of intimates."[35] The fact that pastoral counseling shares this characteristic of gossip means that it often has a subversive agenda not unlike that of the conversations that Spacks had with her friend each morning wherein, among other things, they discussed the politics of their academic department, described the quality of its leadership, and caricatured their offensive colleagues. Pastoral counseling conversation is often similarly irreverent, critical of the powers that be, and often engages in humor at others' expense. Yet, like Spacks' gossip sessions with her colleague, pastoral counseling does not lead to efforts to overthrow the dominant culture by means of political action, but is more quietly subversive, especially as it helps individuals to gain an imaginative freedom from the dominant culture, to devise effective ways to reduce its power, and to develop strategies for gaining small victories over its controlling presence. In the context of pastoral counseling, parishioners often reflect on the power of institutions and groups (for instance, the company they work for, the family they inhabit) to control their lives, affecting their decision making ("I wish I could quit but I need the money"; "I wish I could leave but it wouldn't be right") and emotional state ("My work is so demoralizing"; "I'm treated like a servant"). They seek "that margin of freedom which gives life its savor and its endless possibility for advance."[36]

Still another similarity between pastoral counseling and gossip is the fact that it is a kind of creative play, providing the counselee (and also the pastor) a sense of freedom that they do not experience in the other "language systems" of their lives. Like gossip, it allows the participants to form a kind of partnership, through the use of language which is proscribed or prohibited in other contexts. The parishioner can say things that she would not say directly to her mother for fear of hurting the older woman's feelings, and the pastor can say things that she would never say from the pulpit. Here again, pastoral counseling is not unlike the conversations that Spacks had with her professional colleague and friend, and that their husbands had difficulty appreciating, conversations that clearly served the purposes of self-maintenance in what they experienced as a threatening professional atmosphere. In their conversations together, they could express their frustrations about colleagues for whom they shared a common antipathy and they could entertain themselves by taking "imaginative possession" of these other person's lives, creating stories about what goes on when a male colleague takes a female colleague to lunch. Their gossiping, precisely through its playfulness, contributed to their own self-maintenance. This is also an important feature of pastoral counseling, for much of what occurs in pastoral counseling involves the play of the imagination. For example, the entertainment of options that we are not likely to act upon can, nevertheless, be a helpful exercise in self-maintenance as it "disempowers" the person who is making our life difficult. The parishioner leaves knowing that he will not quit his job or that she will not leave her husband, but each has gained a certain imaginative leverage over the job's or the husband's ability to demean them and to make them feel adequate or inferior.

While it shares these and other characteristics of gossip, pastoral counseling (ideally) differs from gossip as well. While the malicious intent of gossip is often exaggerated, gossip *does* at times degenerate into malice and may, in fact, destroy the reputation of an innocent person. In a pastoral counseling case that I have reported upon before,[37] a woman who knew that she was dying confessed to the pastor that she had done "a terrible thing" several years ago. She had been president of the congregation's women's group for nearly twenty years. Once, "when the girls were going to consider another president, I let them think the other woman was . . . not good enough. Now she's gone, poor soul . . . and I keep thinking about it. It wasn't very Christian, was it Reverend?" This was a clear case of malicious gossip. We are not told what she actually said about the other woman, but whatever it was, it dissuaded "the girls" from choosing the other woman for the presidency.

Pastoral counseling necessarily involves talking about third parties, persons who are often not present and are therefore unable to defend themselves against whatever might be said against them. One of the objectives of pastoral counseling, however, is that of moving beyond malicious and vengeful talk (however cathartic this may be) toward a greater understanding of the person or persons being talked about. Recall Carl Rogers' case of the woman who had very negative feelings toward her mother at the beginning of therapy but these feelings decreased as counseling proceeded, eventually resulting in her own efforts to relate toward her mother as Rogers was relating to her. Thus, one major difference between pastoral counseling and gossip is that the pastor does not enter into an alliance with the counselee against the person or persons who are the object of the counselee's ire. While the pastor is free, even morally obligated, to take sides in cases where the parishioner is the victim of abusive verbal and physical behavior, the pastor does not enter into an alliance in the sense that she joins with the counselee in a common enmity against a third party. In this sense, the pastor maintains a moral neutrality that is not as characteristic of gossip. The pastor's goal is to assist the counselee toward the solving of her problem, or the recognition that the problem cannot be solved and will have to be lived with, and this intention to help the other toward the solving of a problem gives the pastor a different agenda from that of a gossip partner. While gossip will sometimes also result in the solving of problems, it has many other purposes and functions, including mutual expression of antipathy toward another person or persons. While the pastor may be personally acquainted with the third party about whom the two of them are talking, the pastor does not have the same personal agenda against this third party that the counselee may have. By entering into such an alliance, the pastor risks the boundary violations that are all-too-common in pastor–parishioner relationships, boundary violations that often begin in the pastoral counseling setting itself.

The Gospel of Openness

Another difference between pastoral counseling and gossip is that the pastor has greater freedom, even, at times, the obligation, to introduce a values perspective that does not confirm the counselee's own values but instead brings other value considerations to bear. Thus, while the pastor's role is often to confirm and support the values of the parishioner, it is also the pastor's task to call these values into question when, in the pastor's judgment, they are incongruent with essential Christian values. This, of course, raises the very large and complex question of what essential Christian values are, an issue on which Christians exhibit little common agreement. In fact, many of the problems that parishioners bring to pastoral counseling are precisely concerned with these very issues: divorce, sexual orientation, abortion rights, euthanasia, and so forth. When common agreement *does* begin to occur, as in earlier conflicts among Christians regarding alcohol use, autoerotic behavior, or interfaith marriages, they are less likely to become pastoral counseling problems.

A value that is especially important to pastoral counseling, however, is one of openness. An especially illuminating story in this regard is the one to which I have already alluded, the story of the woman who anointed Jesus with an expensive ointment as he was sitting at table in the house of Simon the Pharisee (Luke 7:36-50). What is significant about this story is not only that Jesus is open to the woman and does not turn her away, but also that he is the house guest of a Pharisee. Thus, the story suggests that Jesus was able to integrate persons of very different social and cultural backgrounds, to challenge the traditional social class distinctions and boundaries, and thus to make of Simon's home a locus in which social boundaries became fluid, where social distinctions that were protectively maintained in other contexts were, in this context, broken through and systematically violated.

Thus, what Jesus especially represented and embodied as he traveled throughout Galilee and ate his meals in other people's homes was a value of openness. As represented in the Gospels, he was a man who was remarkably free of the need to maintain traditional social prerogatives relating to race, gender, age, and class. He was also a man who was able to be emotionally open, as when he grieved over a friend who had died or noted that, as an itiner-

ant, homeless person, he had his moments of loneliness, even perhaps of despair. John Dominic Crossan points out that when Jesus
went to the villages, or when he sent his disciples out, they did not
go as beggars for alms, food, clothing, or anything else, but came
with something to give, in exchange for which they received a meal
and a place to sleep over. As he puts it: "They share a miracle and
a Kingdom, and they receive in return a table and a house. Here, I
think, is the heart of the original Jesus movement, a shared egalitarianism of spiritual and material resources."[38] Crossan calls this
arrangement "commensality" (which literally means "eating at the
same table"), and distinguishes it, on the one hand, from almsgiv-
ing or charity, and, on the other, from fees and charges.
(Interestingly, the word *commensual* also applies to an animal or
plant that lives on, in, or with another, sharing its food but neither
parasitic on it nor injured by it.) Crucial to this arrangement, in
Crossan's view, is that it established the inseparability of the spiritual and the material. Jesus and his disciples could not live by miracle alone, and those who shared their food with Jesus and his disciples could not live by bread alone. Crossan draws attention to
Matt. 10:5-9, which concerns Jesus' charge to the disciples whom
he was sending out in pairs to heal the sick, raise the dead, cleanse
the lepers, and cast out demons. They were not to take anything
with them—no money, no bag for soliciting alms—"for laborers
deserve their food" (10:10). This, says Crossan, is not charity, but
commensality. I share with you my power to make you well while
you share with me your food. The next day, I continue on my jour-
ney. I accept no alms, and you owe me no fees.

Crossan goes on to discuss how, after Jesus, the practice of resi-
dency began to replace itinerancy among his followers, and wages
and charity replaced the principles of commensality. But, in Jesus'
own time, his table fellowship reflected this principle, and was the
hallmark of his ministry among the people. It was customary for
wandering preachers to be selective as to whom they would agree to
eat with, so when Jesus placed no restrictions on who was allowed
to come to the table, he received a great deal of criticism, and, as the
story of the woman who anointed him with an expensive ointment
illustrates, this often caused embarrassment and consternation on the
part of his host. None of this would have been a problem had he

stayed in Capernaum and received the sick as clients in Peter's home, as Peter assumed he would do after Jesus healed his wife's mother. But Jesus would then have limited his availability only to those who were physically and financially able to come to him for healing. Thus, the principle of commensality meant that he would open himself to situations that were impossible to control, and would thereby invite close and personal contact with others regardless of race, gender, age, or social class.

A typical story in the Gospels portrays Jesus at table, engaging in conversation with the people gathered around him, when he would be interrupted by someone who, having discovered where he was staying for the night, would request that he come and heal a member of the supplicant's household. Thus, Matthew relates that, in the course of a conversation with his critics, who were not excluded from the house, Jesus was interrupted by a ruler who came to his table and knelt before him, saying, "My daughter has just died; but come and lay your hand on her, and she will live." Matthew says, "And Jesus got up and followed him" (9:18-19). The implication is clear: When Jesus sat at table, he was available for conversation with anyone who happened to be there, but he was also available to those who sought his help. Those who needed him knew where they could find him, and anyone who wanted to see him was permitted to do so, even though he was actually eating in someone else's home. Thus, there was a nonexclusiveness about his table fellowship, which sent a very clear message that he had no need to create a barrier of like-minded persons around him. Homes that had been fortresses designed to keep certain people out were transformed into hospices, where anyone was welcome to enter. As a person who did not have a home himself ("a homeless man") he made no distinction between the private and the public, but undermined this highly valued separation as well.

I suggest that the central value that the pastor represents in the pastoral counseling context is precisely that of openness, and that this value is expressed both in the pastoral counseling role itself and in the perspective that the pastor takes concerning the parishioner's life problems. It is precisely in its openness that pastoral counseling becomes a *gospel* form of gossip. The subject matter of pastoral counseling is still the small talk that prevails in other forms of gossip, but an open atmosphere is created and maintained in every aspect of the counseling process. The counseling process itself reflects an open sharing that is neither parasitic nor injurious to either party. It is neither charity nor brokerage, but is undertaken in a spirit of shared egalitarianism of spiritual and material resources, as the two participants pool their resources—insights, discernment, ideas—toward the task of enabling one of them to solve a personal problem. By the same token, the pastor takes the position that "openness" is the central value of the Christian life and that it should figure significantly in the manner in which pastor and parishioner reflect together on the problem. The parishioner is encouraged to perceive where the same openness that prevails in the counseling setting may become more manifest in the other contexts of her life. As the woman in Carl Rogers's case came to discern, it *was* possible to relate more openly, less defensively, to her mother, and when she did so, her mother responded more openly, less defensively, as well. As a result, a better spirit began to prevail between them, and the woman's daughter was also a beneficiary of the improved, more open atmosphere in the home.

There are times, of course, when the parishioner's needs for self-maintenance will take precedence over the ideal of openness, when the ideal of openness is too threatening for him. What I have called "the remembered self" can be threatened by the demand for too much openness, and the pastor needs to be sensitive to this. Simon the Pharisee was obviously struggling with the fact that a "sinful woman" had been welcomed by Jesus into his home, and his acceptance of Jesus' own reasoning (that "She loves most who has been forgiven most") seems grudging at best. Clearly, this new state of affairs was a threat to the self that Simon had formed through the years, and this self was not as liberated as Jesus' own. Still, Jesus did not abandon his own value of openness in deference to Simon. By his own actions, he quietly challenged Simon to take the more open view that had become the hallmark of Jesus' ministry, the very core of the gospel, and we can only guess whether Simon was sufficiently influenced by Jesus' own commitment to *his* values to reconsider his own. Because such openness is the true mark of the Christian life, one reflected in the very life of Jesus, the pastor hopes that the manner in which the parishioner goes about solving a problem will manifest this value of increased openness to sharing with another what one has to share, including greater emotional availability to the other, less defensiveness, less guardedness, less withholding of one's spirit, of one's capacity to bring joy and pleasure to others.

Other distinctions between gossip and pastoral counseling could be pointed out, but my primary concern has been to suggest that pastoral counseling may be viewed as similar to gossip in its subject matter but different from the more problematic forms of gossip in the atmosphere of openness that it seeks to establish and maintain. Where gossip often serves the values of in-groupism, of exclusivism, of confirming one's own values by denigrating or disowning others who are viewed as the gossipers' moral inferiors, pastoral counseling seeks to exhibit a more generous and open spirit, one that is conducive to the solving of personal problems rather than simply the airing of one's grievances. This does not mean that judgments against other persons are not made, or that accounts of abusive behaviors of other persons are discounted or minimized in a spirit of cheerful optimism. Nor does it mean that the pastor, in the spirit of fair play, must take the side of the person or persons who are being criticized by the counselee. To say, "Have you thought about how Fred feels about this?" is usually perceived by the counselee, and rightly so, as taking Fred's perspective and discrediting her own. The openness that prevails in the pastoral counseling context does not minimize the counselee's real grievances against another, but, in fact, invites greater sharing of these grievances because, in this context, disclosures are encouraged in order that life changes may be effected, that problematic situations may be revised, altered, even eliminated altogether.

Because it models a more open, more gospel-oriented form of gossip than is typical, pastoral counseling contributes significantly to the life of the congregation. It does so by its representation of a more intentional way of talking about and resolving the problems that are so much a part of our everyday small talk. It maintains high standards of confidentiality, it takes the position that insight and discernment are more helpful toward problem resolution than malice and denigration, and it fosters the breaking down of the social and emotional barriers that are so often responsible for the very fact that a problem exists. Thus, pastoral counseling affirms the importance of "small talk" for sustaining the shared values of the congregation, for its own self-maintenance, but it dissociates itself from the more destructive features of gossip, such as gossip's tendencies toward malice, toward self-interested alliances against third parties, and toward unhealthy in-groupism. One indication that pastoral counseling itself is failing to manifest the openness that makes it "gospel-gossip" is when it begins to reflect these more destructive features of gossip. Perhaps the greatest threat to pastoral counseling, precisely because it is the most subtle, is when the pastor joins with the parishioner in a self-interested alliance against a third party. The most obvious example of such an alliance is one where the pastor and parishioner form an alliance against the parishioner's wife or husband, but other examples are alliances against the parishioner's teenage son or daughter, mother or father, or another parishioner.

In short, pastoral counseling as "gospel-gossip" manifests belief "in the importance of the small particular" and a commitment on the part of the pastor never to take exploitative advantage of the invitation to "take possession of another's experience."[39] While the immediate purpose of pastoral counseling is to help individuals solve their problems, its longer-range objective, like any other form or practice of ministry, is to enable others, and oneself, to take fuller possession of the experience of Jesus, to be at table with him, and to share in the life that he, ever the itinerant diner and worker of miracles, continues to offer to anyone who invites him in or seeks him out.

Epilogue

The Art of Holding on Loosely

I have argued that pastoral counseling is essential to the life of the congregation because there is a fundamental need for systematic attention to the ways that we story our experiences so that new understandings of our situation may occur. In chapters 2–4, I presented three of the ways that we envision our life experience acquiring such new understandings—the inspirational, paradoxical, and miracle stories—and I emphasized that each of these story types alerts us to ways in which the listener may assist in enabling these new understandings to emerge. One is the art of the power of suggestion, another is the art of untying knots, and a third is the art of identifying exceptions. In chapter 5, I explored the idea that pastoral counseling is similar to gossip in its focus on the "small particulars" of life.

In this brief epilogue, I want to present the idea that these three "arts" reflect a fact about pastoral power that we tend to overlook, namely, that pastoral power, unlike power in the secular world, is inherently paradoxical. That is to say, pastoral power is greatest when it seems least to be in evidence, and, therefore, the "arts" that I have identified in the preceding chapters are actually powerful resources which, if used appropriately, may have significant beneficial results, and, if used inappropriately, may have serious negative consequences. There is a related paradox in the fact that just because pastoral counseling focuses on the "small particulars" of life, does not mean that it has little real consequence. Instead, its consequences are heightened, even exaggerated, by this very fact. Even as brief therapy is based on the premise that less counseling may effect more change than more counseling, so greater change may be effected through the small talk that occurs in the pastoral counseling context than through the large-scale thinking and long-range planning that occurs in other contexts of the church's corporate life. Human history is replete with stories about how major changes were effected by "small particulars."

The Paradox of Pastoral Power

What do I mean by "the paradox of pastoral power"? In *Sex in the Parish*, Karen Lebacqz and Ronald G. Barton point out that pastors may not feel powerful but they do in fact have power. Moreover, the power that they have is rather unique to their profession. Pastors have *the power of freedom*, that is, the power that comes with not being under continual supervision or surveillance of others. Pastors also have *the power of access and accessibility*, that is, the privileged access to the personal lives of parishioners that comes with being in a profession long associated with giving care.[1] These may not feel like powers, but they decidedly are. I would also add to these two powers a third one that is implied in the second, *the power of knowledge*. Pastors come to know a great deal about the individuals and families in their congregations. They often know the sorts of things that it takes a counselor or therapist several weeks to learn about their counselees. A pastor may not consciously exploit this knowledge, but sometimes he does so unconsciously. If, for example, a male pastor perceives that the husband of a parishioner is inferior to her—and to the pastor—in intellectual and social skills, he may unconsciously "one-up" her husband by meeting her needs for someone who is intelligent and understanding with whom to talk.

Many pastors make a conscious effort to reduce the power differential—the inequality of power—between themselves and the one who has come to them for counseling. These are pastors who do not insist on standing on a pastoral pedestal but who, on the contrary, make an effort to *reduce* the power differential: "Don't call me Reverend Smith, please call me Bob." Yet, what needs to be recognized, but seldom is, is that such efforts to reduce the power differential actually increase it. Why? Because power in ministry is precisely the power of freedom, of access and accessibility, and of knowledge. Thus, as the parishioner shares intimate facts about herself, making her personal life accessible to him, the power differential is actually increased, not decreased, even though it appears otherwise. And, if the pastor proceeds to share intimate facts about himself, this does nothing to counteract the increase in the power differential, for, through these self-disclosures, his access and accessibility to the parishioner are greater than ever. The more successful the pastor becomes in appearing to reduce the power differential, the greater the power differential becomes. This is the paradox of pastoral power.

We in the pastoral care and counseling field must bear responsibility for failing to couple our encouragement of a more "personal" pastoral style with cautions and warnings that this more personal style will *increase*, not *decrease*, the power differential between pastor and parishioner. Also, those of us who have advocated the "empowerment" of the laity, and who have attempted to minimize or even erase the distinction between pastoral and lay ministry—those who have challenged the "clerical paradigm" as it is called—must also bear responsibility, for these initiatives have contributed to the illusion that the power differential between pastor and parishioner may be substantially reduced, if not eliminated altogether.

The "arts" that I have presented in chapters 2–4 reflect this paradox of pastoral power. On the one hand, the arts of the power of suggestion, of untying knots, and of identifying exceptions, do not appear to be powerful methods for eliciting or effecting change. In contrast to the "real" power found in the secular world—the power of money, influence, prestige—these arts do not seem like much. Yet, they do have the capacity to change lives for good, but also, if used inappropriately, for ill. The art of the power of suggestion, if used wisely and thoughtfully, may plant an idea in a parishioner's mind that bears genuine fruit, but, if used thoughtlessly and carelessly, it may prompt a parishioner, especially one who is especially open to suggestion, to act irresponsibly, to place self and others at risk. By encouraging a parishioner to do precisely what she has been trying so hard to avoid, or by proposing a third alternative that she had not considered, the art of untying knots may have a powerful liberating effect, but it may also have unintended negative consequences, including the *successful* enactment of the previously avoided behavior or unforeseen consequences resulting from the seemingly beneficial third alternative. So, too, with the art of identifying exceptions. This method *may* help the parishioner to see where the possibilities for change actually lie, to see that the situation is not as black-and-white as it originally appeared to be. But it may also so highlight the exceptional case that the parishioner becomes overly optimistic that change is possible. Also, by applying it inappropriately, such as by pointing out to an abused wife that her husband does not *always* mistreat her, the pastor may encourage her to remain in a damaging situation instead of taking appropriate measures to extricate herself from it.

Given the power that these "arts" possess, I suggest that the pastor needs one additional art, which is "the art of holding on loosely." As pastors, we often find ourselves unable to influence very much the way things go. A pastor friend of mine says, "I try to figure out where the laity are off to, and then run like hell to get out in front." This being the case much of the time, we may find ourselves trying to compensate in our pastoral counseling efforts for this absence of perceptible influence elsewhere, for surely here, we believe, we stand a fair chance of exerting real influence, of effecting real change. Armed with the arts of the power of suggestion, of untying knots, of identifying exceptions, we may find ourselves taking undue responsibility and excessive initiative for the way the story unfolds, much like an editor who assumes the burden of rewriting a poorly authored manuscript. We take control of the story, assuming that we are absolutely essential to its happy or beneficent outcome. It is not that we seek power for ourselves—if we did, we probably would not have chosen ministry as a profession—but that we so much want the other to feel empowered. Our intentions are good and noble. But they are not necessarily what is needed in this situation.

I suggest, therefore, that pastors who counsel need to develop the art of holding on loosely, of allowing their counselees a great deal of freedom to move about, to think, imagine, and feel for themselves what it would be like to be living in a different kind of story. Steve de Shazer concluded an initial session with a client in this fashion:

Therapist: OK. So what do you think, when should we get back
               together? What do you think—a week, two weeks, three
               weeks, what?
Client: Two weeks.
Therapist: OK. Let's go up front and figure out what's best.[2]

This seemingly casual approach to scheduling is not due to de
Shazer's difficulty in handling an excessively large caseload, but is
consistent with his belief that counseling is for the purpose of helping clients "begin to know their way about," and "to build confidence that they can find their own way about."[3] I believe that the
pastor should take a similarly liberative approach when a parishioner invites her to take possession of some segment of the story of
his life. But pastors are often prone to feel that there is a direct relationship between the energy they expend on a program and its ultimate effectiveness, and this way of thinking tends to influence their
views on pastoral counseling. They are prone to believe that the
harder they work, the more they will achieve.

In *Men at Work*, James E. Dittes begins his chapter entitled
"Conversion and Liberation" with the following story:

> Give two schoolboys the two ends of a rope with a knot in the mid-
> dle. Draw a line on the ground in front of each boy. Tell the boys,
> "You get a nickel every time you can pull the knot across your line."
> For you and for me and for most boys we know and were, this
> becomes competitive tug-of-war. We assume a scarcity of nickels. We
> assume that for me to get my nickel I must keep you from getting
> yours. So we strain and compete. We work. I may drag the knot across
> my line a few times, working against your best efforts, and vice versa.
> In ten minutes maybe one boy wins five nickels and feels triumphant,
> and the other boy wins four nickels and feels defeated. That's the way
> work is.
>
> Give the same rope, draw the same lines, offer the same nickels to
> two other boys, perhaps Latin Americans on the streets of Spanish
> Harlem in New York or somewhere in Central America. They don't
> "work." They play. Probably with music in their voice and dance in
> their step, they saw the rope back and forth across their two lines at a
> great pace and in steady rhythm. In ten minutes they can make twen-
> ty-five dollars each. They are not tricking you or outsmarting you—
> although these encounters between differing cultures can easily make
> both sides feel suspicious or duped. They are following your rules hon-
> estly in the way that makes the most sense to them. They just naturally

envision the situation differently. They assume plenty of nickels, they assume a "user friendly" assignment, and they assume collaboration and partnership. It never occurs to them to make the assumptions that you and I make automatically—the assumption of competition, the assumption that we must wrestle an unwilling and unfriendly piece of work to yield something of personal value, my assumption that you are out to stop me and that I must therefore stop you first, the mentality of preemptive strike, the shoot-out at high noon, which is the essence of machismo, the swagger and bluff of the man who feels that everything is at stake and he does not have what it takes. It doesn't occur to them to "work" with the rope.[4]

Dittes' story is especially applicable to pastoral counseling in the congregational setting, as this situation invites a sense of collaboration and partnership, and should not involve the assumption that the pastor must wrestle and fight—like Jacob with the mysterious nocturnal stranger—and be wounded in the process. The pastor's reputation and sense of professional competence does not rest on this or any other counseling situation. Everything is *not* at stake, and the question of whether the pastor has what it takes is *not* at issue. It is enough that one do what one is able to do within the limits of appropriate expenditure of time and of personal resources.

The art of untying knots is itself illustrative of the art of holding on loosely. When we want to get rid of a knot in a rope or a garden hose, tugging and pulling does not help. It only makes matters worse. Instead, the idea is to *loosen* the rope or hose at the point where the knot has formed. Only then are we in a position to unscramble the knot. Elephants are also illustrative. They follow one another by loosely resting their trunks on the preceding elephant's tail. They are not tethered together, and it never occurs to them that they might need to be chained together—chain gangs are a human creation—yet they manage to find their way, even in the dark. In this regard, we have much to learn from the elephants, who live much longer lives than we humans do.

Problem-Solving vs. Relationship-Oriented Counseling

Yet another way to talk about "the art of holding on loosely" is to contrast the approach to pastoral counseling in the congregational setting that I am advocating here with the ways in which pastoral counseling was represented in the 1960s and 1970s, when the pastoral counseling movement was in its heyday. Back then, considerable emphasis was placed on the pastoral counseling *relationship*, as it was widely believed that change occurred in and through the relationship that was established between counselor and counselee.

This view was supported by client-centered therapy, which emphasized that the relationship between the therapist and client is key to the client's growth and change. As Rogers puts it, the issue for the therapist is: "How can I provide a relationship which this person may use for his own personal growth?" Why is this the issue? Because "change appears to come about through experience in relationship."[5] As Rogers and his colleagues recognized, the development of a helping relationship takes time, and it was therefore not uncommon for client-centered therapy to involve twenty-five or thirty counseling sessions.

The pastoral counseling movement sought to give theological legitimation to this emphasis on the relationship as key to growth and change. An example of this theological justification is William B. Oglesby's *Biblical Themes for Pastoral Care*, published in 1980.[6] He viewed pastoral care as having as its "basic intention" the "reestablishing [of] broken relationships, of healing the wounds of loneliness and grief, of loving and forgiving in the context of truth and grace." Because "the person is always more important than the problem, and the relationship is more important than the solution," the primary focus of pastoral care is on "encounter, on relationships, on reconciliation." Pastoral counseling does not differ in kind, but only in degree, from pastoral care: "Pastoral counseling is that function of ministry wherein the minister and the parishioner or parishioners focus in a concentrated and atypical fashion on the situation of the latter *toward providing the kind of support system and relational encounter* that will enable the person once again to draw nourishment from the ongoing processes of life."[7]

Oglesby views this "relational encounter" between the pastor and parishioner as an expression of the relational encounter that occurs between God and humankind. If the Bible is replete with examples of individuals who, for example, resisted being "found" or "found out" by God, so the parishioner often resists genuine relationships with others, and it is therefore the pastor's role to be

that other person who challenges the parishioner to enter into relationship. As Oglesby puts it, "the minister is aware that if the
encounter does not happen in the relationship with the parishioner,
it is not likely to happen at all. It probably will not occur 'out there'
unless it is experienced 'in here.'" Therefore, "in the encounter with
the minister there is provided an opportunity for the person to relate
in new ways, to respond more openly, not only to the minister but
also to those 'others' who make up his/her world."[8]

Needless to say, this view places considerable emphasis on the
relationship between the pastor and parishioner as the means by
which change is effected. This view envisions that this relationship
may even become, at least temporarily, the primary relationship in a
parishioner's life. As Oglesby puts it, "personal problems are always
relationship oriented, and the primary relationships are certainly
family. Even so, in the relationship between the minister and the
parishioner, significant freedom can be achieved by each person even
though other members of the family do not participate in the
process. . . . Put in biblical terms, once the person experiences love,
s/he is then able to love, and thus becomes a means for reconciliation
with those most closely a part of his/her life."[9]

I suggest that this view of pastoral counseling creates the necessary
conditions for the boundary violations that are now being descried
in books like Marie M. Fortune's *Is Nothing Sacred* and Fortune and
Poling's *Sexual Abuse by Clergy: A Crisis for the Church*.[10] While
some pastors are sexual predators, and are, in fact, self-centered and
narcissistic, many other pastors have gotten themselves into compromising situations because they have taken the relationship model
of pastoral counseling to heart, and have believed that their task is
to mediate or model the love and acceptance of God in a deeply personal way. Recently, a male pastor assured his married female parishioner in a telephone conversation that she was not unloved because,
as her pastor, *he* loves her. Unbeknownst to them, her husband had
bugged their telephone, and used this well-intentioned expession of
pastoral love as grounds for alleging that the pastor had a romantic
interest in his wife. While the pastor had no such interest, the relational model, with its emphasis on the relational encounter and the
pastor's mediation of the love of God to the counselee has a tendency to create conditions where boundary violations may occur.

The fact that this model is given theological legitimation also makes this relational view of counseling considerably more dangerous and subject to abuse than when used by "secular" therapists like Rogers and his followers, as the theological legitimation of this approach raises the stakes much higher. It says, in effect, that if the pastor does not form a deep relationship with the parishioner, she has inadequately mediated or modeled God's love and reconciling grace.

In this book, I have presented the "problem-solving" approach to pastoral counseling which I have advocated in each of my previous books on pastoral counseling.[11] While this approach has been deemed superficial by others, this very judgment fails to take account of the paradox that what appears deeper may not be so. As artists who must learn to paint on a two-dimensional surface well know, one can create the *illusion* of depth.[12] Rarely is Jesus accused of superficiality, and yet, whatever else he may have been, he was surely a solver of problems. People came to him with physical, mental, or spiritual problems—or some combination of these—and he helped them to resolve them. Others came to him over a dispute between them, and he helped them to settle it. It is not necessarily true that counseling that is person centered is deeper than counseling that is problem centered. Moreover, this distinction between the person and the problem is itself a fallacy, for when a parishioner has a problem that prompts her to contact the pastor, this problem *is* her current self-experiencing, for she experiences herself predominantly as one-who-is-troubled-by-such-and-such-problem.

While Jesus is often presented in the pastoral theological literature as deeply relational, with the stories of his encounter with the woman at the well ("He told me everything I ever did") and conversation with Mary ("Mary hath chosen the good part") offered in support of this view, this does nothing to challenge the fact that he is also portrayed in the Gospels as fully attentive to the problem of the person kneeling, sitting, or standing before him. He did not view the identified problem as too mundane for him to give his full attention to, nor did he consider this problem to be merely the proxy for something deeper. He focused on whatever was troubling the other. So, too, with pastoral counseling in the congregational context. A parishioner has a concern, a worry, a problem, a dilemma, a difficulty that he cannot seem to solve without some help. The pastor listens to his story, focuses on its problematic aspect, and helps to resolve it, to the best of her ability. Like Jesus, sometimes she succeeds. Like Jesus, sometimes she fails. But also, like Jesus, she takes it seriously in its own right. It needs no higher or loftier justification to warrant her undivided attention.

This seemingly minimalist view of pastoral counseling may appear to undermine my argument that pastoral counseling is essential to the life of the congregation, that pastoral counseling affords an experience that no other aspect or dimension of the life of the congregation provides. I believe, on the contrary, that it strengthens this argument, for where else in the life of the congregation does a parishioner experience a focused, attentive hearing and response to a concern, a problem, a dilemma, or a difficulty in her life? Does it happen at coffee hour? Usually not, because the pastor has other things on her mind, other claims on her attention. Does it happen during committee meetings, during the worship service, in a class or discussion group? No, because these are settings that have other purposes, other agendas. At best, the concern, problem, dilemma, or difficulty can be mentioned, but it cannot be given the undivided attention that pastoral counseling affords. Even the prayer meeting, where a parishioner may relate her problem in some detail, does not afford the more practical, down-to-earth response that the pastoral counseling context offers. Of course, prayers help. Jesus himself offered us a model in the Lord's Prayer for praying for ourselves and for others. But, more often, he attended to the vexing problems that people brought to him, problems that they had not been able to solve on their own, by doing what he could to make the situation better, either directly (by healing the person) or indirectly (by reframing the problem out of existence).

The one example in this book of my own efforts to provide pastoral counseling (chapter 3) illustrates my point. A student had come to me with a problem. He was having trouble writing a paper for my course. Why did he come to me? Most likely, because I was the professor for whose course he was writing the paper. It made sense that he would come to me, though it would also have made sense if he had chosen someone else, such as a professor in religious education who has specialized knowledge in the educational process, or a professor in communication who actually teaches a course on learning to write more effectively. But he chose me, perhaps because he felt that he might need to ask for an extension of the paper deadline, or perhaps because he felt that at least I would know the material that he was trying to write about. Or maybe because he wanted to keep the matter just between the two of us, whereas going to someone else would get a third person involved.

In any event, I didn't assume that it would be via my pastoral relationship with him that his problem would be ameliorated, nor did it occur to me that I might, through my efforts, mediate or model to him the profound love and reconciling grace of God. As I tend to believe that this particular student is more gifted—and better located, by virtue of his cultural background—to mediate God's love and acceptance to others than I am, the very thought that *I* would do this, be this, for *him* would have been most presumptuous, and, in any case, it would not have helped him with his problem.

Nor did we talk much about his hunch that his recent marriage may have something to do with his problem. As he put it, "Before I got married, I had plenty of time to myself. Now, my wife expects me to spend time with her, and I can't devote as much time to my studies." This helped me to contextualize the problem, and seemed to explain, at least in part, why the problem had suddenly arisen, where it had not been a problem before. If I had been Oglesby-trained, I probably would have seen this as the deeper issue that was disguised by the problem of his being unable to write the paper. Did I do wrong to focus on the surface issue of the paper when there was a deeper issue at stake? I don't think so. He came to me because he was having trouble getting a paper written. He did not come to me to talk about his recent marriage. On the other hand, I indirectly helped him with the "relational" problem by demonstrating that he *could* take less time writing the paper, thus enabling him to meet his wife's needs without feeling quite so resentful. Better, in my view, to tackle the problem that is most amenable to change (writing the paper) than to take on something infinitely more difficult (the alleged relational problem). And why assume that pastoral counseling is the best context, among the many contexts available to him, for addressing the issue of his wife's expectations of him?

About our own relationship to one another, there was nothing that I, or he, could have described as a deep, personal encounter.

When we subsequently encountered one another in passing, we were cordial to one another, but the experience had not made us into anything even approximating soul mates. We did, though, have a meal together, mainly to celebrate his success, and this, as discussed in chapter 5, was something Jesus often did.

In my judgment, pastoral counseling is essential to the life of the congregation when, and if, it respects its own boundaries. If it tries to take the place of the other vital aspects of congregational life, it loses sight of its own unique and distinctive role and function in the life of the congregation, which is to help parishioners tell their own stories in a constructive context. What stories they tell is up to them, but the vast experience of pastors would suggest that the stories parishioners tell are stories about problems or problematic aspects of their lives. Even if they come to talk about their faith in God, this is usually because *it* too has become problematic, and, if so, the pastor as counselor may treat it like any other problem—like the problem of not being able to write a paper—and use the very same "arts" that she would use in assisting the parishioner with a seemingly more mundane problem. Just because the problem may be a "theological" or "spiritual" one does not mean that one need approach it any differently, or with any greater—or lesser—seriousness than if the problem is a "this-worldly" one. As Wittgenstein puts it, "A problem has the form: 'I don't know my way about.'"[13] Whether the problem is a faith struggle or writing a paper, the pastor's role is to assist the counselee in finding her way about.

I have argued in this book that pastoral counseling is essential to the life of the congregation because every congregation needs to have exemplified a constructive modeling of storytelling. Regrettably, pastoral counseling in many congregations becomes, instead, the very locus in which stories are *not* approached in a constructive manner, even one in which destructive stories get created. In congregations where the personal stories of parishioners are treated respectfully, are listened to responsibly, and responded to in a helpful manner, however, the fact that this is how the pastor works becomes known and it becomes a positive example for how parishioners may hear one another's stories. This may appear to be a rather small and insignificant claim for pastoral counseling, but it is actually neither small nor insignificant, for, as many analysts of congregational life have recently pointed out, congregations become known for the way they "story" themselves.[14] Also, as Erik H. Erikson points out, one of the great dangers confronting any group is that it pretends to be something that it is not. It engages in "impersonation," thus creating a large discrepancy between who they are and how they represent themselves.[15] By modeling a constructive storytelling, pastoral counseling can be that element of congregational life through which individuals come to speak truly about themselves. As Erikson writes of Luther, "His style indicates his conviction that a thing said less elegantly and meant more truly is better work, and better craftsmanship in communication."[16] May pastoral counseling set the standard in our congregations for this "better work," this "better craftsmanship in communication." May it be the place where parishioners relinquish the need to be what they are not and embrace the self that they have become. And may it be the place where pastors practice the art of holding on loosely, so that those who come to talk will be enabled to find their own way about in the world.

Notes

Introduction: Counseling in the Congregational Context

1. See Charles V. Gerkin, *The Living Human Document* (Nashville: Abingdon Press, 1984), and *Widening the Horizons* (Philadelphia: Westminster Press, 1986); Edward P. Wimberly, *African American Pastoral Care* (Nashville: Abingdon Press, 1991); Andrew D. Lester, *Hope in Pastoral Care and Counseling* (Louisville: Westminster John Knox Press, 1995); Carrie Doerring, *Taking Care* (Nashville: Abingdon Press, 1995).

2. See, for example, Brian H. Childs, *Short-Term Pastoral Counseling* (Nashville: Abingdon Press, 1990), and Howard W. Stone, *Brief Pastoral Counseling* (Minneapolis: Fortress Press, 1993).

3. Jay S. Efran, Michael D. Lukens, and Robert J. Lukens, *Language, Structure, and Change: Frameworks of Meaning in Psychotherapy* (New York: W.W. Norton, 1990), 93.

4. On the other hand, in *Gossip* (Chicago: The University of Chicago Press, 1985) Patricia Meyer Spacks makes the case that gossip may serve positive social and communal purposes. I will discuss her argument in chap. 5.

5. Cited by Marie M. Fortune in Marie M. Fortune and James N. Poling, *Sexual Abuse by Clergy: A Crisis for the Church* (Decatur, Ga.: Journal of Pastoral Care Publications, 1994), 5. I believe that contextual (i.e., congregational issues) account in part for this difference. See my "Sex in the Parish: Social-Scientific Explanations for Why It Occurs," *The Journal of Pastoral Care* 47 (1993): 350–61.

6. A fairly common response to my earlier book, *Reframing: A New Method in Pastoral Care* (Minneapolis; Fortress Press, 1990), was that I was advocating a counseling method that is incongruent with Christian values (i.e., manipulative). I anticipate that this may well be the response to this book also. While I cannot hope to satisfy all critics on this point, I would draw attention to my earlier statement in *Reframing*, pp. 50–51: "So reframing techniques are not weapons to be used in a manipulative or controlling manner. They are methods that break impasses, making positive change possible. Good reframers are not 'con-artists' who view other people as potential victims; they are 'pro-artists' whose creative imagination is for the sole purpose of enabling others to have fuller, more abundant lives. The real manipulators, the real con-artists, are those who control others through subtle, or not-so-subtle, techniques of double binding. In contrast, good reframers are concerned to help untie the knots, so that victims of such manipulation may experience, at last, the freedom that God had forever intended them to have."

7. See my *Agents of Hope* (Minneapolis: Fortress Press, 1995), and Andrew Lester, *Hope in Pastoral Care and Counseling.*

8. I have set forth my views on premarital counseling in "The Use of Proverbs in Premarital Counseling," chap. 3 of *Biblical Approaches to Pastoral Counseling* (Philadelphia: Westminster Press, 1981).

9. Jay S. Efran et al., *Language, Structure, and Change*, 129.

10. Two books that emphasize the role of innovation or improvisation in women's lives are Kim Chernin, *The Hungry Self* (San Francisco: Harper & Row, 1986), 195–204, and Mary Catherine Bateson, *Composing a Life* (New York: The Atlantic Monthly Press, 1989), 1–18. In effect, I am advocating for pastoral counseling a practice that is especially common to women.

11.Carl R. Rogers, *On Becoming a Person* (Boston: Houghton Mifflin, 1961),26.

12. I make this point in my essay, "The Parabolic Event in Religious Autobiography," *The Princeton Seminary Bulletin*, 4 (1983): 26–38. I also discuss the uses of autobiography for pastoral hermeneutics in *Pastoral Care and Hermeneutics,* Theology and Pastoral Care (Philadelphia: Fortress Press, 1984), chap. 5.

Chapter 1. The Stories Clients Tell

1. Janine Roberts, *Tales and Transformations: Stories in Families and Family Therapy* (New York: W.W. Norton, 1994); Patricia O'Hanlon Hudson and William Hudson O'Hanlon, *Rewriting Love Stories: Brief Marital Therapy* (New York: W.W. Norton, 1991); and Alan Parry and Robert E. Doan, *Story Re-Visions: Narrative Therapy in the Postmodern World* (New York: Guilford Press, 1994).

2. Hudson and O'Hanlon, *Rewriting Love Stories*, 2.

3. Ibid., 4.

4. Roberts, *Tales and Transformations*, xiv–xv.

5. Ibid., 7.

6. Ibid., xv.

7. Ibid., 8.

8. Ibid., 14.

9. Ibid., 21.

10. Ibid.

11. Ibid., 130.

12. Ibid., 146.

13. Hudson and O'Hanlon, *Rewriting Love Stories*, 12.

14. Ibid., 16.

15. Ibid.

16. This story was presented by Hudson and O'Hanlon at the 12th Annual Family Therapy Network Symposium in Washington, D.C. (1989).

17. Ibid., 20.

18. Ibid.

19. Ibid., 21.

20. Ibid., 52–53.

21. Ibid., 48.

22. Parry and Doan, *Story Re-Visions*, chap. 3.

23. Ibid., 44.

24. Ibid., 45.

25. Ibid., 47.

26. Ibid., 86.

27. Michael P. Nichols, *The Self in the System: Expanding the Limits of Family Therapy* (New York: Brunner/Mazel, 1987). For a pastoral counseling text that makes an association of narrative and psychoanalytic object relations theory, see Charles V. Gerkin,

The Living Human Document (Nashville: Abingdon Press, 1984).

28. Carl R. Rogers, *On Becoming a Person*, 314–28.
29. Ibid., 107–24, 163–82.
30. Ibid., 108.
31. Ibid., 109.
32. Ibid., 114.
33. Ibid., 164.
34. Ibid., 176.
35. Ibid., 177.
36. Ibid., 119.
37. Ibid., 181.
38. Ibid., 320.

Chapter 2. The Inspirational Story

1. I have in mind such texts as Gaylord Noyce, *The Art of Pastoral Conversation* (Atlanta: John Knox Press, 1981) and Charles W. Taylor, *The Skilled Pastor: Counseling as the Practice of Theology* (Minneapolis: Fortress Press, 1991). An excellent text by a family therapist on listening is Michael P. Nichols, *The Lost Art of Listening* (New York: The Guilford Press, 1995).

2. Stephen R. Lankton and Carol H. Lankton, *Enchantment and Intervention in Family Therapy: Training in Ericksonian Approaches* (New York: Brunner/Mazel, 1986).

3. Jay Haley, *Uncommon Therapy: The Psychiatric Techniques of Milton H. Erickson* (New York: W.W. Norton, 1973).

4. Lankton and Lankton, *Enchantment and Intervention*, 44.

5. Ibid.

6. David Gordon, *Therapeutic Metaphors: Helping Others Through the Looking Glass* (Cupertino, Calif.: META Publications, 1978), 6. Emphasis in original.

7. Haley, *Uncommon Therapy*, 13. My emphasis.

8. Sidney Rosen, ed., *My Voice Will Go with You: The Teaching Tales of Milton H. Erickson* (New York: W.W. Norton, 1982).

9. Ibid., 21.
10. "Foreword" to ibid., 13.
11. Ibid., 13–14.
12. "Editor's Note" to ibid., 20.
13. Haley, *Uncommon Therapy*, 24–39.
14. Rosen, *My Voice Will Go with You*, 20.
15. Quoted by Rosen, 211.
16. Harvey Mindess, *Makers of Psychology: The Personal Factor* (New York: Insight Books, 1988), 141–42.
17. Rosen, 149–50.
18. Ibid., 150.
19. Ibid.
20. Ibid., 25.
21. Ibid., 150.
22. Ibid., 47–48.
23. Ibid., 50.
24. Ibid., 51.
25. Ibid., 110–11.
26. Ibid., 112.

27. Lankton and Lankton suggest that Erickson may have gotten the "confusion technique" from his father, Albert, whom they describe as practical, hard-working, but also a bit enigmatic. When he proposed marriage to Erickson's mother, Clara, she said she want-

ed some time to think about it. When Albert caught her underneath a tree a couple of days later, he said to her, "You know, when I proposed to you I didn't ask you to make a single decision." She accepted at that point, "totally confused" (*Enchantment and Intervention*, 8).

28. Rosen, *My Voice Will Go with You*, 123–24.

29. The Lanktons note, however, that Erickson and Frankl came by the therapeutic use of paradox independently of one another (*Enchantment and Intervention*, 11). See also their *The Answer Within: A Clinical Framework of Ericksonian Hypnotherapy* (New York: Brunner/Mazel, 1983).

30. Rosen, *My Voice Will Go with You*, 124–25.

31. Ibid., 125.

32. Ibid., 125–26.

33. Ibid., 80–81.

34. Ibid., 198.

35. Ibid.

36. Ibid., 198–99.

37. Ibid., 209.

38. Ibid., 209–10.

39. Ibid., 210.

40. Ibid., 52.

41. Ibid., 53.

42. Ibid., 28.

43. Ibid.

44. On this point, see James E. Dittes's chapter on "Seeing Through Expectations to Find Ministry" in *When The People Say No: Conflict and the Call to Ministry* (San Francisco: Harper & Row, 1979), 70–93. I discuss this chapter in chap. 4.

45. Rosen, *My Voice Will Go with You*, 126–27.

46. See Mary Louis Bringle, *The God of Thinness: Gluttony and Other Weighty Matters* (Nashville: Abingdon Press, 1992).

47. In his essay, "The Analysis of Rumor," in *Personality and Social Encounter* (Boston: Beacon Press, 1960), 311–26, Gordon W. Allport shows that as stories travel, they tend to grow shorter, more easily grasped and told. In successive versions, more and more of the original details are *leveled* out; fewer words are used and fewer items are mentioned. On the other hand, as this leveling of details proceeds, the remaining details are necessarily *sharpened*. Sharpening denotes the selective perception, retention, and reporting of a few details from the originally larger context. While sharpening always occurs, the same details are not always emphasized. Much depends on the constitution of the group in which the story is transmitted, for those items will be sharpened which are of particular interest to the reporters. Why are some details obliterated and others emphasized? The answer is to be found in the process of *assimilation*, which results from the powerful attractive force exerted by habits, interests, and sentiments already existing in the listener's mind. In the telling and retelling of a story, for example, there is marked assimilation to the principle theme. Items become sharpened or leveled to fit the leading motif of the story, and they become consistent with this motif in such a way as to make the resultant story more coherent, plausible, and well rounded. Ernest L. Abel has applied Allport's theory (developed together with Leo Postman) to stories in the Gospels. See "The Psychology of Memory and Rumor Transmission and Their Bearing on Theories of Oral Transmission in Early Christianity," *Journal of Religion* 51 (1971): 270–81.

Chapter 3. The Paradoxical Story

1. Jay Haley, *Uncommon Therapy: The Psychiatric Techniques of Milton H. Erickson* (New York: W.W. Norton, 1973), 9.

2. Paul Watzlawick and John H. Weakland, eds., *The Interactional View* (New York: W.W. Norton, 1977), xi.

3. *Webster's New World Dictionary of the American Language* (Cleveland: World Pub. Co., 1966), 1060.

4. This and other examples of the "double bind" are found in Dan Greenburg, *How to Be a Jewish Mother* (Los Angeles: Price/Stern/Sloan, 1964).

5. Paul Watzlawick, *Münchausen's Pigtail* (New York: W.W. Norton, 1990), 27–28.

6. Ibid., 28. This and preceding examples imply that the parent, especially the mother, is the primary cause of schizophrenia in the child. While Bateson's theory that schizophrenia is essentially due to communication "binds" created by the parent was quite popular in the 1950s, it was not universally accepted then, and is even less accepted today. In *Childhood and Society* (New York: W.W. Norton), originally published in 1950, Erik H. Erikson was extremely careful *not* to blame the mother in his own case of a young schizophrenic girl (chap. 5). He was, in fact, criticized for seeming to blame the child herself for her affliction. This criticism led him to add a footnote to the 1963 revised edition of the text, emphasizing both that the etiology of any emotional disturbance is necessarily multicausal and that the study of childhood schizophrenia is still very much in its infancy (p. 207). In any case, I believe that parental communication styles have *some* influence on children's emotional development, and the fact that some parents use "double-binding" communication styles did lead the Bateson group to discover ways in which such communication styles could be used therapeutically. The therapeutic use of Watzlawick's paradoxical story type and the art of untying knots does not require the acceptance of the Bateson group's original explanation for how schizophrenia itself develops.

7. Paul Watzlawick, John Weakland, and Richard Fisch, *Change: Principles of Problem Formation and Problem Resolution* (New York: W.W. Norton, 1974), 63. The foreword to this book was written by Milton H. Erickson. Owing to his ill health, it is brief, but concludes: "I am pleased that my own work has contributed to the ideas represented in this book. I appreciate having had the opportunity to make this small comment on it. *Perhaps, here as elsewhere, such a small gesture is all the expediting one needs do*" (x; my emphasis).

8. Paul Watzlawick, Janet Beavin Bavelas, and Don D. Jackson, *Pragmatics of Human Communication: A Study of Interactional Patterns, Pathologies, and Paradoxes* (New York: W.W. Norton, 1967), 187–256.

9. Ibid., 187–88.

10. Ibid., 198.

11. Paul Watzlawick, *The Language of Change: Elements of Therapeutic Communication* (New York: Basic Books, 1978), 109.

12. Watzlawick et al., *Pragmatics of Human Communication*, 213.

13. Ibid., 198–99.

14. Erik H. Erikson, *Young Man Luther: A Study in Psychoanalysis and History* (New York: W.W. Norton, 1958), 23–48.

15. Watzlawick et al., *Pragmatics of Human Communication*, 202.

16. Ibid.

17. Paul Watzlawick, "Self-Fulfilling Prophecies," in *The Invented Reality*, ed. Paul Watzlawick (New York: W.W. Norton, 1984), 95–116. The illustration is on pp. 95–96.

18. Watzlawick et al., *Pragmatics of Human Communication*, 231–32.

19. Ibid., 235.

20. Ibid., 236.

21. Ibid.

22. Ibid., 236–37.

23. Ibid., 241.

24. Paul Watzlawick, *Ultra-Solutions: How to Fail Most Successfully* (New York: W.W. Norton, 1988), 42.

25. Ibid., 42–43. My case of weight loss in chap. 2 is also an illustration of the third alternative. Presented with advice that I either exercise or diet, and finding myself resisting both options, I found a third alternative that I did not resist, that of sleeping an inordinate number of hours per day. This third alternative differs significantly from the usual tendency to combine exercising and dieting because it introduces an entirely different behavior, not a combination of the two original behaviors which were individually rejected. It seems implausible that one would embrace a combination of behaviors that were singly rejected.

26. Ibid., 44.

27. Watzlawick et al., *Change*, 81.

28. Haley, *Uncommon Therapy*, 225–27.

29. Paul Watzlawick, *The Language of Change*.

30. Ibid., 73.

31. In *Change*, Watzlawick et al. discuss this distinction between first- and second-order reality as a basis for determining the type of change one is seeking to achieve. They note the human tendency to use first-order change techniques in cases where second-order change is desired (pp. 77–91). I have discussed this issue at some length in *Reframing: A New Method in Pastoral Care* (Minneapolis: Fortress Press, 1990).

32. Oscar Wilde, *The Soul of Man and Prison Writings*, ed. Isobel Murray (New York: Oxford University Press, 1990), x.

33. Watzlawick, *The Language of Change*, 77.

34. Burton L. Mack, *The Lost Gospel: The Book of Q and Christian Origins* (San Francisco: HarperSanFrancisco, 1993), 73–80. The translations are Mack's.

35. Watzlawick, *The Language of Change*, 75.

36. John Dominic Crossan, *In Fragments: The Aphorisms of Jesus* (San Francisco: Harper & Row, 1983).

37. Ibid., 6.

38. Ibid.

39. Ibid.

40. Ibid.

41. Ibid., 20.

42. Ibid., 22. Crossan's *The Dark Interval: Towards a Theology of Story* (Niles, Ill.: Argue Communications, 1975) makes a very similar comparison between myth and parable, and emphasizes the paradoxical nature of the latter. He also analyzes selected parables of Jesus according to the chiastic structure noted above in our discussion of Watzlawick. See especially chap. 4 entitled, "Jesus as Parabler."

43. In *African American Pastoral Care* (Nashville: Abingdon Press, 191), Edward P. Wimberly identifies *thickening* as one of four properties or functions of "the eschatological plot" that "undergirds the faith story of black Christians" (13). The others are unfolding, lining, and twisting. In this eschatological plot, thickening "refers to those events that intrude into God's unfolding story and seek to change the direction of that story for the ill of all involved" (15). Thus, plot thickening is essentially a disruption of the unfolding story which, as a consequence of the thickening, now needs to be *twisted* back "to God's original intention, despite the thickening that hindered the plot" (15–16). In contrast to Wimberly, I suggest that God may be the agent of plot thickening, which also implies that God is capable of paradoxical intentions. I make this point in *Reframing*, 167–68.

44. Paul Ricoeur, "Listening to the Parables of Jesus," in *The Philosophy of Paul Ricoeur: An Anthology of His Work*, eds. Charles E. Reagan and David Stewart (Boston: Beacon Press, 1978), 239–45.

45. Crossan, *The Dark Interval*, 57.

46. Donald Capps, "The Pursuit of Unhappiness in American Congregational Life," *Pastoral Psychology* 39 (1990): 3–23.

47. Paul Watzlawick, *The Situation Is Hopeless but not Serious: The Pursuit of Unhappiness* (New York: W.W. Norton, 1983).

48. In "Intolerable Language: Jesus and the Woman Taken in Adultery," Patricia Klindienst Joplin comments on the fact that this story can easily be ignored or escaped because it is a "homeless pericope." The Revised Standard Version places this story in a footnote and notes that other ancient authorities place it at the very end of the Gospel of John or after Luke 21:38, just prior to the account of Jesus' death. Joplin notes that, in taking responsibility for the resolution of this social crisis, Jesus linked his fate to hers. The location of this "homeless pericope" in Luke carries this very implication. In *Shadow of Spirit: Postmodernism and Religion*, eds. Philippa Berry and Andrew Wernick (New York: Routledge, 1992), 226–37.

Chapter 4. The Miracle Story

1. Steve de Shazer, *Putting Difference to Work* (New York: W.W. Norton, 1991), 26–27.
2. Ibid., 32.
3. Ibid., 33.
4. Ibid., 34.
5. Ibid., 35.
6. Ibid., 72-73.
7. Ibid., 73.
8. Ibid.
9. Ibid., 74.
10. Ibid., 64.
11. Ibid.
12. Ibid., 64–65.
13. Ibid., 65.
14. Ibid., 66.
15. Ibid.
16. Ibid., 67.
17. Ibid., 63–65.
18. Ibid., 66.
19. Ibid., 68–69.
20. Ibid., 69.
21. Ibid., 91.
22. Ibid., 91–92.
23. Paul Watzlawick, *The Situation Is Hopeless, but not Serious* (New York: W.W. Norton, 1983), 51.
24. De Shazer, *Putting Difference to Work*, 92.
25. Ibid., 93.
26. Ibid., 93–94.
27. Steve de Shazer, *Words Were Originally Magic* (New York: W.W. Norton, 1994), 13.
28. Ibid., 18. De Shazer is quoting here from Bandler and Grinder's *The Structure of Magic* (Palo Alto, Calif.: Science and Behavior Books, 1975), 43.
29. Ibid.; quoting from Bandler and Grinder, 44.
30. Ibid., 21–22.
31. Ibid., 29.
32. Ibid.
33. Ibid., 30.
34. Ibid., 31.
35. Ibid.
36. Ibid., 31–32.
37. Ibid., 32.

38. Ibid.
39. Ibid.
40. Ibid.
41. Ibid., 33.
42. Ibid., 34.
43. Ibid.
44. Ibid., 73.
45. Ibid., 87.
46. Ibid., 90.
47. Ibid., 48.
48. While de Shazer views Wittgenstein as his philosophical mentor, it is worth noting that Wittgenstein was influenced by William James, and that this particular idea—that variety and diversity are the essence of things—is directly attributable to James's *The Pluralistic Universe* (New York: Longmans, Green, 1909).
49. De Shazer, *Words Were Originally Magic*, 95.
50. Ibid.
51. Ibid., 96.
52. De Shazer, *Putting Difference to Work*, 113.
53. Ibid., 114–15.
54. Ibid., 115.
55. De Shazer, *Words Were Originally Magic*, 92.
56. Ibid.
57. Ibid.
58. Ibid., 93.
59. Ibid., 94–95.
60. Ibid., 90.
61. Ibid., 250–51.
62. Ibid., 272.
63. Ibid. My use of sleeping as a means to lose weight is a case in point. I did not need to be taught or coached how to sleep, as I had been doing this all my life. It may also be noted that this case illustrates the value of identifying exceptions, for I had already observed that while I usually gained weight during waking hours, I rarely gained weight during sleeping hours. Usually, I lost weight while sleeping. By extending the number of hours that I was asleep, I devoted more hours of the day to the "exception," leaving fewer hours in the day for the problem to manifest itself. Furthermore, unlike exercising or dieting, there was a less obvious relationship between the "solution" and the "problem."
64. Ibid., 273.
65. Ibid. Carl Rogers makes a similar point. In order to determine whether measurable progress was being achieved in client-centered therapy, Rogers used a technique called the Q-technique, developed by William Stephenson, which involved having clients rank order a set of cards at various intervals in the course of therapy. The cards containing brief self-descriptions were sorted twice, once to describe their "self" as currently experienced and once to describe the "self" they aspired to be. In the course of therapy, both descriptions changed. Therapeutic progress was therefore defined as the realization of greater congruence between the "real" and "ideal" self, not as the realization of the "self" to which one originally aspired at the beginning of therapy. See his *Client-Centered Therapy* (Boston: Houghton Mifflin, 1951), 140.
66. De Shazer, *Words Were Originally Magic*, 273.
67. Paul Watzlawick, John Weakland, and Richard Fisch, *Change: Principles of Problem Formation and Problem Resolution* (New York: W.W. Norton, 1974), 84.
68. William James, *The Principles of Psychology*, 2 vols. (New York: Dover Publications, 1950), 2:634.
69. Ibid., 1:298.

70. Ibid., 1:299.

71. Ibid., 1:253. The foregoing discussion of James's views on experience has been informed by an essay by John Capps entitled, "The Bedrock of Experience: An Assessment of James's Proposals for a Critical Science of Religion," in Donald Capps and Janet L. Jacobs, eds., *The Struggle for Life: A Companion to William James's* The Varieties of Religious Experience (West Lafayette, Ind.: Society for the Scientific Study of Religion Monograph Series No. 9, 1995), 238–49.

72. James E. Dittes, "The Mitigated Self," in Richard K. Fenn and Donald Capps, eds., *The Endangered Self* (Princeton, N.J.: Princeton Theological Seminary Monograph Series No. 2, 1992), 79–87.

73. William James, *The Varieties of Religious Experience* (New York: Penguin Books, 1982), 478–83.

74. Michael P. Nichols, *The Self in the System: Expanding the Limits of Family Therapy* (New York: Brunner/Mazel, 1987), chap. 1.

75. Telephobia is not uncommon. In a brief reply to a criticism of their use of telephone survey methods to study social phobics (which the critic likened to interviewing people at the top of the Empire State Building to estimate the prevalence of height phobia), Murray B. Stein and his colleagues acknowledged that 50 percent of their socially phobic clients often avoided initiating telephone calls, while about one-third of these also avoided answering phone calls (in *American Journal of Psychiatry* 152 [1995]: 653–54). This may account in part for the fact that whereas about half of the persons suffering from agoraphobia seek professional treatment, fewer than 10 percent of social phobics do. See C. A. Pollard, "Help-seeking Patterns of Anxiety-disordered Individuals in the General Population," *Journal of Anxiety Disorders* 3 (1989): 131–38.

76. Watzlawick et al., *Change*, 80–81.

77. Gershen Kaufman and Lev Raphael, *Coming Out of Shame: Transforming Gay and Lesbian Lives* (New York: Doubleday, 1996), 60–61.

78. James E. Dittes, *When the People Say No: Conflict and the Call to Ministry* (San Francisco: Harper & Row, 1979), chap. 5.

79. Ibid., 77.

80. Ibid., 74.

81. De Shazer, *Putting Difference to Work*, 112.

82. Watzlawick, *The Situation Is Hopeless but not Serious*, 31–33.

83. See, for example, *Therapy as Social Construction*, ed. Sheila McNamee and Kenneth J. Gergen (London: Sage Publications, 1992). In her contribution to this volume, Lynn Hoffman cites Kenneth Gergen's case for "the social construction of the self," noting that it rejects the idea of the self as "a kind of irreducible inner reality represented by words like cognitions or the emotions" (p. 10). In his contribution, William Lax writes: "This narrative or sense of self arises not only through discourse with others, but *is* our discourse with others. There is no hidden self to be interpreted. We 'reveal' ourselves in every moment of interaction through the on-going narrative that we maintain with others" (p. 72).

84. Erik H. Erikson, *Identity: Youth and Crisis* (New York: W.W. Norton, 1968).

85. Saint Augustine, *The Confessions*, trans. John K. Ryan (Garden City, N.Y.: Image Books, 1960), 229. My emphasis.

86. Quoted by Erik H. Erikson, "The Galilean Sayings and the Sense of 'I,'" *The Yale Review* 70 (1981): 361.

87. Donald Capps, "The Discerning Heart: The Psalms as Pastoral Resource in Ministry to Potential Organ Recipients and Their Families," *Journal of Health Care Chaplaincy* 5 (1993): 123–36.

88. Troels Nørager, *Hjerte og Psyke: Studier i den Religiose Oplevens Metapsyologi og Diskurs Forlaget* [*Heart and Psyche: The Metaphysicality and Discourse of Religious Experience*] (Frederiksberg, Denmark: Forlageer ANIS, 1996), 361.

89. Ibid., 362.

90. See James B. Ashbrook, *Minding the Soul: Pastoral Counseling as Remembering* (Minneapolis: Fortress Press, 1996). Ashbrook writes: "What we are learning about the human brain makes more understandable the longings of the human heart. To speak of the heart and its longings is to think experientially. We know what we know from the inside, all at once, in ever more significant ways. . . . The language of the heart is closest to that which is particularly congruent with pastoral counseling. On first impression the language of the brain seems irrelevant to our task, yet the implicit and moving meanings of the heart can become more explicit and certain with knowledge of the brain. We can think about what we feel is true. We can reflect on what we know is real. We can join our subjectivity with the subjectivity of the other" (p. xviii).

91. De Shazer, *Words Were Originally Magic*, 274.

Chapter 5. Social Gossip and Pastoral Counseling

1. John Dominic Crossan, *The Historical Jesus: The Life of a Mediterranean Jewish Peasant* (San Francisco: HarperSanFrancisco, 1991).

2. Patricia Meyer Spacks, *Gossip* (Chicago: University of Chicago Press, 1985), 25.

3. Ibid., 26.

4. Jack Levin and Arnold Arluke, *Gossip: The Inside Scoop* (New York: Plenum Press, 1987), 19.

5. Max Gluckman, cited in Ralph L. Rosnow and Gary Alan Fine, *Rumor and Gossip: The Social Psychology of Hearsay* (New York: Elsevier Press, 1976), 90.

6. Ibid., 91.

7. Ibid.

8. Levin and Arluke, *Gossip: The Inside Scoop*, 24.

9. Ibid.

10. Ibid., 27.

11. Ibid., 24.

12. Ibid.

13. Spacks, *Gossip*, ix.

14. Ibid., x.

15. Ibid.

16. Ibid., 15.

17. Ibid.

18. Ibid., 16–17.

19. Kierkegaard, quoted in ibid., 18.

20. Ibid., 29.

21. Ibid., 19–20.

22. Ibid., 22.

23. Ibid., 57.

24. Ibid., 63.

25. Ibid., 63–64.

26. Ibid., 231.

27. Ibid.

28. Ibid.

29. Ibid., 231–32.

30. Gordon W. Allport and Leo Postman, *The Psychology of Rumor* (New York: Holt, 1847).

31. Spacks, *Gossip*, 232.

32. Ibid., 248.

33. Ibid., 258–59.

34. Ibid., 15.

35. Spacks, *Gossip*, 15.

36. David Riesman, *Individualism Reconsidered* (New York: The Free Press, 1954), 27.

37. See Donald Capps, *Life Cycle Theory and Pastoral Care*, Theology and Pastoral Care (Philadelphia: Fortress Press, 1983), 94–96.

38. Crossan, *The Historical Jesus*, 341.

39. Spacks, *Gossip*, 15, 22.

Epilogue: The Art of Holding On Loosely

1. Karen Lebacqz and Ronald G. Barton, *Sex in the Parish* (Louisville: Westminster/John Knox, 1991), 98–102.

2. Steve de Shazer, *Words Were Originally Magic* (New York: W.W. Norton, 1994), 155.

3. Ibid., 272.

4. James E. Dittes, *Men at Work: Life Beyond the Office* (Louisville: Westminster/John Knox Press, 1996), pp. 83–84.

5. Carl R. Rogers, *On Becoming a Person: A Therapist's View of Psychotherapy* (Boston: Houghton Mifflin, 1961), 32–33.

6. William B. Oglesby Jr., *Biblical Themes for Pastoral Care* (Nashville: Abingdon Press, 1980).

7. Ibid., 41–42. My emphasis.

8. Ibid., 87.

9. Ibid., 88.

10. Marie M. Fortune, *Is Nothing Sacred? When Sex Invades the Pastoral Relationship* (San Francisco: HarperSanFrancisco, 1989); Marie M. Fortune and James N. Poling, *Sexual Abuse by Clergy: A Crisis for the Church* (Decatur, Ga.: Journal of Pastoral Care Publications, 1994).

11. See Donald Capps, *Pastoral Care: A Thematic Approach* (Philadelphia: The Westminster Press, 1979), chap. 3; *Pastoral Counseling and Preaching: A Quest for an Integrated Ministry* (Philadelphia: The Westminster Press, 1980), chap. 2; *Reframing: A New Method in Pastoral Care* (Minneapolis: Fortress Press, 1990), chap. 8.

12. As noted earlier, Reinhold Niebuhr is said to have said that "surfaces are not superficial." Erik H. Erikson makes much the same point in his essay, "The Dream Specimen of Psychoanalysis," in Erik H. Erikson, *A Way of Looking at Things: Selected Papers from 1930 to 1980*, ed. Stephen Schlein (New York: W.W. Norton, 1987), 237–79. He writes: "The psychoanalyst, in looking at the surface of a mental phenomenon, often has to overcome a certain shyness. So many in his field mistake attention to surface for superficiality, and a concern with form for lack of depth. But the fact that we have followed Freud into depths which our eyes had to become accustomed to does not permit us, today, to blink when we look at things in broad daylight. Like good surveyors, we must be at home on the geological surface as well as in the descending shafts. . . . One might say that psychoanalysis has given new depth to the surface" (246–47).

13. Quoted in de Shazer, *Words Were Originally Magic*, 272.

14. See James F. Hopewell, *Congregation: Stories and Structures*, ed. Barbara G. Wheeler (Philadelphia: Fortress Press, 1987).

15. Erikson discusses impersonation in *Toys and Reasons: Stages in the Ritualization of Experience* (New York: W.W. Norton, 1977), 102–3. I discussed this issue in my chapter, "The Ritual Coordinator," in *Life Cycle Theory and Pastoral Care*, Theology and Pastoral Care (Philadelphia: Fortress Press, 1983), where I use Erikson's theory of ritual to differentiate the "healthy" from the "unhealthy" congregation (55–80).

16. Erik H. Erikson, *Young Man Luther: A Study in Psychoanalysis and History* (New York: W.W. Norton, 1958), 220.

Index